Palgrave Studies in Democracy, Innovation, and Entrepreneurship for Growth

Series Editor
Elias G. Carayannis, The George Washington University, Washington, DC, USA

The central theme of this series is to explore why some areas grow and others stagnate, and to measure the effects and implications in a trans-disciplinary context that takes both historical evolution and geographical location into account. In other words, when, how and why does the nature and dynamics of a political regime inform and shape the drivers of growth and especially innovation and entrepreneurship? In this socio-economic and socio-technical context, how could we best achieve growth, financially and environmentally?

This series aims to address such issues as:

- How does technological advance occur, and what are the strategic processes and institutions involved?
- How are new businesses created? To what extent is intellectual property protected?
- Which cultural characteristics serve to promote or impede innovation? In what ways is wealth distributed or concentrated?

These are among the key questions framing policy and strategic decision-making at firm, industry, national, and regional levels.

A primary feature of the series is to consider the dynamics of innovation and entrepreneurship in the context of globalization, with particular respect to emerging markets, such as China, India, Russia, and Latin America. (For example, what are the implications of China's rapid transition from providing low-cost manufacturing and services to becoming an innovation powerhouse? How do the perspectives of history and geography explain this phenomenon?)

Contributions from researchers in a wide variety of fields will connect and relate the relationships and inter-dependencies among (1) Innovation, (2) Political Regime, and (3) Economic and Social Development. We will consider whether innovation is demonstrated differently across sectors (e.g., health, education, technology) and disciplines (e.g., social sciences, physical sciences), with an emphasis on discovering emerging patterns, factors, triggers, catalysts, and accelerators to innovation, and their impact on future research, practice, and policy.

This series will delve into what are the sustainable and sufficient growth mechanisms for the foreseeable future for developed, knowledge-based economies and societies (such as the EU and the US) in the context of multiple, concurrent and interconnected "tipping-point" effects with short (MENA) as well as long (China, India) term effects from a geo-strategic, geo-economic, geo-political and geo-technological set of perspectives.

This conceptualization lies at the heart of the series, and offers to explore the correlation between democracy, innovation and growth.

More information about this series at
https://link.springer.com/bookseries/14635

Andrée Marie López-Fernández ·
Antonia Terán-Bustamante
Editors

Business Recovery in Emerging Markets

Global Perspectives from Various Sectors

Editors
Andrée Marie López-Fernández
Facultad de Ciencias Económicas y
Empresariales
Universidad Panamericana
Mexico City, Distrito Federal, Mexico

Antonia Terán-Bustamante
Facultad de Ciencias Económicas y
Empresariales
Universidad Panamericana
Mexico City, Mexico

ISSN 2662-3641　　　　　　　　　ISSN 2662-365X (electronic)
Palgrave Studies in Democracy, Innovation, and Entrepreneurship for Growth
ISBN 978-3-030-91531-5　　　　　ISBN 978-3-030-91532-2 (eBook)
https://doi.org/10.1007/978-3-030-91532-2

© The Editor(s) (if applicable) and The Author(s), under exclusive licence to Springer Nature Switzerland AG, part of Springer Nature 2022
This work is subject to copyright. All rights are solely and exclusively licensed by the Publisher, whether the whole or part of the material is concerned, specifically the rights of translation, reprinting, reuse of illustrations, recitation, broadcasting, reproduction on microfilms or in any other physical way, and transmission or information storage and retrieval, electronic adaptation, computer software, or by similar or dissimilar methodology now known or hereafter developed.
The use of general descriptive names, registered names, trademarks, service marks, etc. in this publication does not imply, even in the absence of a specific statement, that such names are exempt from the relevant protective laws and regulations and therefore free for general use.
The publisher, the authors and the editors are safe to assume that the advice and information in this book are believed to be true and accurate at the date of publication. Neither the publisher nor the authors or the editors give a warranty, expressed or implied, with respect to the material contained herein or for any errors or omissions that may have been made. The publisher remains neutral with regard to jurisdictional claims in published maps and institutional affiliations.

Cover illustration: © Alex Linch/shutterstock.com

This Palgrave Macmillan imprint is published by the registered company Springer Nature Switzerland AG
The registered company address is: Gewerbestrasse 11, 6330 Cham, Switzerland

Preface

The COVID-19 pandemic, caused by the SARS-CoV-2 virus, has certainly taken a toll on most every aspect of life; its ubiquitousness has meant that its effects and those of its collateral crises have been shared globally. The latter has triggered an unprecedented global health, social, and economic collapse. While harsh conditions and adversity are globalized, some countries, specifically emerging markets and developing countries, have been struggling to survive with little to no resources and infrastructure, which has cost millions of lives and strained entire healthcare systems. Health policies, such as lockdown at the beginning of the pandemic and social distancing, while necessary, have had important global implications on social and business growth and development and, in turn, on the economy.

Emerging markets are, in many ways, in transition as they build and adopt necessary infrastructures to ensure not only economic growth but also social development. They are key partners, rich in diversity, as well as the backbone of global supply chains, and show promising growth rates. That being said, they are also at great risk as significant social, political, and economic issues permeate these markets. This means that, during the pandemic, these economies have had to navigate the new challenges in less than favorable conditions. A clear example of this, healthwise, has been noted in the lack of PPE (Personal Protective Equipment) and oxygen tanks, as well as water shortage, and electric power interruptions, among others. Moreover, their societies also face persistent inequality, political instability, conflict, and lack of safety and security. Thus, emerging markets, as well as developing countries, have their work cut out for them in terms of effective recovery.

The first step in recovery is to understand the context and environment; in this sense, analyzing emerging markets' sectors' stages of recovery in which they currently operate. The second step requires comprehending the underlying reasons that have impeded recovery and, the third, proposing new ways to operate for business and social growth and development for a global recovery. Accordingly, this collaborative work offers a panorama of the different current challenges faced by various sectors and organizations, in the wake of the new normal, as well as potential approaches to respond to the health and collateral crises.

There are many different challenges triggered by the pandemic, which are analyzed in the book from various perspectives. In reference to public policy, this health-financial crisis presents great challenges for governments and decision-makers for a quick recovery. Short-term policies are required to help the population in need, preserve jobs, mitigate health complications, guarantee safety and security, and support the productive structures of these markets. At the same time, countries require structural economic measures, among which are fiscal, health, and telecommunications. Strategic decisions made by both government and company leaders in a crisis must take all factors of a complex and fragile environment into account. Accordingly, organizations need to hone their ability to make strategic decisions, and at the same time, they must make the most of their skills to develop strategic alliances and generate innovative and sustainable business models which positively impact organizations and society's quality of life.

It is noteworthy that even a decade after the fulfillment of the 2030 Agenda, or lack thereof, the COVID-19 pandemic is going to have a substantial impact on its outcome. These impacts may be both positive, as is the case of climate change, and negative, with a particular focus on the detriment of health and the increase in inequalities due to the global economic slowdown. The COVID-19 pandemic has shown that there can be no sustainable economy without universal social and health protection and that environmental and biodiversity crises directly affect sustainable development and the global economy. For such matter, the crisis is an important opportunity to transform current economic and social models to promote and enable global sustainable development, by achieving the Sustainable Development Goals.

The COVID-19 pandemic is an important reminder; albeit nondiscriminatory, painful, and distressing, the pandemic has reminded us that the many unpredictable events in the future will require proactivity for effective prevention and preparation. Moreover, tackling pre-pandemic conditions, particularly in emerging markets and developing countries, is essential. This book presents its content in three different approaches: public policy, innovation and decision-making, and business ethics and social responsibility; and given the theoretical and practical approach of the chapters, the discussions may be useful for business management and economic scholars, researchers and practitioners.

Mexico City, Mexico Andrée Marie López-Fernández
October 2021 Antonia Terán-Bustamante

Contents

1 **Introduction**   1
Andrée Marie López-Fernández

2 **The Secondary Economic Sector's Role in Post-pandemic Recovery: Analysis in the Neoliberal Capitalism Context**   7
José Anselmo Pérez Reyes and Ananya Rajagopal

3 **Perspectives for Recovery of VAT Collection Derived from Imports of Goods**   23
Javier Moreno Espinosa and Leovardo Mata Mata

4 **Public Policy for the Application of 5G in Mexico Within a Context of COVID-19**   41
José Luis Solleiro, Rosario Castañón, David Guillén, and Norma Solís

5 **The Structural Impact of COVID-19 on Employment: The Role of Skills and Gender in an Industrialized Local Economy**   61
Cecilia Y. Cuellar and Jorge O. Moreno

6 **Finally Back to Campus? Motivations for Facemask Adoption in the Higher Education Sector**   85
Paolo Morganti, Antonia Terán-Bustamante, and Enrique Murillo

7	The K-shape Economic Recovery and a New Company Classification Salvador Rivas-Aceves and Mauricio Maawad Morales	109
8	Business Model Innovation and Decision-Making for the Productive Sector in Times of Crisis Antonieta Martínez-Velasco and Antonia Terán-Bustamante	129
9	Innovation in Knowledge-Intensive Businesses: A Collaborative Approach for Post-pandemic Recovery Ananya Rajagopal and José Anselmo Pérez Reyes	157
10	Communicating with Stakeholders via Twitter: From CSR to COVID-19 Jorge Arturo León y Vélez Avelar	181
11	Unethical Supply Chains Delaying Recovery: Analyzing Pre and Mid COVID-19 Conditions Andrée Marie López-Fernández and Alejandra Sánchez-Rosales	201
12	The Pandemic Driving Socially Responsible Work-Family Performance in the Transportation Sector Max Daniel Revuelta-López	223
13	Machine Learning Sustainable Competitiveness for Global Recovery Andrée Marie López-Fernández, Antonia Terán-Bustamante, and Antonieta Martínez-Velasco	241

Index 269

Notes on Contributors

Rosario Castañón is a Researcher at Institute for Applied Sciences and Technology, National University of Mexico (UNAM). She is a Chemical Engineer, specialist in competitive intelligence and transfer of technology.

Cecilia Y. Cuellar is a Ph.D. Candidate in Economics at the Universidad Autónoma de Nuevo León (UANL), holds a Master's degree in Industrial Economics, UANL (2019), and a B.A. degree in International Affairs (UANL, 2017). She is Junior Researcher in Economics and has served as a Visiting Researcher at the Hibbs Institute at the University of Texas, Tyler. She is currently an Adjunct Professor (Lecturer) at UANL and at the Tecnológico de Monterrey. She is the winner of the "Consuelo Meyer L'eppe Award" for the best Master's Thesis. Her work has been published in national and international academic journals. Her research areas are Labor Economics, Gender Economics, and Applied Economics.

Javier Moreno Espinosa is a Research Professor at the School of Economics and Business Administration at the Universidad Panamericana. He has a Ph.D. in Strategic Management and Development Policies from Anahuac University and is a member of the National System of Researchers level candidate in Mexico; his research areas are focused on Economic Theory, Public Finance, Artificial Intelligence, and Text Mining applied, in the area of social sciences.

David Guillén is a Researcher at Cambiotec, A.C. He is an Industrial Engineer, specialist in intellectual property and competitive intelligence. He has been business consultant for Latin American firms.

Jorge Arturo León y Vélez Avelar is a full-time Professor and Director of the Bachelor's degree in International Business at the Universidad Panamericana, where he held the position of Director of Postgraduate Studies (2013–2021). He is currently studying a Ph.D. at the University of Antwerp (Belgium). Jorge Arturo holds a Master's degree in Business Administration from the Instituto Panamericano de Alta Dirección de Empresa (IPADE), a Bachelor's degree in Computer Engineering from the Universidad Panamericana, and a specialty in Philosophical Anthropology from the same institution. His research is focused on sustainability, influenced by various positions in the Scout Movement, of which he is currently an Inter-American Committee member.

Andrée Marie López-Fernández is a Professor and Researcher at the School of Economics and Business Administration at the Universidad Panamericana. She studied Business Administration at the Tecnológico de Monterrey, obtained a Ph.D. in Administrative Sciences from the EGADE Business School, and a specialty in Philosophical Anthropology from the Universidad Panamericana. Her research areas of interest include corporate social responsibility, social media and viral marketing, governance, and consumer behavior. The latter has resulted in the presentation of her work at International Conferences and publications in International Refereed Journals, as well as a couple of books and book chapters. Dr. Andrée Marie is an Associate Editor for Emerald Emerging Markets Case Studies Journal and has been conferred as a member of the Mexican National System of Researchers by CONACYT.

Antonieta Martínez-Velasco is a Researcher and Professor at the Faculty of Engineering, Universidad Panamericana. She has a Master's degree in computer sciences from the Instituto Politécnico Nacional, and Ph.D. in Engineering from the Universidad Panamericana. Her research is focused on Machine Learning applied in health care, welfare, and social sciences.

Leovardo Mata Mata is a Professor-Researcher at the Faculty of Economics and Business at Universidad Anáhuac México, has a Ph.D. in Financial Sciences from the EGADE Business School at the Tecnológico de Monterrey and is a member of the National System of Researchers Level-I in Mexico; his research areas are Economic Theory, Numerical

Analysis, Earth Sciences, and interdisciplinary quantitative tools applicable to the area of Social Sciences.

Mauricio Maawad Morales is a Bachelor degree student of the School of Economics and Business Administration at the Universidad Panamericana; he specializes in International Business analysis and micro, small, and medium size company studies.

Jorge O. Moreno holds a Ph.D. and Master's in Economics from the University of Chicago, a Master's in Economics from El Colegio de México, and a B.A. in Economics at the Universidad Autónoma de Nuevo León (UANL). He has served as Deputy Director in the Ministry of Public Finance in Mexico, Economist JPA in the Human Development Sector at the World Bank, Visiting Researcher at the General Directorate for the Analysis of the Financial System of the Banco of Mexico (Banxico), Adjunct Professor at El Colegio de Mexico, Lecturer at the University of Chicago, and Professor at the ITAM School of Business. He is currently a Professor and Researcher at the Faculty of Economics, UANL. He has published multiple books, chapters, papers, reviews, and received multiple honors nationally and internationally for his research work and academic career including the prestigious "Wayne C. Booth" Award for Excellence in Teaching at the University of Chicago, among other recognitions. His research areas are Applied Econometrics, Human Capital Theory (Education, Health, and Labor), Financial Economics, and Developmental Economics of Mobility and Transportation.

Paolo Morganti is a Professor of Economics at the Universidad Panamericana, School of Economics and Business Administration. He has a Ph.D. in Economics from the New York University (USA). His research is focused on Industrial Organization and Microeconomic Theory. He has conducted studies where he analyzes firms' conducts in imperfectly competitive markets with product differentiation. His work has appeared in *Quantitative Economics, Análisis Económico, and Revista Mexicana de Economía y Finanzas*.

Enrique Murillo is a Professor of Marketing (tenured) at the Universidad Panamericana and member of the National System of Researchers in Mexico. He received his Ph.D. in Management from Bradford University School of Management (UK) and a Postdoc in Organizational Behavior from the Freeman School of Business at Tulane University

(USA). His research centers on Internal Branding, which strives to identify the psychological drivers of employees' positive attitudes toward the service brand, a requirement for brand-aligned service encounters. He has undertaken studies in various organizations in Latin America, including restaurant chains, airlines, fashion retailers, drugstore chains, and ride-sharing services. His most recent work appeared in the *International Journal of Contemporary Hospitality Management, Journal of Product and Brand Management, Journal of Service Management*, and *Journal of Business Research*.

Ananya Rajagopal holds a position of Research Professor at Universidad Anáhuac Mexico and has been conferred the recognition of National Researcher Level-I by the Government of Mexico. She holds a Ph.D. in Administration with focus on Entrepreneurship and Marketing Strategies from the EGADE Business School, Tecnológico de Monterrey. Ananya Rajagopal has published several papers in international journals of repute and contributed research works in international conferences and edited books. Ananya Rajagopal is the author of three books with Palgrave Macmillan. She is a reviewer of several journals of international repute including *Emerald Emerging Markets Case Studies, Journal of Transnational Management*, and *Journal of Strategy and Management*. She is also a member of the advisory panel of Elsevier Insights.

Max Daniel Revuelta-López is a Professor and Researcher at the Universidad La Salle. He is an Industrial Engineer from the Universidad Panamericana and holds a Master's degree in business administration, marketing, and finance from the EGADE Business School. And, he is the project leader and Senior Consultant-Advisor-Instructor specializing in strategic planning of the value-service supply chain at AJR logistics services and Logistics Intelligence.

José Anselmo Pérez Reyes has a Ph.D. in Business Administration, graduated from the EGADE Business School, Tecnológico de Monterrey, with focus on corporate finance and behavioral economics. He has obtained a Master's in innovation for enterprise development from the Escuela de Ingeniería y Ciencias, Tecnológico de Monterrey, where he graduated with honors. He also has a Bachelor's degree in Geophysical Engineering from the Universidad Nacional Autónoma de México (UNAM). His current research interests include behavioral economics, innovation, and the relationship between financialization and decision-making process. He has ample experience in innovation, business development, business strategies, and strategic operational processes. Currently, he serves as Professor at the Tecnológico de Monterrey, Business Division—Entrepreneurship, Toluca campus. He has published in various international journals of repute and has contributed to chapters in edited books. He has participated in various international conferences and is a reviewer of indexed international journals.

Salvador Rivas-Aceves has a Ph.D. in Economic Sciences, a Master's degree in Economic Sciences, a Bachelor's degree in Economics by the Universidad Autónoma Metropolitana, México, and a specialty in Anthropology by the Universidad Panamericana. He is an Economics, Finance, and Politics Analyst and, since 2006, he has been a Research Professor. He was Chief of the Economics Academy at the School of Economics and Business Administration during 2013–2105; From 2015 to 2019, he was the Academic Dean as well as Research Dean of the Government and Economics School at the Universidad Panamericana. Since 2020, he has been the Research Dean at the School of Economics and Business Administration. Salvador has published research on Economic Growth, Technological Change, Financial Regulation, and Risk Analysis on the Financial Sector in several scientific papers, books, and chapters in scientific books since 2005. He is a member of the National Research System of Mexico since 2010.

Alejandra Sánchez-Rosales is a Management and International Business student at the Universidad Panamericana. She is currently working as a research assistant at the School of Economics and Business Administration, focusing on sustainability and CSR-related topics.

Norma Solís holds a degree in Communication and Journalism from UNAM. She works at Institute for Applied Sciences and Technology, National University of Mexico in research and training projects on innovation management and technology transfer.

José Luis Solleiro is a Researcher at Institute for Applied Sciences and Technology, National University of Mexico (UNAM). He is an Industrial Engineer, specialist in public policies related to technological innovation. He is a professor at National University of Mexico and is leader of Strategic Innovation Management Group.

Antonia Terán-Bustamante is a Researcher and Professor at the School of Economics and Business Administration at the Universidad Panamericana and is a member of the Mexican National System of Researchers by CONACYT. She has a Ph.D. in Administration Sciences and Master's in Administration International Business from the Universidad Nacional Autónoma de México (UNAM). Her research is focused on Human Capital, Competitiveness, Innovation, and Entrepreneurship.

List of Figures

Fig. 2.1　Multidimensional economic recovery decision model (*Source* Authors)　17

Fig. 3.1　Evolution of VAT on foreign trade and imports of intermediate, final consumption and capital goods (million dollars) (*Source* Own elaboration with data from SAT [2021], INEGI [2021] and BANXICO [2021])　30

Fig. 4.1　Mobile subscriptions by technology (*Source* Own elaboration with Ericsson [2021, p. 4] information)　44

Fig. 4.2　Ranking of average fixed broadband speed in selected countries (*Source* Own elaboration with data from Swain et al. [2020, p. 11])　45

Fig. 4.3　Distribution of the interviewees by the institution of belonging and Distribution of the interviewees by area of knowledge　49

Fig. 5.1　COVID-19 shock and formal labor employment in Nuevo Leon, by skill level (*Notes* Trend estimation uses VAR Model 1. The data of employment observed of 2020:Q2 was calculated of ETOE. *Source* Own estimations with time series constructed and homologized of employment surveys [ENEU-ENE-ENOE])　74

Fig. 5.2	COVID-19 shock on employment in Nuevo Leon, by skill level and gender (*Notes* Trend estimation uses a VAR model. The data of employment observed of second 2020 quarterly was calculated of ETOE. *Source* Own estimations with time series constructed and homologized of employment surveys [ENEU-ENE-ENOE])	75
Fig. 5.3	VAR model: estimation and Impulse-Response Functions (IRLs) (*p*-value: 0.001***, 0.01**, 0.05*. *Source:* Own estimations with time series constructed and homologized of employment surveys (ENEU-ENE-ENOE). Seasonally adjusted series presented by growth rates)	80
Fig. 7.1	Economic recovery shapes (*Source* Own elaboration based on Hansen [2020], Clark [2020], and IX. Exchange Staff [2020] information)	115
Fig. 7.2	Bankruptcy business declarations % change compared with the previous quarter and business bankruptcy index by activity, seasonally adjusted of the Europe Union, available countries (2015–2021) (*Source* Own elaboration based on Eurostat [2021] information)	117
Fig. 8.1	Business model innovation (*Source* Own elaboration based on Wirtz et al. [2016], Wirtz and Daiser [2017, 2018], Wirtz (2020), Baden-Fuller and Mangematin [2013], Boons et al. [2013], Bocken et al. [2014], and DaSilva and Trkman [2014])	134
Fig. 8.2	Scheme of the Business model innovation: variables and nodes (*Source* Authors)	140
Fig. 8.3	BMI Bayesian Network (*Source* Authors)	147
Fig. 9.1	Strategic growth perspectives in Knowledge-intensive firms (*Source* Authors)	172
Fig. 11.1	Socially responsible resilient supply chain governance model (*Source* authors)	214
Fig. 12.1	Equity performance model	230
Fig. 13.1	Global sustainable competitiveness framework	261

List of Tables

Table 3.1	Unit root test	31
Table 3.2	Andrews-Ploberger and Zivot-Andrews tests	33
Table 3.3	Johansen test	35
Table 4.1	Specialized events attended to gather information	48
Table 5.1	VAR model: tests and selection criteria	71
Table 6.1A	Sample descriptives: sociodemographic variables versus comparable official data	93
Table 6.1B	Sample variables that lack an official data comparison	94
Table 6.2	Regression of SVO over trust and gender	95
Table 6.3	Regressions of facemask wearing conducts	97
Table 7.1	Business bankruptcy by economic sector in Canada, 2019–2020	119
Table 7.2	Number of bankruptcies in the U.S. by industry and bankrupt companies by sector as a percentage of total companies for Mexico	120
Table 8.1	Definition of variables and nodes	141
Table 8.2	Variables classification	146
Table 8.3	Global confusion matrix for BMI model	148
Table 8.4	Metrics for the model variables	149
Table 10.1	Complete list of companies analyzed by size, sector, and Tweets	190
Table 10.2	Source of tweets	193
Table 10.3	Classification of tweet words according to ESR badge	194
Table 10.4	Likes and retweet analysis	195
Table 11.1	Years to close the gender gap per region	210

Table 12.1	Equity performance model descriptive statistics $[n = 607]$	232
Table 12.2	Equity performance model regression coefficients $[n = 607]$	232
Table 12.3	Equity performance model correlation coefficients $[n = 607]$	233
Table 13.1	GCI cluster analysis	251
Table 13.2	GII cluster analysis	254
Table 13.3	IGI cluster analysis	256
Table 13.4	HDI cluster analysis	257

CHAPTER 1

Introduction

Andrée Marie López-Fernández

In 2020, the pandemic caused panic, fear, and a great deal of uncertainty. Government and business leaders were mostly forced to make initial decisions to ensure people's safety and security which, in general, meant lockdowns. This decision has ultimately caused global economic and social setbacks; however, the end of 2020 brought hope as vaccines were approved and, in December, the first person was vaccinated. By the beginning of 2021, the strain on the economy was the main driver for government and business leaders' decision-making. However, successful economic recovery is only viable as business and society both sustain growth and development.

Lockdowns have been lifted and sectors reopened with an urgency to go back to "normal." The pandemic caused by COVID-19 continues, yet, it seems as though the health emergency has taken a backseat as decision makers push for a pre-COVID-19 context in education, business,

A. M. López-Fernández (✉)
Facultad de Ciencias Económicas y Empresariales, Universidad Panamericana, Mexico City, Mexico

© The Author(s), under exclusive license to Springer Nature Switzerland AG 2022
A. M. López-Fernández and A. Terán-Bustamante (eds.), *Business Recovery in Emerging Markets*, Palgrave Studies in Democracy, Innovation, and Entrepreneurship for Growth,
https://doi.org/10.1007/978-3-030-91532-2_1

and society at large. The rationale has been: Some have been vaccinated, thus, we are ready to begin recovering from the crisis. Two things come to mind, (i) the crisis has not ended; its end will begin when people are not in danger and the pandemic becomes an epidemic; and (ii) only about thirty percent of the population worldwide has been vaccinated. That being said, it makes complete sense to assess the current situation to formulate a strategic plan for a safe, suitable, fair, and satisfactory recovery.

Globally, we are on a learning curve in terms of the effects of the pandemic on business dynamics. As such, the more research is conducted, the better we are able to tackle the collateral effects on society, business, and the environment. The book is a collaborative work which analyzes the recovery process of different sectors, from the pandemic as well as its collateral effects. The chapters are approached from a global perspective and emerging markets' perspective by means of conceptual and empirical studies. The research questions guiding the collaborative work include: have industries and sectors recovered from the pandemic? How have industries and sectors recovered—if at all—from the pandemic and its collateral crises? And, what underlying aspects have impeded industries and sectors recovering from the pandemic and its collateral crises? The book explores the parameters of business and economic perspectives for the construction of effective models to pursue an effective recovery. The collaborative work is sectioned in a three-part analysis of social and economic recovery: public policy, innovation and decision-making, and business ethics and social responsibility.

Economic recovery is arguably government and business leaders' current primary focus; there are multiple variables that are hindering its fulfillment including, but not limited to: primary and secondary sector growth, value-added tax collection, telecommunications, bankruptcy, unemployment, and communication. The first section includes discussions on public policy for social and economic recovery. Chapter 2 discusses the importance of governments' economic actions toward recovery from the effects of COVID-19 in emerging markets. The study highlights basic Keynesian economic model assumptions to bridge socioeconomic market gaps in the context of the global health crisis. It is debated that to confront the challenges, public policies ought to be strategically assigned to both primary and secondary sectors to drive a sustainable economic recovery. The following chapter analyzes the correlation between elasticity of value-added tax collection and imports of goods. It is argued that economic recovery will be significantly impacted by the magnitude in which sectors contribute to gross added value. This is particularly important for emerging markets in which tax collection is not exceptionally effective.

Public policy-making and funding related to the fifth-generation mobile network (5G), as discussed in Chapter 4, is elemental for growth and development; however, emerging markets tend to lag behind in taking action. Results indicate that the 5G network (technologies, network design, and standards, among others) characteristics have important applications for digital health, digital education, digital government, industry 4.0, among others. Therefore, significant investments in technology, research, and development are required, and digital skills ought to be fostered; further, policies and regulations are needed to close users' connectivity gap. Moreover, such policy-making and investments are key for the development solutions of social, business, and economic problems and, thus, elemental to recovery from the effects of COVID-19.

Collaborators are perhaps the most important internal stakeholders as without them a firm could not operate. As such, ensuring their well-being is elemental to their satisfaction, productivity, and individual and organizational performance. The labor force is essential to economic performance and, moreover, it and the gender gap have a significant impact on social and economic performance, particularly in emerging markets as the gender gap is larger. Chapter 5 includes a discussion on formal employment by skill segment and the gender gap amid the first COVID-19 pandemic shock. The author(s) argue that the crisis requires the development of public policy for the investment in human capital focused on the achievement of high-skill labor market and gender equity.

Social distancing has changed organizational dynamics around the world, and universities are not the exception. Universities, like all schools, took to online learning and, once returning to campus was on the table, safety measures began to be discussed. The next chapter analyzes the effects of health protocols in response to the pandemic on the education sector. As behavior is impacted by trust and social value orientation, public health communications will prove to be key to ensure facemask adoption and a safe return to campus on the road to recovery. The second section of the book includes discussion on studies related to innovation and decision-making to drive social and economic recovery. It is common for decision makers to avoid investing in innovation when uncertainty rules over daily operations. The argument boils down to profit for survival and, therefore, any aggregated cost could jeopardize organizations' permanence in the market. That being said, innovation is an excellent response to a crisis; in addition, when there is a crisis, innovation tends to have the ability to remove obstacles previously considered very difficult to overcome.

Social distancing, a required health protocol, saves lives and yet has had significant effects on social, business, and economic recovery. Chapter 7 consists of an analysis of the economic recession caused by bankruptcy and increased unemployment, triggered by the pandemic. Face-to-face interaction intensity has notably impacted economic activity decline, impacting unemployment and bankruptcy, and led to a new company classification. Further, firms that have innovated their production and distribution processes have overcome these challenges and may successfully impact business and economic recovery.

Given the shifts caused by the pandemic, organizations are facing challenges related to their business models. For such matter, Business Model Innovation (BMI), discussed in Chapter 8, seeks to enhance consumer value proposition by means of improved decision-making. By doing so, organizations may improve their consumers' satisfaction, lead to improved business growth, and, therefore, aid in the recovery from the COVID-19 crisis. Knowledge-intensive organizations are elemental to growth and development as they provide critical data and information for decision-making. These organizations offer supply to services industries such as: education, finance, health, information and technology, and business. Chapter 9 includes a discussion on knowledge-intensive firms' process of coping with global pandemic in emerging markets. As opposed to traditional organizations which are profit oriented, knowledge-intensive firms focus on business processes' professional knowledge. The authors have posited that innovative business practices in these firms may positively impact economic recovery from the COVID-19 crisis.

The third section of the book includes discussion on the impact of business ethics and Social Responsibility on business, social, economic, and environmental recovery. Over the past two decades, the United Nations' leaders called businesses leaders to action. They have exhorted them to proactively work toward the achievement of global sustainable development. At the very least organizations must act ethically, however, in order to comply with the call to action, organizations need to design and execute objectives and strategies aligned with the 2030 agenda, and corporate social responsibility (CSR) aligned with the 2030 agenda is certainly one way of moving toward sustainable development.

Effective and transparent communication with stakeholders is one of the key elements of corporate social responsibility. Since the beginning of the pandemic, organizations' communication with stakeholders has naturally tended to focus on the COVID-19 crisis. Chapter 10 includes a discussion on organizations' socially responsible communication on social media, specifically Twitter, during the COVID-19 outbreak. Interestingly, organizations genuinely engaged in corporate social responsibility have not forgotten their commitment to sustainable development which may, ultimately, positively impact business and social recovery.

Focal companies are not the only firms affected by lockdowns and social distancing, as entire supply chains have been impacted. Chapter 11 includes a discussion on how inequality, which permeated global supply chains before COVID-19 emerged, has been hindering social growth and development and will, therefore, impede effective recovery. Closing the inequality gap will require organizations to engage in socially responsible supply chain governance and proactively work to guarantee global equality, not just within focal companies. Simply put, economic and social growth and development are not plausible if the inequality gap endures.

Pre-pandemic, most the work-family relationship was unbalanced and leaned toward work; that is, collaborators would spend much more time working than with their family, ultimately, negatively impacting their family performance. During COVID-19, social distancing and lockdowns shifted the work-family relationship, as discussed in Chapter 12, toward the family. Finding the adequate balance in such relationship may successfully drive family and organizational performance and, in turn, positively impact their recovery from the effects of COVID-19.

The final chapter of the book deals with global perspective on recovery; five global indexes and their related economies were assessed to determine a path for organizations to work toward sustainable competitiveness. The authors posited that there are particular variables, pertaining to human development, innovation, impunity, sustainable development goals, and competitiveness, that may be tackled at a micro-level (i.e., by organizations) to, in turn, impact at a macro-level (i.e., countries). As such, through a socially responsible approach to business dynamics (i.e., social, economic, and environmental performance), organizations may positively impact nations' sustainable competitiveness and, thus, influence global recovery from the pandemic and its collateral effects.

Decision makers around the world, as previously mentioned, have weighed the outcomes and decided to take the risk and reopen for the sake of economic recovery. Although there is a social argument (i.e., people need to socialize, lockdown is not healthy), social growth and development requires much more than socialization. The only way we will successfully recover from the COVID-19 crisis is by means of both business and social growth and development; in other words, it may not be achieved by merely tackling financial and economic variables.

Interestingly, all aspects analyzed through the looking glass of COVID-19, indicate that successful recovery across sectors and industries, as well as from a macro- and micro-perspective, requires tending to pre-pandemic issues permeating business, society, and the economy. The reality is that before the crisis we had been globally dealing with a series of areas of opportunity that were hindering economic and social growth and development. Put simply, all aspects that are currently impeding recovery from COVID-19 are pre-pandemic variables which need to be strategically addressed and solved to set the process of recovery in motion. Given the previous state of affairs, why would we choose to simply go back the way things were? On the road to recovery, going back to the status quo will not suffice; a new and improved approach to organizational dynamics is needed.

CHAPTER 2

The Secondary Economic Sector's Role in Post-pandemic Recovery: Analysis in the Neoliberal Capitalism Context

José Anselmo Pérez Reyes and Ananya Rajagopal

INTRODUCTION

The recent global health crisis, the pandemic caused by COVID-19, has brought a systemic human development crisis affecting the economic and social dimensions of development (United Nations, 2020). In reference to the concept of systemic crisis (Trichet, 2007), it is established that an economic system enters into crisis when it collapses due to incapacity, saturation, or lack of instruments to solve the problems created by its own

J. A. P. Reyes (✉)
Tecnológico de Monterrey, Toluca, Mexico
e-mail: josea.perezre@tec.mx

A. Rajagopal
Universidad Anáhuac México, Mexico City, Mexico
e-mail: ananya.rajagopal@anahuac.mx

© The Author(s), under exclusive license to Springer Nature Switzerland AG 2022
A. M. López-Fernández and A. Terán-Bustamante (eds.), *Business Recovery in Emerging Markets*, Palgrave Studies in Democracy, Innovation, and Entrepreneurship for Growth,
https://doi.org/10.1007/978-3-030-91532-2_2

dynamics. The global health crisis will probably bring with it the most disruptive economic effects in modern history. Such disruptive economic effects can be seen in political and economic actions witnessed around the world, which demonstrate the uncertainty toward the most relevant operations. Thus, in a global conceptual framework analyzing the economic impact of the pandemic, it is predicted that the economy will enter into recession, which will tend to have negative effects on employment, income, and inequality in the socioeconomic structure of the country. This can be attributed to social-distancing measures adopted globally that have caused limited supply of labor and restricted the ability to operate in many large sectors of the economy such as tourism, entertainment, and commerce (Hevia & Neumeyer, 2020).

The social norms and limited market dynamics mentioned above put pressure on countries' financial and economic variables, and motivate access to financing from international markets. In view of these movements toward alternative financing options, Guillén (2020) discusses that the costs implied during the process of market lockdown are not enough to explain the current economic decline. According to the study conducted by Guillén (2020), the economic decline has other profound causes associated with different triggers originated since the economic-financial crisis of 2007 that affect the systemic contradictions of capitalism. The study also explains that such financing plays a preponderant role evident in the recent behavior of the stock markets, in which an upward trend can be observed despite the collapse of productive activities among various sectors of the market. According to Georgieva (2020), the human costs of the pandemic make it necessary to emphasize three fundamental elements of analysis:

(a) In the global growth prospects, priority should be given to the adoption of fiscal measures aimed at flexible monetary policy for affected workers and companies, with a view to strengthen the healthcare systems around the world.
(b) Concern toward emerging economies with reference to their economic debt and the level of economic impact caused by the pandemic.
(c) The measures that the International Monetary Fund (IMF) will adopt in a multilateral-cooperation framework to support its member countries.

These policies should include emergency financing and replenishment of the Trust Fund for Disaster Relief and Containment with a focus on emerging economies. Within the framework of these economic recovery measures, the IMF (2021) predicts that support for policies and the recent application of vaccines at the international level will project a growth of the world economy of around 5.5% for 2021 and 4.2% for 2022. The projections for 2021 have been revised upwards by 0.3 percentage points with respect to the first forecast (IMF, 2020), attributed to the expectations of a strengthening in economic output and the support for the measures proposed by the IMF. However, these forecasts are projected with some degree of uncertainty due to the new variants of the virus and the lack of knowledge of their impact on the health and socioeconomic systems. It can be foreseen that, as part of the strategic economic reactivation plan for developing countries, a series of public policies should be implemented with the aim of reducing vulnerabilities and fostering the necessary capacities to face the health crisis. Nevertheless, with reference to the secondary sector of the economy, governments have opted for maintaining operations among various associated activities aimed at generating long-term social returns.

In view of the above assumptions, economic activities in different countries slowed down as a result of a series of public-health-safety-led decisions to suspend all those activities that are considered as non-essential. As a result, several manufacturing and service sectors were affected. However, some important sectors such as mining, construction, and the automobile industry were defined as essential activities as they incite basic-necessity activities in society. Therefore, it can be conferred that the demand for goods and services is associated with employment levels in reference to vigorous public investment. Such vision assumes that public spending is a way to ensure the use of factors of production, especially the labor force. Thus, a government investment program would stimulate the economy and invigorate the market from the movement of resources, which may come from different fiscal schemes but also from public debt.

García and García (2020) explain that the crisis caused by the pandemic is a systemic, economic, health, energy, food, and environmental crisis, which cross-examines the economic development considering the aforementioned dimensions to facilitate economy recovery. Consequently, the stock markets, economy, and the employment sector have been highly vulnerable to such unprecedented health crisis in the modern economic ambiance. Therefore, the neoliberal orthodoxy of the free market has been adversely affected, leading to the existence of a world recession with a prior origin and the probable need to apply policies directed toward large public investments to reactivate the economy.

Based on the above discussion, this research proposes a conceptual approach for the development of an effective strategy, based on the economic-recovery decisions adopted by governments in emerging economies, aimed at a multidimensional vision that involves political, social, and cultural factors. The study also focuses on the emerging economies whose recovery decisions are aimed at the specialization of labor-intensive activities and government intervention order to promote effective implementation of market policies. Such policy implementation is considered as one of the effective ways to face a crisis and recover economic growth. The conceptual development of this research will make it possible to assess the public policy response, exercised by the government, which will bring positive effects toward economic recovery. Therefore, this study contributes to the existing literature by understanding the impact of the global pandemic in emerging economies, in reference to the political response and its impact on the overall employment rate. The study also discusses strategies that can be implemented to mitigate the economic consequence of the pandemic in emerging economies and the response of the market considering the following questions:

RQ_1: What would be the impact of public spending of the secondary sector on the emerging economies?
RQ_2: Can the economic recovery strategies implemented by the governments help drive the growth of the countries to their pre-pandemic performance?

LITERATURE REVIEW

According to Stoyanova (2019), supporters of government non-intervention are neoclassicists and liberals. They believe that the market with foreign and outer interference, i.e., a maximum free market and minimum government interference, is perfect; where the market by itself partially maintains balance. On the other hand, supporters of Keynesian theory believe that the market needs government intervention to regulate the demand-supply process. However, the Hayekian approach (Hayek,

1960) assumes that Keynesian policies only contribute to increase inflation, displacement of private investment, and imbalance in public finance. In view of the above discussion, this approach disturbs the functioning of the market, resulting in a total loss of the country's wealth due to failures in government policies. Therefore, encompassing previous arguments, the idea that the secondary economic sector plays an important role in the economies of countries based on directed public spending is not new. The Keynesian model, which insists on government interventionism as the best way to face a crisis, seeks to increase public spending for the construction of social and labor services with an aim to increase productivity and employment (Keynes, 1978).

Keynesian economics is based on the concept of increase in the government spending through socioeconomic variables to improve the production output and employment rate, and attain stability in the inflation rate. Such economic outlook focuses on improving the economy based on short-term strategies implemented by the government through an increase in expenditure and decrease in taxes in order to stimulate demand. Hence, the optimal economic performance attained by implementing strategies tends to increase government spending. Implementation of deficit spending not only encourages consumers to increase their spending capacity, but also compensates for the loss of foreign direct investment within the economy (Asada & Yoshida, 2001). One of the principal causes of economic downturn in any crisis situation is not the lack of knowledge, labor skills, or market inadequacy, but insufficiency of aggregate demand leading to adjusting the impact of consumer-market fluctuations in business cycles. The impact of aggregate variables like income and employment observed in market adjustments explains the fluctuations in the business cycles, as these form a part of intrinsic consumer-market phenomenon taking place during the economic crisis (Gori et al., 2018; Naimzada & Pireddu, 2014).

The Keynesian model implies that government expenditure through the implementation of public policies and public equity is an exogenous tool used to significantly influence market dynamics to promote economic growth in the short-term. Keynes (1978) proposes that fiscal stimulus through government expenditure acts as the primary driver for economic growth in the post-crisis era. Developed nations possess economic resources to implement fiscal policies, such as subsidies, tax-cuts, unemployment benefits, and tax holidays among others, to maintain the market dynamics and delay any economic stagnation. However, emerging economies are very restricted in providing such economic resources that are aimed at delaying the economic downturn, leading to economic recession (Srinivasan, 2013). Hence, the Keynesian model explains that by increasing government spending and maintaining constant consumption and investments, the overall economic output increases. Additionally, an increase in government spending through various economic stimulus packages and subsidies on taxes has been the standard approach of the government expenditure to tackle the economic recession. In view of the above discussion, government expenditure can be determined as one of the most important and effective tools to implement fiscal policies and public expenditure to drive economic growth in the post-crisis era.

The New Keynesian Model is an extension of the "demand-crisis" model, which incorporates the intrinsic factors of employment fluctuation on the labor-intensive market. Fluctuation in business cycles not only affect the asymmetric patterns of the New Keynesian Model, but also explores the interaction among employment opportunities, job rationing, rigidity in increasing wages, lack of regulations to control inflation flux, and labor-capital resource allocations (Casares et al., 2014). The New Keynesian model also discusses the role of public investment through fiscal policies aimed at stimulating short-term market reactivation strategies and long-term economic growth perspectives. Public consumption-expenditure and public-investment strategies act as an effective transition mechanism between the high-growth period prior to the crisis, and the low-growth post-pandemic era. Such outlook allows the governments in the emerging economies to use short-term market reactivation strategies to stabilize the economic impact. The public investment is inversely proportional to the business cycles, i.e., during the high-growth period of the business cycle the public investment is relatively lower than the low-growth period such as post-pandemic economy. In the short-term, public investment has a significant effect on generating employment, whereas the public consumption expenditure has a high impact on the country's Gross Domestic Product leading to an increase in the private spending capacity (Petrović et al., 2021).

Framework of Propositions

It has been argued by some authors that the current global economic decline is a new stage of the capitalistic crisis accentuated by COVID-19.

However, it is complex to evaluate the public policy response exercised by governments for economic reactivation under these conditions. According to García and García (2020), the crisis caused by the pandemic is a systemic crisis with an economic, health, energy, food, and environmental scope that questions economic reproduction in the same dimensions. Consequently, such effects may be present in all countries and, especially in relation to some of the core variables such as the stock markets, economy, and employment rate. The above discussion negatively reveals the neoliberal free market orthodoxy, leading to the recognition of the emergence of a worldwide economic recession and probable need to apply policies toward large public investments to reactivate the economy. According to Esquivel (2020), economic activities slowed down significantly as a result of the decision to suspend all those activities considered non-essential, which affected several manufacturing and service sectors that had to be temporarily closed to guarantee social distancing. However, some important sectors such as mining, construction, and the automotive sector came to be defined as essential activities. This is consistent with the demand for goods and services being associated with employment levels in a context of vigorous public investment. In other words, this vision assumes that public spending is a way to ensure the use of productive factors, especially the labor force.

Guillén (2020) argues that, during economic crisis, the best alternatives for recovery lie in multidimensional vision involving development of economic, political, social, and cultural factors. The study also proposes that a feasible strategy for recovery lies in the specialization of labor-intensive activities that increase its international competitiveness, which would involve a systemic intervention of the government aimed at application of fundamentalist market policies. Therefore, the proposal discussed in the study assumes that the best way to face a crisis lies in an internal strategy aimed at recovering growth, raising employment levels, satisfying the basic needs of the population, and eliminating extreme poverty. In reference to the above discussion, the solution could be analyzed from a technical and political perspective, encompassing a more systemic intervention from the government to promote public initiatives. Taking into consideration both the approaches discussed in this section toward the implementation of public policies aimed at recovering growth, the secondary economic sector becomes highly relevant as it uses inputs from productive sectors such as metals, cement, and wood, among others. Hence, the secondary economic sector is assumed to be the main economic driver that benefits different branches of society.

Accordingly, under such a directed spending scheme caused by the pandemic, governments in emerging countries have implemented large plans for discretionary spending and/or tax-cuts that seek to mitigate the fall of the economic activity. Consequently, central banks of different countries have facilitated the financing of these government policies with purchases of assets in the secondary market, encouraging the predominant use of credit channels. However, such strategy could cause a part of the invested money to get stuck in the asset markets, which would not become real investment impeding economic growth. This particular concept is called "liquidity trap."

Moreno-Brid (2020) proposes a monetary policy in strong coordination with the fiscal policy that considers an enormous support from the central- and development banks with an aim to channel funds to the private sector. Such policy is directed toward emerging countries that lack significant automatic stabilizers such as unemployment insurance. The study also indicates that the pandemic should motivate a reflection about public finances in a countercyclical manner, on the priorities of the central bank and the monetary policy with a focus on long-term economic gains. In view of the above discussion, the following proposition has been framed:

> P_1: The negative effects caused by systemic crisis in emerging economies can be solved by public policies directed towards investment in the secondary economic sector.

As discussed above, it is clear that the aim of the governments is to resolve the economic crisis originated by the pandemic. However, according to Mendoza (2016), the profitability for large companies does not only come from their productive activity, but also from financial rating. In view of the previous argument, financial rating affects the actions and strategies of the business growth, because large corporations seek the participation of external capital in their economic decisions, especially for those located in a very dynamic and strategic economic sector, as in the case of the secondary sector.

In view of the above discussion, government intervention can be referred to discretionary acts by government to intervene in the market dynamics and the economy. According to Stoyanova (2019), the concept of government intervention was put in place long-time ago, but during the 1940s, it became one of the most attractive concepts within the scientific community, as it was provoked by the first commercial crises. Government interference has its supporters and opponents in several schools over the years that continue in the present. Marinova (2015) assumes that governments can create buffer stocks of production by buying it from the saturated market and thus preventing or mitigating the development of crisis, while the private market cannot afford such action. In this perspective, government functions influence market relations toward an increase or a decrease of aggregate production in industrial sector and thus tend to restore market equilibrium.

It should be noted that, according to Stiglitz (2013), government intervention is often used in emerging countries, where the market defects are larger and the government's ability to cope with them is relatively smaller. The study by Stiglitz (2013) identifies five key components of the government intervention as explained below:

(a) Education
(b) Technologies supporting the financial sector
(c) Investing in infrastructure
(d) Preventing environmental degradation
(e) Creating and maintaining a social security network.

In accordance with the above elements considered for the emerging economies, the government intervention is applied with greater intensity in the secondary sector than other sectors of the economy. The primary reason behind this is foundations of the Keynesian school, where scientists are inclined toward more active government intervention in relation to the financial attributes. It should be emphasized that the main intention of the government intervention is to create a positive economic environment in order to provide the necessary financial resources for the activities in the secondary sector. However, such government intervention aids in the process of employment generation among the other sectors of the economy. Taking into account the previous points, it can be considered that the government intervention seeks the balance incomes in different sectors of the economy. According to Stoyanova (2019), another reason for government interference is the possibility of eliminating part of the price shocks resulting from the conditions of international markets by protecting the internal market. In reference to the above discussion, according to Rodríguez-Moreno (2015), the financial markets by themselves do not always work properly, as they present faults like any other market. Therefore, these failures justify the presence of the government through the use of regulation and supervision processes, thus allowing markets to behave properly generating not only efficiency, but also equity. On the other hand, emerging government investments encourage the growth of the secondary sector and, consequently, of the production chain. This would lead to an increase in the rate of exploitation of workers, as well as stagnation or decline in their current wages, as a result of the detriment of a real economic recovery. Based on the above arguments, the following proposition has been derived:

> P_2: Investment in the secondary sector translates into economic sectoral interdependence due to the stimulation of factors of production, especially the labor force.

Conceptual Model

One of the major contributions of government participation in overcoming any systemic crisis is through strict enforcement of capital controls on all public and private sector contracts. Such strategy not only maintains the traditional diversification strategies, but also stimulated an intraasset correlation leading to a decrease in the short-term impact of the crisis in the emerging economies. The countries with economic stability contribute positively to the systemic crisis as compared to the emerging economies, which mainly withhold negative effects such as increase in unemployment rate, income disparity leading to an increase in the gaps among social structures, and socio-cultural inequality. Such risky terrain needs careful navigation by implementation of public policies and government investment programs in order to decrease the probability of long-term economic downturn (Steinkamp & Westermann, 2018). Hence, public policies directed toward investment in the secondary economic sector tend to mitigate the negative effects caused by systemic crisis in emerging economies (P_1) as illustrated in the Fig. 2.1.

The primary sector of the economy provides raw materials and other supplies to the secondary sector for its production process. However, during the economic recovery process, the secondary industrial sector detonates the industrial activity and involves the primary sector in the economic reinitiating process. The support provided by the secondary sector to the primary and tertiary industrial sectors generates more

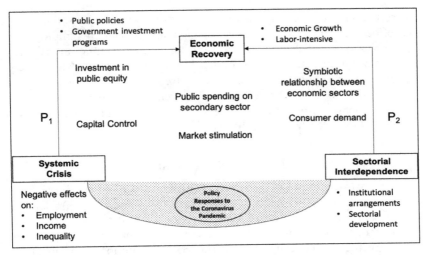

Fig. 2.1 Multidimensional economic recovery decision model (*Source* Authors)

employment opportunities, reduces income barriers within the marketplace, and promotes institutional alliances. Labor-intensive industries in alliance with sociopolitical support tend to improve the business cycle leading to economic recovery. Therefore, investment in the secondary sector translates into economic sectoral interdependence due to the stimulation of productive factors, especially the labor force (P_2). The symbiotic dynamics between production and marketability optimizes the production capacity, reinforces employee skills, and maximizes productivity. The adoption of analytical perspectives promotes the secondary sectors toward effective management of risks-opportunities, competition-demand, and competitive advantage-supply chain management (Alamá-Sabater et al., 2016).

Emerging markets are based on the support from public equity, which is aimed to support the social structure to acquire equity, trade equity, and promote participation of private firms to raise substantial capital from many small market players. However, such practice has been evolved from individuals to institutions, paving the way for increased public participation in order to increase economic growth (Kalcheva et al., 2020). However, such government support stimulates consumer-market relationship boosting the market dynamics and promoting growth prospects in the recession-led economy. Such market stimulation reverts the negative effects of the systemic crisis through an increase in employment rate, enhanced social governance, and promotes mutual interdependence among primary and secondary industrial sectors. Accordingly, the process of rebooting the economy strengthens the labor-intensive production process through effective management of labor competences, knowledge-based production process, and skills management process (Llorente-González & Vence, 2020).

General Discussion

The crisis caused by COVID-19 accentuated a systemic crisis, origin of which can be seen in the inconsistencies of neoliberalism. As Guillén (2020) said, the pandemic is associated with different triggers that affect the contradictions of capitalism in the context of the increasing tensions of disagreements between elites. In this context, the intervention of the government to stabilize the economy points to support the large companies in the secondary sector without taking help from other important sectors like agriculture, transportation, commerce, etc. Therefore, the decisions made by governments to control the pandemic lie in social distancing and shrinking of the production capacity resulting in a negative impact to the economy. Such decisions were implemented in view of the unforeseen impact on the associated costs of a prolonged crisis. For these reasons, the intervention by the government to support the secondary sector is a kind of emergent Keynesianism to sustain the economy, particularly to support the large companies of these sectors by slightly altering the neoliberal model. However, it will be interesting to see the strategies taken up by the governments to maintain the production chains of the economy, particularly the stability of the working class, as the current decisions made by the government has had a direct impact to the accumulation of capital.

As Antentas (2020) said, if the neoliberal theses prevail, this second wave of massive bailouts to sustain the economy, after the first one in 2008 oriented toward the financial system, may simply be the prelude to a more virulent phase where a crises of legitimacy, social reproduction, and of the global forms of governance of neoliberalism are interwoven. The study indicates that such policies would imply a strengthened neoliberalism toward increasing authoritarian interventions in domestic politics in the midst of greater geopolitical tensions. Such outlook explains the growing fractures between different fractions of the political and financial conglomerates. Probably, this means that we are facing the main structural contradictions of neoliberalism and the beginning of a new kind of economic model similar to Keynesianism arguments.

Conclusions

To separate the economy from the government is ineffective, as the relationship between government and economy is a dialectic process of interdependence. In such interdependence, the debate between neoliberalism and statism in the global economy under said health crisis is difficult to solve because such political and social crisis has never been seen before. The discussions in the chapter indicate that specific policies pursued by governments will vary according to countries' political and social contexts. For emerging economies, the public support is exclusively directed to the secondary sector, generally limited toward large and consolidated enterprises due to their high public spending capacity.

Taking into account the global uncertainty, the only thing that appears to be clear is that one era is running out and another with high ambiguity is yet to come. The post-crisis world will be the result of the balance of forces in an international dimension, between the various sociopolitical projects in play. Every crisis starts with the application of misguided policies and ends with a process of economic reorganization, which results in a social and political collision. The current situation shows a crisis of legitimacy of capitalism and the contradictions of the neoliberal model, which highlights its flaws in terms of the efficiency of public health systems, dependency on inputs, reduction of government financing for social systems (health, education, etc.), and the economic instability created from the above-mentioned flaws. In accordance with the above, it is not certain that supporting the secondary sector is the correct solution. Hence, this chapter suggests that the right policies to confront the pandemic involve that the public spending can be assigned not only to the secondary sector, but also to the primary sector of the economy in order to drive government efforts toward quick and sustainable economic recovery. The characteristic of the present systemic crisis is based on the assumptions that current government regulations are heading to overcoming the pandemic by increasing the profitability based on public spending in the secondary sector. Also, it is important to contrast the sources of income for large companies in terms of compatibility with the assumptions of previously discussed economic reactivation plans. However, this perspective can be explored with the scope of future research.

The study highlights the basic assumptions of the Keynesian economic model and its role in bridging the socioeconomic gaps in the market due to the recent global health crisis. In view of this premise, future studies may focus on the imperfect nature of the market competition and the imperative role of public funding to coordinate the socioeconomic variables, driving them toward economic growth. Also, the rigidity of prices aimed at reducing the impact on the profit margins of the financial and industrial conglomerates can be explored. Such inflexibility is based on the assumptions of consumer expectations adapted to the convenience of the market players, leading to an economic downturn rather than uplifting the local economy. The imperfection in the capitalistic market drives asymmetries of information leading to limitations or rationing of public equity. Such risk-averse nature of the capitalistic market leads to credit-rationing policies by financial institutions and public funds. Therefore, future research may also tend to understand the limitations faced by the market players, which puts them in a position of risk. Also, the symbiotic relationship of interdependence between public investment and private participation may affect the equilibrium level of various variables outlined within the theory of business fluctuations, which can be explored in other research studies.

REFERENCES

Alamá-Sabater, L., Heid, B., Jiménez-Fernández, E., & Márquez-Ramos, L. (2016). What drives interdependence of FDI among host countries? The role of geographic proximity and similarity in public debt. *Economic Modelling, 58*, 466–474. https://doi.org/10.1016/j.econmod.2016.06.007

Antentas, J. M. (2020). Coronavirus: Notes on crisis, borders and the future of neoliberalism. *Geographica Helvetica, 75*(4), 431–436. https://doi-org.pbidi.unam.mx:2443/10.5194/gh-75-431-2020

Asada, T., & Yoshida, H. (2001). Stability, instability and complex behavior in macrodynamic models with policy lag. *Discrete Dynamics in Nature and Society, 5*(4), 281–295. https://doi.org/10.1155/S1026022600000583

Casares, M., Moreno, A., & Vázquez, J. (2014). An estimated New-Keynesian model with unemployment as excess supply of labor. *Journal of Macroeconomics, 40*, 338–359. https://doi.org/10.1016/j.jmacro.2014.01.010

Esquivel, G. (2020). Los impactos económicos de la pandemia en México. *Journal of Economic Literature, 17*, 28–44. https://doi.org/10.22201/fe.24488143e.2020.51.543

IMF. (2020, April). *World economic outlook, April 2020: The great lockdown*. International Monetary Fund. https://www.imf.org/en/Publications/WEO/Issues/2020/04/14/weo-april-2020

IMF. (2021, January). *World economic outlook update: Policy support and vaccines expected to lift activity*. International Monetary Fund. https://www.imf.org/en/Publications/WEO/Issues/2021/01/26/2021-world-economic-outlook-update

García, P., & García, Z. R. (2020). *2020: La pandemia del capitalismo global*. Machdohnil Ltd.

Georgieva, K. (2020, March 23). *The great lockdown: Worst economic downturn since the great depression us*. International Monetary Fund. https://www.imf.org/en/News/Articles/2020/03/23/pr2098-imf-managing-director-governmentment-following-a-g20-ministerial-call-on-the-coronavirus-emergency

Gori, L., Guerrini, L., & Sodini, M. (2018). Disequilibrium dynamics in a Keynesian model with time delays. *Communications in Nonlinear Science and Numerical Simulation, 58*, 119–130. https://doi.org/10.1016/j.cnsns.2017.06.014

Guillén, R. A. (2020). La economía mexicana en el marco de la pandemia y de la crisis económica global. In P. C. Medel, N. A. Rodríguez, B. G. Jiménez, & R. R. R. Martínez (Eds.), *México ante el COVID-19: acciones y retos* (pp. 215–224). Consejo Nacional Editorial de la H. Cámara de Diputados.

Hayek, F. A. (1960). *The constitution of liberty*. Chicago: University of Chicago Press.

Hevia, C., & Neumeyer, A. (2020). *Un marco conceptual para analizar el impacto económico del COVID-19 y sus repercusiones en las políticas*. Universidad Torcuato Di Tella. Serie de documentos de política pública. PNUD LAC C19 PDS No. 1. https://www.latinamerica.undp.org/content/rblac/es/home/library/crisis_prevention_and_recovery/a-conceptual-framework-for-analyzing-the-economic-impact-of-covi.html

Kalcheva, I., Smith, J. K., & Smith, R. L. (2020). Institutional investment and the changing role of public equity markets: International evidence. *Journal of Corporate Finance, 64*. https://doi.org/10.1016/j.jcorpfin.2016.06.007

Keynes, J. (1978). *The collected writings of John Maynard Keynes (the collected writings of John Maynard Keynes)* In. E. Johnson & D. Moggridge (Eds.), Royal Economic Society. https://doi.org/10.1017/UPO9781139524261

Llorente-González, L. J., & Vence, X. (2020). How labour-intensive is the circular economy? A policy-orientated structural analysis of the repair, reuse and recycling activities in the European Union. *Resources, Conservation and Recycling, 162*. https://doi.org/10.1016/j.resconrec.2020.105033

Marinova, N. (2015). The problems of unifying the conditions of competition in the European Union. In *Eleventh international scientific conference of young scientists*. UNWE, Sofia, Bulgaria.

Mendoza, A. (2016). Financiarización y ganancias de corporaciones en México. *Ola Financiera*, 5(3), 161–192. ISSN 1870–1442. http://www.revistas.unam.mx/index.php/ROF/article/view/23068/21877

Moreno-Brid, J. C. (2020). Pandemia, política pública y panorama de la economía mexicana en 2020. *Journal of Economic Literature*, 17(51). http://revistaeconomia.unam.mx/index.php/ecu/article/view/569/602

Naimzada, A., & Pireddu, M. (2014). Dynamics in a nonlinear keynesian good market model Chaos. *DEMS Working Paper Series*, 24(1), 1–21. https://doi.org/10.1063/1.4870015

Petrović, P., Arsić, M., & Nojković, A. (2021). Increasing public investment can be an effective policy in bad times: Evidence from emerging EU economies. *Economic Modelling*, 94(1), 580–597. https://doi.org/10.1016/j.econmod.2020.02.004

Rodríguez-Moreno, E. L. (2015). Intervención Del Estado en El Sector Financiero. *Principia Iuris*, 12(24), 109–125. http://revistas.ustatunja.edu.co/index.php/piuris/article/view/1081

Srinivasan P. (2013). Causality between public expenditure and economic growth: The Indian case. *International Journal of Economics and Management*, 7(2), 335–347. https://papers.ssrn.com/sol3/papers.cfm?abstract_id=2376143

Steinkamp, S., & Westermann, F. (2018). Systemic crisis and growth revisited: Has the global financial crisis marked a new era? *Economics Letters*, 170, 50–54. https://doi.org/10.1016/j.econlet.2018.05.032

Stiglitz, J. (2013). The price of inequality. *New Perspectives Quarterly*, 30, 52–53. https://doi.org/10.1111/npqu.11358

Stoyanova, D. (2019). The need for state intervention in the economy and in particular in the agricultural sector—Arguments for and against. *Trakia Journal of Sciences*, 17(Supplement 1), 440–444. https://doi-org.pbidi.unam.mx:2443/10.15547/tjs.2019.s.01.071

Trichet, J. C. (2007). Welcoming remarks. In European Central Bank: Simulating financial instability. In *Conference on stress testing and financial crisis simulation exercises*. Frankfurt am Main, July 12–13, 2007, pp. 16–18. https://www.ecb.europa.eu/pub/pdf/other/simulatingfinancialinstability200809en.pdf?f6427026bcf400e849ff88415b1386ba

United Nations. (2020). *Nuevos datos revelan enormes diferencias entre los países para enfrentar y recuperarse de la crisis de COVID-19*. México. https://www.onu.org.mx/nuevos-datos-revelan-enormes-diferencias-entre-los-paises-para-enfrentar-y-recuperarse-de-la-crisis-de-covid-19/

CHAPTER 3

Perspectives for Recovery of VAT Collection Derived from Imports of Goods

Javier Moreno Espinosa and Leovardo Mata Mata

INTRODUCTION

In Mexico, public finances have Value-Added Tax (VAT) as the second source of income. From 2010 to 2020, VAT collection had an average share of 34.1% concerning the Federal Government's tax revenues. By 2020, tax revenues reached 3 trillion 338.9 billion current pesos, representing 14.5% of the proportion of the gross domestic product (GDP); on the other hand, VAT at current pesos was equivalent to 4.2% of GDP (SAT, 2020). The uncertainty experienced in 2019, which worsened

J. M. Espinosa
Facultad de Ciencias Económicas y Empresariales, Universidad Panamericana, Mexico City, Mexico
e-mail: jmorenoe@up.edu.mx

L. M. Mata (✉)
Facultad de Economía y Negocios, Universidad Anáhuac, Mexico City, Mexico
e-mail: leovardo.mata@anahuac.mx

© The Author(s), under exclusive license to Springer Nature Switzerland AG 2022
A. M. López-Fernández and A. Terán-Bustamante (eds.), *Business Recovery in Emerging Markets*, Palgrave Studies in Democracy, Innovation, and Entrepreneurship for Growth,
https://doi.org/10.1007/978-3-030-91532-2_3

throughout 2020, had clear effects on different sectors in the economy, such as: information, agriculture, energy, communications, among others; public finance and tax collection were no exception, of course, and were also affected by this uneasiness. Under these circumstances, the main goal of the book is to analyze how different sectors and industries have bounced back, are in the process of doing so or have failed to restore their pre-pandemic operational levels. To this end, determining the elasticity of tax collection, our government's second source of income facing capital, intermediate and final consumption goods is truly relevant because it will enable us to identify the degree of dependence on VAT facing imports' behavior in a ten-year period, specifically 2020, with the aim of determining if VAT income is currently at pre-pandemic levels or well below them.

Studies published by the Tax Administration Service (SAT) on tax evasion allow the assertion that in the case of VAT, there is no consensus among researchers on the trend of the evasion rate; some studies state that the evasion rate shows a downward trend while others, working with different methodologies and in different periods of time, mention that, on the contrary, this rate shows an upward trend. The Instituto Tecnológico y de Estudios Superiores de Monterrey (Fuentes, 2009) estimated that the VAT evasion rate showed a tendency to decrease from 23.22% in 2000 to 17.77% in 2008, which meant a decrease of 5.45% points. When comparing evasion with GDP, the study estimated that it represents just under a one percentage decreasing point of the GDP. In 2000, the proportion was 0.97%, while in 2008, the ratio was 0.81%. The behavior of both the potential VAT and the VAT collected explained the estimated evasion. Observed VAT collection stood at 3.19% of GDP in 2000 and 3.74% in 2008. The maximum VAT collected back then was limited by the existing special treatments and by the non-causation of VAT on some goods and services. Another study (Fuentes, 2013) found that the VAT evasion rate showed a downward trend from 34.88% in 2004 to 24.28% in 2012, decreasing more than ten percentage points. When comparing evasion as a proportion of GDP, the latter represented a figure close to 1.5% in the period 2004–2012, since at the beginning of this period it registered the figure of 1.76% while in 2012 it decreased to 1.20%.

In its 2017 Global Evasion study, The University of the Americas (San Martín, 2017) established that the evasion rate showed a downward trend from 2005 to 2016, moving from 33.6 to 16.4%. Consequently, the amount of uncollected tax was equivalent to 161,228.7 million current pesos (MCP) in 2005 and 188,589.4 MCP in 2016. Both events represented an evasion equivalent to 1.7% of the GDP in 2005, and 1.0% in 2016, respectively. According to the National Autonomous University of Mexico (UNAM, 2019), VAT evasion, in addition to the tax authority's estimates, went from 40,097.2 million pesos (MCP) in 2015 to 77,318.6 MCP in 2018; during this period, the annual average was 60,605.0 MCP, showing a clear upward trend.

The review of VAT evasion studies showed that VAT collection has not exceeded the threshold of 4% as a proportion of GDP at constant prices (Moreno, 2019). Since the rate of evasion has shown both downward and upward trends, no consensus has been reached as to which trend predominates. However, different sources clearly concur that the proportion of VAT evasion as a percentage of GDP is between 1 and 2% points. Given that the total VAT collection during 2020 amounted to 987,252 MCP, of which 60% stemmed from foreign trade operations, specifically from imports of goods and services, it is advisable to estimate the sensitivity of VAT collection for foreign trade concerning imports by type of good. Thus, measuring intermediate goods (IG), final consumption goods (FG), and capital goods (CG) will allow calculating the sensitivity in the collection of VAT for foreign trade in order to improve forecasts on the behavior of imports.

This chapter is structured as follows: Section I briefly explains the customs legislation and the VAT Law that regulates foreign trade operations, a regulatory framework that allows establishing the direct relationship between imports of goods and services, and the collection of VAT for foreign trade. In addition, there is also a brief explanation of the behavior of VAT collection for foreign trade and imports by type of good. Section II describes the data used in this investigation, which covers the period from 2010 to 2020, supported by monthly information and estimates the sensitivity of VAT collection for foreign trade concerning imports of intermediate, final consumption and capital goods. Finally, our conclusions are submitted at the end.

VAT Collection for Foreign Trade and Imports by Type of Good

According to the Brussels Cooperation Council, customs regime is understood as the destination that goods subject to customs control may have; therefore, selecting individuals for a customs procedure requires compliance with the various customs obligations specific to each procedure (Cisneros, 2019). The Customs Law (CL) states that goods that are introduced into or removed from the national territory may be assigned to a customs procedure of the following: (a) definitive, (b) temporary, (c) tax warehouse, (d) transit of goods, (e) elaborating, processing or repairing in a controlled area, and (f) strategic controlled area (Ponce de León, 2021).

Specifically, the CL defines the definitive import regime as the entry of goods of foreign origin to national territory, remaining for an unlimited period of time. In accordance with this definition, it can be stated that the obligation to pay contributions is generated by the entry of goods which will remain on national territory for an unlimited time (Ponce de León, 2021). With regard to the temporary imports procedure, it is defined by the CL as the entry of goods to national territory with the aim of remaining in it for a limited time and having a specific purpose; in this regime, neither taxes on foreign trade, nor the Value-Added Tax will be paid, with the exception of IMMEX[1] companies, which are exempted from this benefit.

The VAT Law states that those subject to the payment of VAT are natural and legal persons who, on national territory, carry out the following acts or activities: they dispose of goods, provide independent services, grant the temporary use or enjoyment of goods, and import goods or services (López, 2021). From the definition of the liable parties obliged to pay VAT, it follows that the import of goods is subject to payment of this tax, a legal obligation that results from the causality in tax collection for the import of goods or services that is made on national territory (López, 2021). The VAT Law considers that the import

---

[1] Decree for the Promotion of the Manufacturing, Maquiladora and Export Services Industry, published on November 1, 2006, which allows the temporary import of goods to be used in an industrial or service process intended for elaborating, processing or repairing goods of foreign origin temporarily imported for export or for the provision of export services, without covering the payment of general import tax, value-added tax and, where appropriate, countervailing duties, reformed in 2013 to modify profits.

of goods or services occurs when goods are introduced into national territory. Importation takes place when the goods are destined for temporary import customs procedures, for elaborating, processing or repairing in maquila or export programs; tax warehouse to undergo the process of assembly and manufacture of vehicle export programs, transformation or repair of supervised enclosure and strategic controlled enclosure (López, 2021).

Importation also takes place when people who reside in national territory acquire intangible assets which are alienated by persons resident in some other country; the temporary use or enjoyment, in national territory, of intangible assets provided by persons not resident in the country; the temporary use or enjoyment, in national territory, of tangible goods whose delivery was made abroad; the use of independent services in national territory when they are provided by non-residents of the country, except for international transport; when a certain good temporarily exported returns to its country of origin having added value by repair abroad, attachments or any other concept involving additional value (López, 2021). Exempt imports shall be those which, in terms of customs legislation, are not consummated, are temporary, have the character of return of goods temporarily exported, or are subject to transit or transshipment, with some exceptions (López, 2021).

Normally, VAT must be paid on imports except in the following cases: those which, in terms of customs legislation, are not consummated, are temporary, have the character of return of goods temporarily exported, or are subject to transit or transshipment. This exemption shall not apply when goods are put under temporary import customs procedures for working, processing or repair in maquila or export programs; tax warehouse to undergo the process of assembly and manufacture of vehicles; of elaboration, transformation, or repair in a supervised enclosure and strategic supervised enclosure (López, 2021). From these definitions and obligations established in customs legislation and the VAT Law, it follows that the behavior of imports has a significant impact on VAT collection and that there is a direct link between imports of goods and the collection of VAT on foreign trade.

The main argument for studying VAT collection behavior derives from the definition of the Economy's Gross Value Added, which includes the added value of all resident economic units plus taxes on products (less subsidies on products); that is, aggregate production at basic prices minus intermediate consumption valued at buyer prices, plus taxes minus subsidies on products. This implies that the value added should be related in a constant proportion to the VAT; however, since there are differentiated rates, zero rate, and exemptions, the basic theoretical concept is not fulfilled and the distortions generated by the current VAT tax structure are a relevant argument to carry out a sectorial analysis of the tax, through the calculation of VAT collection elasticities with respect to the type of goods that are imported (intermediate, final consumption or capital), in order to identify their contribution to indirect tax collection and their participation in the gross added value of an economy (Moreno, 2019).

The economic relevance of this tax is fundamentally due to the fact that it represents the second source of tax revenue of the Mexican Public Treasury. Although it was established in 1980, its tax collection has not exceeded 4% as a proportion of GDP, at constant pesos, even though changes have been made in the tax rate (Moreno, 2019). From 2010 to 2020, total VAT collection represented on average 34% of the Federal Government's tax revenues; in 2020, the total VAT reached the figure of 987,525 MCP, which meant a share of 29.6% of the total tax revenue. In the same period, VAT on foreign trade, generated mainly by imports, represented 62% of the total VAT collected. In 2020, VAT collection for foreign trade amounted to 594,364 MDP, representing 60% of the total VAT collected (SAT, 2021).

Econometric Analysis

The Data

The monthly time series for the collection of VAT on foreign trade and imports by type of good [intermediate consumer goods (I.G), final consumer goods (F.G), and capital goods (C.G)] are official figures obtained from the open data portal of the Tax Administration Service (SAT) and the Economic Information Bank (BIE) of the National Institute of Statistics and Geography (INEGI). The values of imports remained in millions of dollars. The collection of VAT on foreign trade operations was converted to millions of U.S. dollars at the exchange rate to settle obligations in foreign currency published by the Bank of Mexico.

In the figure, you can see the close relation between imports by type of good and VAT collection generated by foreign trade operations; you can also note the seasonal behavior of the figures, which is why they were seasonally adjusted through the Census X12-ARIMA procedure. In Fig. 3.1, the positive relation and upward trend between VAT collection and intermediate goods imports is shown, with the exception of year 2020; imports of these goods represented 76% of all goods during the period 2010–2020 in average. Even though intermediate goods are very relevant in terms of value, import wise, customs legislation establishes some exemptions in tax payment which could lessen their impact on VAT collection.

In Fig. 3.1, the positive relation between VAT collection and final consumption goods imports can be seen as well; imports of these goods represented 14% of total imports in average during the time studied in this paper. However, in spite of the fact that they rank second place in value terms, it is estimated that their impact on VAT collection is relevant because customs legislation clearly states that all final consumption goods imports must pay VAT without exceptions.

A positive relation between VAT collection and imports of capital goods is clearly shown as well in Fig. 3.1; imports of these goods represented 10% of total imports on average for the ten-year period analyzed in this paper. These goods rank third place, right after intermediate and final consumption goods. Even if their impact might not seem relevant in value terms, their effect on VAT collection could well be significant due to the fact that they represent machinery and equipment coming into national territory, which can be considered as definitive imports that must pay VAT. The Figure shows the direct relation between imports and VAT collection. This relation is best appreciated in 2020 when imports were affected by the phenomenon of COVID-19, which impacted global value chains and caused a decrease in the demand for imported goods in Mexico due to the cutback in national economic activity.

Integration Order and Control Variables

Before making any estimate on the sensitivity of the collection of VAT for foreign trade concerning imports by type of good, it is necessary to know if the time series is stationary, on the one hand, and their order of integration, on the other (Enders, 2014). To this end, the generalized Dickey-Fuller hypothesis tests (DF-GLS), Phillips-Perron (PP) and Kwiatkowski–Phillips–Schmidt–Shin (KPSS) were used in order to verify the stationarity condition of the seasonally adjusted time series, both in levels as well as in first difference. Table 3.1 shows the test results for the

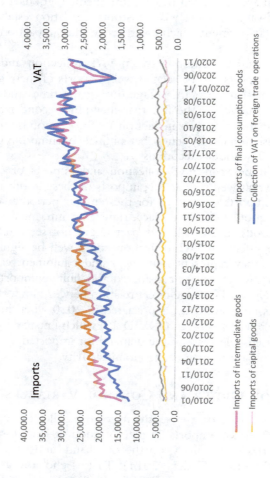

Fig. 3.1 Evolution of VAT on foreign trade and imports of intermediate, final consumption and capital goods (million dollars) (*Source* Own elaboration with data from SAT [2021], INEGI [2021] and BANXICO [2021])

Table 3.1 Unit root test

Variable	Level			First difference		
	DF-GLS	PP	KPSS	DF-GLS	PP	KPSS
ln(IVA)	−2.81	−2.79	0.61***	−15.13***	−16.61***	0.001
ln(BI)	−2.75	−2.71	0.59***	−17.19***	−17.09***	0.011
ln(BF)	−3.18	−3.21	0.66***	−15.71***	−13.32***	0.023
ln(BC)	−3.84	−3.72	0.81***	−13.14***	−18.95***	0.018

Note *, **, ***: 10, 5 and 1% in significance level, respectively
Source Own elaboration with figures from INEGI (2021) and SAT (2021)

time series, both in levels and in first differences.

The results of the DF-GLS tests show that, with a confidence level of 99%, there are not enough elements to reject the existence of a unit root; on the other hand, with a confidence level of 99%, the unit root null hypothesis is rejected for the series in first differences. Therefore, it can be stated that the variables are integrated by order one $I(1)$, while they are not stationary in level since they have unit root, they are stationary in their first difference $I(0)$ (Tsay, 2015).

The relation between the different variables can change over time for different reasons, including regulatory or collection modifications, among others. Therefore, two binary control variables were included in this study: dart24 (to capture the legal change to Article 24 of the VAT Law, which asserts that when goods are introduced into national territory and destined for the customs regimes of temporary importation, this will be considered an import of goods) and dart27 (in order to consider the legal modification to article 27 of the VAT Law, which stipulates the value or taxable base to be taken into account for the import of goods by making an analogy which would correspond to the disposal of goods, use or enjoyment of goods or provision of services, in national territory, as the case may be).

$$\text{dart24} = \begin{cases} 1 & \text{if the observation is to be found in the period 2014–2020} \\ 0 & \text{other case} \end{cases}$$

Similarly, a dichotomous variable is added to consider the recent impact of the pandemic due to COVID-19:

$$\text{covid19} = \begin{cases} 1 & \text{if the observation is to be found in the year } 2020-2021 \\ 0 & \text{other case} \end{cases}$$

In this sense and in order to estimate this cointegration relation in a sturdy way, the likely structural change captured by *COVID-19*, based on Andrews and Ploberger (1994) and Zivot and Andrews (1992), was analyzed. The findings of these authors estimate an endogenous rupture under different specifications, where the null hypothesis states that the time series has no structural change. Andrews and Ploberger (1994) carried out the hypothesis test on a time window $[T_1, T_2]$, assuming that there is a structural change. Then they looked for evidence to prove the rejection of H_0 through a sequence of chi-squared estimators $\chi^{2(1)}, \chi^{2(2)}, \ldots, \chi^{2(N)}$ which compare data variation in interval partitions. AP statistical testing was used to measure the corresponding p-value.

$$\text{AP} = \log\left[\frac{1}{N}\sum_{i=1}^{N} e^{\frac{1}{2}\chi^{2(i)}}\right]$$

In contrast, the Zivot and Andrews (1992) test poses as null hypothesis the existence of unit root with trailing and provides as alternative hypothesis the presence of stationary processes with tendency ruptures. In other words, it searches for the unknown sequential rupture, be it as an interception or a tendency or both. This procedure consists in estimating equations by least squares generalized in a sequential mode, with the aim of verifying if there actually is a structural change in the deseasonalized time series ln(IVA) with regard to the window of time.

In Table 3.2, the results of the hypothesis tests for VAT's natural logarithm are shown. It can be seen that there are structural changes in the tendency and an intercept in the time series from March to June 2020, because the p-value in brackets is lower than the significance levels. In this case, the point average effect of these structural changes can be captured by the binary variable *COVID-19* in the window of time 2020–2021, as suggested by Joyeux (2001) for this intercept and slope break scenarios.

The following section shows the results for the model specification based on the information available.

Table 3.2 Andrews-Ploberger and Zivot-Andrews tests

Variable	Andrews-Ploberger			Zivot-Andrews		
	Intercept	Slope	Both	Intercept	Slope	Both
ln(VAT)	2020/2003*** 2020/2006*** (34.65)[0.009]	2020/2003*** 2020/2006*** (21.52)[0.000]	2020/2003*** 2020/2006*** (36.67)[0.000]	2020/2003* 2020/2006* (−4.42)[0.067]	2020/2003* 2020/2006* (−4.54)[0.059]	2020/2003* 2020/2006* (−4.87)[0.097]

Note *, **, ***: 10, 5 and 1% in significance level
Source Own elaboration with figures from INEGI (2021) and SAT (2021)

Estimates and Results

In the previous section, unit root testing on time series in levels and first difference was carried out. These tests yielded evidence suggesting that these variables constitute built-in series of order one. In this case, there are several procedures to estimate long-term elasticities. An outstanding one is the Autoregressive Distributed Lag (ARDL) Model and the Vector Error Correction (VEC) Model (Tsay, 2015). In this study, long-term elasticities are estimated using a VEC model. This specification considers the cointegration relations between variables (Hamilton, 2000). The specification has also been considered because it allows pondering multiple cointegration relations under different specifications in the Johansen test (Lütkepohl, 2013). Specifically, the long-term relation is defined as a logarithmic, linear equation that seeks to estimate the response elasticities:

$$\ln(\text{VAT}_t) = \beta_0 + \beta_1 \ln(\text{IG}_t) + \beta_2 \ln(\text{FG}_t) + \beta_3 \ln(\text{CG}_t) + u_t$$

where:

- $\ln(\text{VAT}_t)$ it is the natural logarithm of VAT collection derived from foreign trade operations in millions of dollars;
- $\ln(\text{IG}_t)$ it is the natural logarithm of imports of intermediate consumer goods, in millions of dollars;
- $\ln(\text{FG}_t)$ is the natural logarithm of imports of final consumer goods, in millions of dollars;
- $\ln(\text{CG}_t)$ is the natural logarithm of imports of capital goods, in millions of dollars;
- u_t is the random perturbation.

The specification of the VEC model (Enders, 2014) is given by:

$$\Delta Y_t = \sum_{k=1}^{m} \beta_k \Delta Y_{t-k} + \sum_{k=1}^{m} \gamma_k X_k + \sum_{k=1}^{n} \text{MCE}_k + u_t$$

where Y_t is a 4×1 size vector containing the following variables $\ln(\text{VAT}_t)$, $\ln(\text{IG}_t)$, $\ln(\text{FG}_t)$, $\ln(\text{CG}_t)$; X_k is an exogenous variables vector (covid19, dart24, and dart27), MCE_k stands for the error correction terms, and finally u_t is a vector of random disturbance having the same dimension as Y_t. In order to estimate the VEC model, the number of optimal lags was determined using the Akaike (AIC), Schwarz (BIC), and Hanna-Quinn (HQIC) information criteria which correspond to the implicit VAR specification. In this case, the number of lags is one determined by the minimum criteria of the BIC and HQIC test.

Given the number of optimal lags, Johannsen's test was carried out in order to verify the cointegration and find the number of cointegration vectors to be considered within the VEC model (Tsay, 2015). Table 3.3 shows the trace test results and the maximum eigenvalue; there is evidence of two or three cointegration relations. In this case, the estimates were made with two and three cointegration vectors. The model whose Schwarz information criterion was smaller, was chosen, corresponding to the linear trend case with three cointegration relations.

Based on the results of Johansen's test, there is evidence to assert that the variables $\ln(VAT_t)$, $\ln(IG_t)$, $\ln(FG_t)$ and $\ln(CG_t)$ are cointegrated, which implies a long-term equilibrium relation under a common trend. Furthermore, if the cointegration vector concerning $\ln(VAT_t)$ is normalized, long-term elasticities can be obtained, as depicted in the following equation:

$$\ln(IVA_t) = 2.57 + 0.381 \ln(IG_t) + 0.606 \ln(FG_t) + 0.362 \ln(CG_t)$$

In this case, the elasticities have a positive sign and are inelastic (less than the unit). Specifically, if the consumption of intermediate goods increases

Table 3.3 Johansen test

Specification		None	None	Linear	Linear	Quadratic
		No intercept No trend	Intercept No trend	Intercept No trend	Intercept Trend	Intercept Trend
Test type	Rank					
Trace/maximum eigenvalue	0	87.813	143.501	134.662	163.961	152.361
	1	31.167	65.861	79.028	74.049	73.592
	2	4.739*	22.319	24.458	26.087	25.589
	3	0.351	1.99*	4.189*	5.758*	5.066
	4	0.279	1.298	3.287	2.128	4.017

Note *Indicates the number of cointegration ratios
Source Own elaboration with figures from INEGI (2021) and SAT (2021)

by 1%, then VAT collection rises to 0.38%. Similarly, there are 0.61 and 0.36% increases for final consumer goods and capital goods, respectively.

Considering that intermediate goods are raw materials in primary or semi-finished state, with which final goods—final consumption and capital goods—will be manufactured, it can be implied that the global demand on final goods determines a certain growth rate in intermediate goods; hence, the demand for intermediate goods will not depend exclusively on the internal market but also on the economy's ability to import. The main feature of intermediate goods is that a part of them is destined for the manufacture of consumer goods, others for the production of capital goods and others for the elaboration of such intermediate goods. In most cases, a single intermediate good is simultaneously used in the three ways mentioned above, or at least in two of them. This fact poses a classification problem when it comes to differentiating the uses ascribed to a given intermediate good. Due to the relevance of these type of goods, analyzing imports' behavior given a certain level in final demand, is deemed necessary because it determines to a large extent the structure supporting domestic production of final and intermediate goods (CEPAL, 1957).

This way, the import of intermediate goods has effects on the structure of production and this, in turn, on VAT collection, whereby estimating the sensitivity of VAT collection facing the import of intermediate goods is so relevant. During the 10 years analyzed in this paper, imports of these goods represented 76% of total imports, a very high percentage when compared to capital and final consumption goods. Nonetheless, the effect of this type of goods on VAT collection is lower than the one estimated for final consumption and capital goods. In other words, a 1% increase in imports corresponds to a 0.38% increase in VAT collection. This result allows us to assert that the import of intermediate goods is achieved through customs procedures which do not contribute to VAT collection, because they are integrated to the production of final consumption or capital goods.

In contrast, in spite of only representing 14% of total imports during the aforementioned 10 year-period, the import of final consumption goods has an effect on VAT collection which is 1.59 times higher than that of intermediate goods. Thus, a 1% increase in imports value for final consumption goods would mean a 0.606% increase in VAT collection. This result concurs with the definitions by law, which state that all definitive imports on final consumption goods must pay VAT. Therefore, a strategy to increase indirect VAT collection would be the tax audit of tariff items that register definitive imports of final consumption goods.

Capital goods, understood as the machinery and equipment used in the processes of production, can be imported under customs regimes which imply VAT payment or in those cases where machinery is brought into national territory temporarily and must not necessarily pay this tax. This way, the elasticity obtained under the proposed model is low for capital goods, with only 10% of total imports, it reaches a sensitivity of 0.362, similar to the one obtained for the import of intermediate goods, whose elasticity is also low.

It is important to point out that the dummy variables that seek to capture the modifications to Articles 24 and 27 of the VAT Law in its 2013 and 2016 reforms are not significant. However, they reflect important changes in the regulatory framework on imports and VAT collection. In contrast, the variable associated with the COVID-19 pandemic is significant and has a negative coefficient.

Moreover, if the elasticities were estimated during the pandemic using the VEC model, it will be observed that the elasticities decrease, on average, 14.13%. Specifically, the elasticities under the COVID-19 period are 0.313 for intermediate goods, 0.332 for capital goods, and 0.506 for final consumer goods; this means that, during the year of the pandemic and in the face of an imports increase of 1%, tax collection was much lower than estimated throughout the entire study period. This result is consistent with those obtained through the structural change tests developed by Andrews and Ploberger (1994) and Zivot and Andrews (1992), while supporting our estimates on the binary variable *COVID-19*.

Conclusions

In this document, a VEC model was estimated to determine the elasticity of value-added tax collection resulting from foreign trade operations based on imports' transactions for capital goods, intermediate goods, and final consumption. For this purpose, the effect of COVID-19 in 2020 and the amendments to Articles 24 and 27 of the VAT Law were considered. Results indicate an inelastic relation, where final consumer goods stand out with 0.606%, followed by intermediate goods at 0.381%, and capital goods at 0.362%. It should be duly noted that the impact on the collection of VAT for foreign trade in the face of imports' transactions of consumer goods is lower; that is, an increase in consumer goods' imports sharply rises VAT collection to a (0.606%) proportion, a sensitivity that can be explained by the fact that these are final consumer goods which are commonly manufactured using definitive imports. Finally, focusing on the recent time period and due to COVID-19, a clear reduction in the corresponding elasticities was found: 14.13%, on average.

From the point of view of a sectorial analysis of the public finances of the Mexican economy, specifically of the collection of the second source of Mexican tax revenue, the obtained results in this research paper clearly shows that the relation between the import of goods and VAT collection is inelastic. This means that sensitivity is higher than zero but lower than one, which implies that when there is a percentage increase in the import of goods, the rise in VAT collection due to foreign trade operations will be lower in proportion.

This result is relevant because VAT collection derived from foreign trade operations represented approximately 62% in the 2010-2020 period, as VAT collection presents an inelastic elasticity with respect to goods' import (intermediate, of consumption and capital) it cannot be concluded that through imports of goods the recovery of the collection of this tax is expected in the short term; therefore, the recovery of indirect tax revenue collection must come from internal consumption in the Mexican economy. The increase in recovery should be carried out by strengthening internal audits and foreign trade operations' audits, specifically imports of intermediate goods, since upon entering the country with the promise of integrating into a final good and therefore not being subject to the payment of VAT, the incentive to change the regime to sell these products in the national market is significant and through these operations it is possible to contribute to tax evasion.

As mentioned in previous paragraphs, indirect taxes are a component of the gross added value of the economy, in the absence of distortions (differentiated rates, zero rate or exemptions) their participation would be a constant that makes up the added value; however, in the Mexican economy this theoretical concept is not fulfilled, therefore, it is relevant to determine the magnitude in which the different sectors contribute to the growth of the gross added value of the economy, in this case the imports of goods that, as the results show its contribution to the VAT recovery is less than proportional as it shows inelastic elasticity.

References

Andrews, D. W., & Ploberger, W. (1994). Optimal tests when a nuisance parameter is present only under the alternative. *Econometrica: Journal of the Econometric Society*, 1383–1414.

BANXICO. (2021). Tipo de cambio promedio del periodo (CF86) para solventar obligaciones pagaderas en moneda extranjera, Sistema de Información Económica. Retrieved April 23, 2021 from Banco de México: https://www.banxico.org.mx/SieInternet/consultarDirectorioInternetAction.do?accion=consultarCuadro&idCuadro=CF86&locale=es

Cisneros, J. R. (2019). *Derecho Aduanero Mexicano* (Tercera edición ed.). Ciudad de México: Editorial Porrúa.

CEPAL. (1957). *El desequilibrio externo en el desarrollo económico latinoamericano, El caso de México*. Comisión Económica para América Latina, Consejo Económico y Social, Séptimo periodo de sesiones. Retrieved July 23, 2021 from: https://repositorio.cepal.org›handle›S5700476_es.

Enders, W. (2014). *Applied econometric time series* (2nd ed.). Wiley.

Fuentes, H. (2009). *Evasión Global de Impuestos: Impuesto sobre la renta, Impuesto al Valor Agregado e Impuesto Especial sobre Producción y Servicio no Petrolero, Instituto Tecnológico y de Estudios Superiores de Monterrey, Servicio de Administración Tributaria*. Retrieved April 30, 2021 from: http://omawww.sat.gob.mx/cifras_sat/Documents/2009_eva_glob_imp_isr_iva_ieps.pdf

Fuentes, H. (2013). *Estudio de Evasión Global de Impuestos, Instituto Tecnológico y de Estudios Superiores de Monterrey, Campus Ciudad de México, Servicio de Administración Tributaria*. Retrieved April 30, 2021 from: http://omawwww.sat.gob.mx/cifras_sat/Documents/Evasion%20Global%20de%20Impuestos.pdf

Hamilton, J. (2000). *Time series analysis*. Princeton University Press.

INEGI. (2021). *Valor de las importaciones por tipo de bien, bienes de uso intermedio, Banco de Información Económica (BIE), Instituto Nacional de Estadística y Geografía*. Retrieved April 23, 2021 from: https://www.inegi.org.mx/app/indicadores/?tm=0#divFV33865

Joyeux, R. (2001). *How to deal with structural breaks in practical cointegration analysis* (Vol. 112). Macquarie University, Department of Economics.

López, J. (2021). *Ley del Impuesto al Valor Agregado, last reform published DOF 23 April 2021, Servicio de Administración Tributaria*. Retrieved April 23, 2021 from: https://www.sat.gob.mx/personas/normatividad

Lütkepohl, H. (2013). *Introduction to multiple time series analysis*. Springer Science & Business Media.

Moreno, J. (2019). *Impuesto al Valor Agregado: Variables que condicionan su recaudación* (U. A. Norte, Ed.) Ciudad de México. Retrieved March 30, 2021 from: https://anahuac.primo.exlibrisgroup.com/discovery/fulldi

splay?docid=alma993734079005016&context=L&vid=52ANAHUAC_INST:UAMX&lang=es&adaptor=Local%20Search%20Engine

Ponce de León, E. (2021). *Ley Aduanera, last reform published DOF 6 November 2020, Servicio de Administración Tributaria.* Retrieved April 23, 2021 from: https://www.sat.gob.mx/personas/normatividad

SAT. (2020). *Informe Tributario y de Gestión, cuarto trimestre 2020, Servicio de Administración Tributaria.* Retrieved April 23, 2021 from: http://omawww.sat.gob.mx/cifras_sat/Documents/ITG_2020_4T.pdf

SAT. (2021). *Recaudación por operaciones de comercio exterior, datos abiertos, Servicio de Administración Tributaria.* Retrieved April 23, 2021from: http://omawww.sat.gob.mx/cifras_sat/Paginas/datos/vinculo.html?page=RecDerImp.html

Tsay, R. (2015). *Analysis of financial time series* (2nd ed.). Wiley.

San Martín, J. (2017). *Evasión Global 2017. Universidad de las Américas Puebla. Servicio de Administración Tributaria.* Retrieved April 30, 2021 from: http://omawww.sat.gob.mx/cifras_sat/Documents/Evasi%C3%B3n%20Global%202017.pdf

UNAM. (2019). *Evasión en IVA: análisis de redes, Servicio de Administración Tributaria.* Retrieved April 30, 2021 from: http://omawww.sat.gob.mx/cifras_sat/Documents/Evasi%C3%B3nenIVA_An%C3%A1lisisdeRedes.pdf

Zivot, E., & Andrews, D. W. K. (1992). Further evidence on the great crash, the oil-price shock, and the unit-root hypothesis. *Journal of Business and Economic Statistics., 10*(3), 251–270.

CHAPTER 4

Public Policy for the Application of 5G in Mexico Within a Context of COVID-19

José Luis Solleiro, Rosario Castañón, David Guillén, and Norma Solís

INTRODUCTION

The most recent generation in the evolution of standardized specifications for mobile communication (technologies, network design, standards,

J. L. Solleiro (✉) · R. Castañón · N. Solís
Universidad Nacional Autónoma de México, Mexico City, Mexico
e-mail: solleiro@unam.mx

R. Castañón
e-mail: rosarioc@unam.mx

D. Guillén
CamBioTec A.C, Mexico City, Mexico
e-mail: d.guillen@cambiotec.org.mx

© The Author(s), under exclusive license to Springer Nature Switzerland AG 2022
A. M. López-Fernández and A. Terán-Bustamante (eds.), *Business Recovery in Emerging Markets*, Palgrave Studies in Democracy, Innovation, and Entrepreneurship for Growth,
https://doi.org/10.1007/978-3-030-91532-2_4

among others) is the so-called 5G network (ITU, 2019). The characteristics of 5G networks allow the enabling of relevant and unpublished products and services to this day; many of them for critical applications, for example: high transfer speed (enhanced mobile broadband or eMBB) applications in augmented and virtual reality, systems of massive machine communications (mMTC) that allow a massive volume of devices to be connected simultaneously (Internet of Things and uses of Internet in industry with a large number of sensors and devices such as streaming video cameras, etc.), as well as ultra-reliable and low latency communications (URLLC) applications that require real-time responses (assisted remote surgery, driverless cars). The transformative impact on businesses derived from 5G technology is such that it is considered essential for the fourth industrial revolution (I4.0) since it is at the center of digital transformation as it is the main channel through which people communicate with each other and access the Internet and online applications (GSMA, 2019).

Since the beginning of 2020, the world has faced an unprecedented crisis, derived from the COVID-19 pandemic, which has made it clear that technology and innovation are necessary to overcome problems in the most diverse areas: education, health care, productive systems, etc. The pandemic highlighted the need to improve connectivity to access more and better services at all levels (from the individual to large organizations). Just to cite one example, it is estimated that data traffic increased by 50% in just a couple of weeks after the pandemic began (Swain et al., 2020).

Data traffic not only occurred in large cities but also in suburbs and rural areas; and the largest share of traffic was absorbed by the residential fixed network (Saldaña et al., 2021). Greater connectivity implies a greater demand for bandwidth and solving the problems associated with a higher response speed. These situations will encourage worldwide efforts to deploy 5G-related technologies sooner than expected.

Mexico, as the rest of the world, has been facing many healthcare, economic, and societal challenges due to the COVID-19 pandemic.[1] Some guidelines to prevent the spread of the virus introduced by the Mexican Government included the following: schools were closed, remote work was promoted, malls and stores were closed, and people

---

[1] By the end of July 2021, Mexico recorded over 2.7 million positive cases and over 239 thousand deaths (JHU, 2021).

were persuaded to stay home. Some of these new routines will stay even if COVID-19 is under control. To face these challenges, new technologies will be developed and implemented. One of them is 5G, which is an enabling technology that fosters innovations in other areas such as Internet of things and artificial intelligence because of its improved characteristics.[2] It provides crucial capabilities to develop solutions to alleviate many pandemic-related problems.

The so-called 5G is the fifth (5) generation (G) of mobile or wireless communication technologies that derive from the evolution of this type of system whose origin dates back to the 1970s (ITU, 2020). 5G is not only proposed as a tool for communication between people, but it goes a step further and is proposed as an instrument for connectivity between machines, in line with the implementation of the Internet of Things. Unlike humans, who can tolerate long waits for data transmission, communication between machines require great speed when carrying out this information transfer (Muñoz et al., 2018, p. 18).

According to the most recent mobility report of Ericsson, around the world "5G subscriptions with a 5G-enabled device grew by 70 million during the first quarter, to around 290 million. We estimate that there will be close to 580 million 5G subscriptions by the end of 2021" (Ericsson, 2021, p.4), in addition to the fact that the trend is notably upward, as observed in Fig. 4.1.

In Latin America, 5G penetration is still incipient, but several countries have already taken various actions to accelerate it. Mexico is not the exception, but it needs to intensify its intervention to overcome different challenges like, for example, that in the matter of fixed broadband speed, Mexico is ranked 75th out of 180 countries (Fig. 4.2).

Swain et al. (2020) estimate that by 2035, the incorporation of 5G in Mexico would allow the generation of US$ 730 billion, mainly through Information and Communication Technologies (ICT) industries (USD 137 billion), manufacturing (USD 134 billion), services (113 billion), retail (75 billion), real estate (52 billion) and construction (51

---

[2] 5G networks target delivering 1000× higher mobile data volume per area, 100× higher number of connected devices, 100× higher user data rate, 10× longer battery life for low-power massive machine communications, and 5× reduced End-to-End (E2E) latency (Siriwardhana et al., 2021).

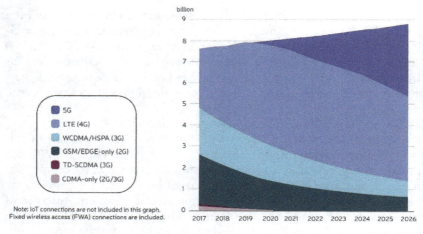

Fig. 4.1 Mobile subscriptions by technology (*Source* Own elaboration with Ericsson [2021, p. 4] information)

billion); and 134 billion in other industries.[3] But realizing these forecasts and obtaining the maximum benefit from this technology requires that Mexico take a more active stance and not limit itself to being a buyer of solutions offered by leading companies.

Main Applications of 5G

Mobile networks are designed to generate a high level of connectivity, for which the data is required to be contextualized, structured, and processed in the cloud, which requires a storage infrastructure with large capacity, transmission equipment, and development of algorithms and software for

---

[3] Different studies that analyze this macroeconomic impact agree that the wide range of solutions that will be developed from 5G will generate employment and outstanding economic value in the coming years. In this sense, the World Economic Forum (WEF) estimates by 2035, the generation of some USD $13.2 billion in economic value and 22.3 million jobs just in the global 5G value chain (WEF, 2020).

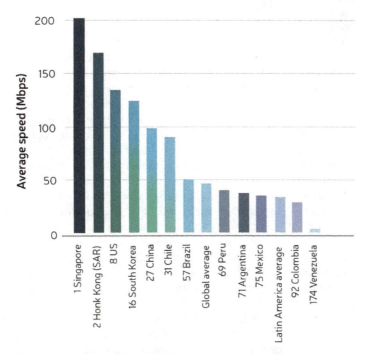

Fig. 4.2 Ranking of average fixed broadband speed in selected countries (*Source* Own elaboration with data from Swain et al. [2020, p. 11])

the treatment of large volumes of data. This platform opens many application options. Huawei (2021) recently prioritized the next top ten, based on market size and the relevance of 5G technologies to those applications.

1. Virtual and augmented reality in the cloud. These are visualization and simulation applications that can have a large benefit in the educational, entertainment, and industrial process simulation sectors.
2. Connectivity in the automotive sector. The introduction of autonomous vehicles, the use of the Internet of Things for remote fleet monitoring, automated systems for fault detection and maintenance, and connectivity between devices represent a revolution in mobility that is just beginning.

3. Smart manufacturing. In this area, applications are multiple and are aimed at increasing productivity, using interconnected robots, production monitoring systems, warehouses, and transportation equipment, data analysis, artificial intelligence, and machine learning to optimize processes and quality analysis using sensors and the Internet of Things.
4. Interconnected energy. Incorporation of renewable sources to the smart grid through the Internet of Things and artificial intelligence, the synergy between sources through interconnected sensors, and optimization of consumption through analysis of large volumes of data (Big data).
5. Electronic health (eHealth) with wireless connections. Intensive use of sensors, artificial intelligence, and the Internet of Things to make remote diagnoses, patient monitoring, and analysis of special epidemiological situations by evaluating large volumes of data.
6. Entertainment with wireless connection. With higher bandwidth, transmission speed and latency are optimized, which opens up great improvements to streaming systems, video games, and higher quality, without the need for a cable connection.
7. Interconnected drones. The use of these devices for professional inspection and security, increasing their precision, the capacity for data and image transmission, communication between drones, and the processing of large volumes of data.
8. Social networks. Sensitive increase in transmission quality and speed with ultra-high definition, with great opportunities for new applications.
9. Personal assistants and wearables with artificial intelligence. Intelligent applications are developed for personal use devices such as work clothes (helmets, safety glasses, etc.) and other devices, taking advantage of the greater information processing capacity, special algorithms, sensors, and connectivity.
10. Smart cities. Intensive use of sensors and wireless video devices for supervision and surveillance of issues such as pollution, traffic, activity in public offices and hospitals, public transport, parking lots.

We can see that a large part of these applications may have a favorable impact on overcoming the health crisis and economic recovery. The objective of this article is to describe the reforms necessary to have a public policy that facilitates the optimal adoption of 5G in Mexico.

Methodology

To identify, for the specific case of Mexico, the key elements to address in terms of public policies for the deployment of 5G, the following methodology has arisen: (1) Review of specialized literature on the subject, as well as reports from different stakeholders (government institutions, companies, autonomous institutes, and researchers) where the status of 5G, its impact on different economic sectors, and the necessary conditions for its adoption and deployment were analyzed. (2) Attendance at specialized events related to the plans for the deployment of 5G in different regions and their implications (Table 4.1).

(3) Interviews. To contrast, the elements collected from literature and specialized events, as well as to give the issue a national dimension, 19 interviews with specialists were conducted. The distribution of these by sector and area of specialization is shown in Fig. 4.3.

And, (4) Organization of a discussion forum in collaboration with the Commission of Science, Technology, and Innovation of the Chamber of Deputies, which aimed to discuss the main measures that the Mexican government should take to have a more adequate participation in this wave of innovation. Deputies, members of the commission, representatives of the telecommunications industry, relevant government entities (Ministry of Communications and Transportation -SCT, for its acronym in Spanish- and IFT), non-governmental organizations, and academics participated in the forum.

Results, Discussion, and Analysis

Based on the consultations made to the specialists, it was concluded that to fully realize the benefits of 5G, laws and policies need to be adjusted, as the scope and quality of 5G services largely depend on governments and regulators allowing timely access to the portion and type of spectrum that is adequate and affordable, under the right conditions (GSMA, 2019).

In the case of Mexico, the starting point for defining a policy should be what is established in Article 6 of the Political Constitution. "The

Table 4.1 Specialized events attended to gather information

Event	Organizer
Date: 2021	
Mexico FTTx Industry Development Strategy Summit	Huawei, Digital Policy and Law
Chile 5G	Digital Policy and Law * The regulatory and public policy authorities of the sector participated
European 5G Conference	Forum Europe * Organized to discuss 5G opportunities
Innovation and digital economy for recovery	Economic Commission for Latin America and the Caribbean (ECLAC), National Telecommunications Association (ANATEL, for its acronym in Spanish) and Huawei
Technology for citizen protection	Digital Policy and Law
The 5G Action Plan Review	Forum Europe * Organized to discuss 5G implementation plans in Europe
Date: 2020	
Challenges of the competition in a digital environment	Federal Institute of Telecommunications (IFT, for its acronym in Spanish), Mexico
Next Generation Networks and 5G Network Perspectives	Federal Telecommunications Institute (IFT)
Prospects of the telecommunications and broadcasting sectors in the economic reactivation of the new normal	IFT
Seventh conference on spectrum management in Latin America	Forum Europe
Neutrality of Mobile Devices	IFT
Forum Neutrality of the network in Mexico. Analysis and debate	IFT
6th Asia–Pacific Spectrum Management conference	Forum Europe

State will guarantee the right of access to information and communication technologies, as well as to broadcasting and telecommunications services, including broadband and internet" (Cámara de Diputados del H. Congreso de la Unión, 1917). This statement clearly defines that access to ICT is an essential condition to guarantee human rights and other constitutional rights (right to education, work, health, culture, security, free movement) to move toward the "digital rights" related to quality connectivity, data protection, privacy, cybersecurity, and digital literacy, among

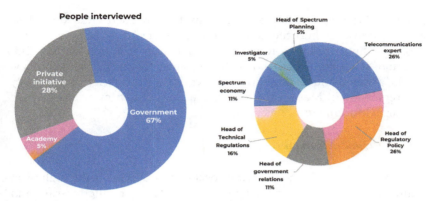

Fig. 4.3 Distribution of the interviewees by the institution of belonging and Distribution of the interviewees by area of knowledge

others. But the policy on the matter does not only imply giving access to the spectrum but also tending to the following elements: spectrum allocation and cost, cybersecurity, infrastructure, digital literacy, investment promotion, promotion of the digital economy and innovation, and protection of health and the environment. Addressing public policies in all these areas is not an easy task, but it is essential to incorporate 5G more effectively in Mexico.

As a result of the interviews, specialists also identified six principles that should govern the issuance of national policy: (i) Enhance the socioeconomic benefit and its wide distribution; (ii) Evidence-based decisions; (iii) Contribute to a competitive development of the industry; (iv) Promotion of innovation with a technology-neutral approach; (v) Evaluation of risks; and (vi) Adherence to the national and international legal framework. They are aimed at using technology to promote the maximum benefit for society, creating conditions for its application in fair and competitive conditions, with a decision-making environment based on the generation of evidence and not on discretionary preferences. In this sense, the law and the policy, as well as the institutions to implement them must remain neutral in terms of the types of technology and its development process. Decisions must be made based on objective performance criteria and guided by the pursuit of the public good and sustainable competitiveness.

Likewise, all the interviews highlighted the fact that a national digital agenda is required that offers the set of high-level objectives in which public policies are framed since at this time Mexico lacks one. This absence translates into the lack of concrete goals to be achieved in the short, medium, and long-term, and even a clear definition on how 2G, 3G, and 4G technologies should be managed to co-exist with the new 5G in a well-planned evolution. The critical elements for a 5G policy and regulation in Mexico based on the analysis of the interviews and the specialized forum are summarized below.

a. *Spectrum access and cost*

The cost of using the radioelectric spectrum in Mexico is the highest in Latin America, which translates into a disincentive for the industry and a high price of the service for the end-user, which can widen the country's digital gap. The Ministry of Finance and Public Credit (SHCP, for its acronym in Spanish) has seen a collection opportunity that generates a perverse incentive. Evidence of this is that, recently, some bands have been returned by operators because the cost of spectrum reduces the competitiveness of the industry. A high price of the spectrum can be a significant obstacle for 5G deployment, which is why consensus was reached in recommending:

- To focus the policy on promoting the use and allocation of spectrum and not on the collection; that is, to license spectrum at values following real market dynamics and not with a collection approach that only contributes to short-term goals at the cost of development goals.
- A long-term broadband development plan must be made public that gives rise to a roadmap for the release of low and medium spectrum bands that allow companies to plan their investments, operations, and benefits derived from the use of the spectrum.
- To offer regulatory clarity regarding the possibility and type of authorization to outsource infrastructure as a business model (secondary spectrum market for small operators).
- To develop a permanent inventory of disused bands and set clear rules regarding what can be done with bands that are out for tender and are not being used.

- To accelerate the bidding processes so that operators can take advantage of them in periods consistent with the dynamics of telecom industry.

b. *Construction of infrastructure*

There is full consensus that an unprecedented deployment of infrastructure is required which can, with current criteria and costs, be profitable in large urban centers, but not in suburbs or rural areas. There is a lack of standardization of the norms for the deployment of telecommunications infrastructure throughout the country (both at the state and municipal level). Therefore, a policy is required that includes the following elements:

- Intensify and offer incentives for government cooperation with the private sector at different levels: Internet and telecommunications service providers; owners and operators of infrastructure and manufacturers of network equipment; and large users of the industrial sector (automotive and aerospace companies e.g.).
- The generation of public–private partnerships should be promoted to generate works with a long-term perspective and a broad regional scope.
- To allow and promote sharing agreements (mainly to deploy passive infrastructure) that provide regulatory clarity to network operators and independent infrastructure providers.
- To facilitate the coexistence of community networks or Wireless Active Server Pages (ASP) that allows the connection of rural communities with adequate quality.
- To promote the national development of low-cost equipment and systems (radio base stations, antennas, etc.).
- To eliminate unnecessary obstacles and charges to the deployment of network infrastructures, simplifying the procedures for concession, granting of permits and facilities to mobilize equipment and workers in the municipalities.
- Homologation and cooperation between municipal, state, and federal governments regarding costs, times, and concession processes in telecommunications matters.
- To increase investment for greater deployment of fiber-optic infrastructure.

c. *Cybersecurity and data protection*

Although the Federal Telecommunications Institute has generated guidelines on this matter, there is still no entity focused on the protection of systems and devices related to networks and software and the data they contain. Given the dynamics of technological change and the exponential increase in data flows, it is necessary to define protocols for the protection of technical infrastructure, procedures and workflows, physical assets, national security, and the confidentiality, integrity, and availability of information (Wiley, 2021).

That is why the great challenges in cybersecurity of 5G demand a review of the current policy framework applicable to the telecommunications sector and its ecosystem, as well as the development of cybersecurity[4] technologies. All this requires, from all the actors involved, especially manufacturers, operators, and government agencies, timely response, and continuous innovations, for which it is recommended:

- To create a legal framework that specifies the powers of surveillance, security, and data protection for:
    - Protection of physical infrastructure.
    - Security protection.
    - Consumer protection against fraud (identity theft, financial fraud, illegitimate collection of confidential data).
    - Data protection and consumer privacy (accessibility and disclosure by unauthorized persons, entities, or processes).
- To strengthen collaboration processes between judicial bodies, competent authorities, and the digital and telecommunications industry.
- To consider "regulatory testing grounds" for the development of innovative services with high levels of security.
- To promote active cooperation between the government and international regulators to create an exchange and coordination mechanism on cybersecurity and data protection.

---

[4] In this context, during 2018, the 3rd Generation Partnership Project (3GPP) SA3 held seven meetings in which experts from 74 companies participated, in order to formulate security standards for 5G.

d. *Digital Literacy to Extend the Benefits of 5G Adoption*

The potential of 5G cannot be realized if there is not enough knowledge to apply this technology in the various fields previously mentioned. At this time, in Mexico, there are shortcomings in the training of professionals who can competitively integrate into industries that incorporate 5G. At the end-user level, there is also a lack of teaching digital skills to exploit technologies in all their magnitude and potential. Given this, it is necessary to collaborate with the Ministry of Public Education, universities, companies, and training institutes to improve digital skills at different levels. For this, the recommendations of the specialists consulted are:

- To incorporate basic training in 5G knowledge and its applications within study programs from the middle level.
- To incorporate intensive training of professionals for the management and development of solutions based on the Internet of Things, artificial intelligence, simulation, data science, etc.
- To design continuous training programs for the training, updating, and specialization of professionals in different industries capable of using information technologies based on 5G.
- To promote and finance research for the development of information technology applications based on 5G in fields such as: education, health, Industry 4.0, smart cities, mobility.

e. *Reduction of the digital gap*

There are important differentials in the management of information technologies and digital skills from a geographical point of view (the north of the country is better connected than the south); generational (young people are better at technology than older adults); and regional (urban centers have better services than rural areas), to mention some of the most obvious manifestations. The widening of this digital gap does not benefit the country, since it deepens inequality and social and regional differences. Therefore, the following recommendations have been issued:

- Connectivity must be provided to everyone with the best possible quality (depending on their requirements), to comply with the

mandate of Article 6 of the Constitution and, from that, enable other fundamental rights of the population
- One option that has been pursued is to offer unlicensed use of the spectrum, with the idea that this can bring low-cost Internet to underserved communities. This is the case of the Red Compartida (shared network) managed by the company Altan Redes, which has entered into a commercial bankruptcy process. One of the objectives of the Red Compartida is to bring telecommunications services to areas not currently covered by commercial networks. However, according to the Shared Network Coverage Viewer of Promtel, as of March 2021, Altán had coverage of 99% in Mexico City, 94% in Nuevo León, and 92% in the State of Mexico. In contrast, coverage in Chiapas was 29%, in Guerrero and Oaxaca 5% (Bravo, 2021). This shows that it is not enough to offer unlicensed use, since it is necessary to ensure that the companies that obtain such a concession have competitive performance and ensure the quality of services and connectivity. Given this, the recommendation is that the authority takes measures to seek a better balance between economy, quality of service, and price of access in remote communities. Working in various modalities of licensed spectrum and collaboration with large operators and technology generating companies can be more effective in closing the digital divide.
- To develop public–private mechanisms and technological solutions that support the obligation to invest in the deployment and coverage of infrastructure and quality services throughout the country.
- To rebalance taxes to promote digital inclusion, so that more users have access to mobile services and the affordability barrier is lowered.

f. *Promotion of investment in networks*

We have already mentioned that the extension of 5G networks implies a much greater investment in fiber-optic networks and better equipment for managing information flows. The policy should promote the existence of adequate economic conditions to favor investments in this area so that the specialists consulted agree on:

- To encourage long-term investment, offer long-term licenses, clear procedures for their renewal, and roadmaps for spectrum assignment.
- To promote the rational reallocation of network assets following long-term objectives that should be included in a National Digital Agenda.
- To apply the criterion of technological neutrality to make decisions regarding the development of networks.
- To design economic and fiscal incentives to favor private investment in networks.
- The regulatory framework should promote infrastructure sharing to increase territorial coverage and serve unattractive segments for large companies.
- To promote research focused on optimizing the use of networks.

g. *Promotion of the digital economy*

There is consensus that the State must improve the drive to digitize the country at individual, industrial, and governmental levels. This must be done under a Digital Agenda that sets objectives and general strategies. The COVID-19 pandemic has made it clear that the introduction of ICTs must be promoted in multiple aspects of government administration, business activity, and daily life, as connectivity has been critical to prevent its collapse. Therefore, the following policy recommendations have been issued:

- A sufficient amount of spectrum needs to be released in such a way as to encourage the digitization of businesses and ensure high-quality and widespread affordable services for all industries.
- To generate incentives for research and development of 5G solutions applicable to health, education, financial management, industrial and logistics operations, etc.
- To promote cooperative agreements between companies, governments, universities, and research centers for the development of new 5G applications to solve specific problems.
- To promote the construction of research infrastructure on 5G applications is essential, as well as the undertaking to have local

technology-based companies dedicated to offering innovative and cost-effective applications and solutions.

h. *Protection of health and the environment*

Scientific evidence on risks associated to the relationship between health, environment, and telecommunications is currently limited, but there are concerns about the risk of increased radiation exposure. In this sense, the IFT has developed the Agreement by which the Plenary of the Federal Telecommunications Institute issues Technical Provision IFT-007-2019: Maximum exposure limits for human beings to non-ionizing radiofrequency electromagnetic radiation in the 100 kHz interval at 300 GHz in the environment of radiocommunication stations or broadcast sources. This provision was issued to provide that, in areas of exposure to electromagnetic fields produced by the operation of radiocommunication stations, where people live, said maximum exposure limits are not exceeded for the frequency range of 100–300 GHz.

In Mexico, there is also the Official Mexican Standard NOM-013-STPS-1993 issued by the Ministry of Labor and Social Welfare (STPS, for its acronym in Spanish), whose objective is to establish preventive and control measures in work centers where non-ionizing electromagnetic radiation is generated. This NOM establishes preventive and control measures in work centers where non-ionizing electromagnetic radiation is generated, to prevent risks to the health of workers that involve exposure to such radiation; therefore, it establishes the maximum power density, energy density, magnetic field, and electric field limits for exposure to microwave and radiofrequency radiation. "This, however, is insufficient since its objective and field of application is limited to work centers where non-ionizing radiofrequency electromagnetic radiation is generated. Furthermore, no measurement or conformity assessment procedures are established" (IFT, 2019, p. 2). It can be observed that risk scenarios have already been addressed, but it is necessary, in the opinion of the specialists consulted, to consider the trend in terms of the density of facilities that are expected to emerge in the framework of the deployment of 5G, so it is recommended to complement this regulatory framework by:

- Actions aimed at minimizing the possible impacts of the deployment of the new 5G infrastructure, carrying out good planning and

risk assessment, sharing infrastructures, and involving all the agents involved in the process of the responsibility of following standards and guidelines issued by the authority
- To promote the development of a code of good practices for the deployment of facilities in urban environments.
- To promote that all mobile operators develop management programs for their electronic waste (based on sustainability and responsibility criteria).
- The set of systems that integrate 5G must adopt the limits of exposure to radio frequencies under what is established by the International Commission on Non-Ionizing Radiation Protection (ICNIRP) and the standards that arise from the revision of Technical Provision IFT-007-2019 (which should occur in 2024).
- Evidence of risk and mitigation measures must arise from scientific research, so the implementation of projects in this area should be supported.

Conclusions

The creation of a national digital agenda is key to enable 5G and capitalize its benefits for the country. Under the current government, this strategic framework does not exist, and it should be considered as soon as possible, especially since it would identify short, medium, and long-term national goals. This would be the backbone on which vertical strategies for the application of 5G are inserted in areas such as digital health, digital education, digital government, industry 4.0, among others.

The coordination of federal, state, and municipal governments is essential to generate coherent policies and regulations and harmonize, as far as possible, costs, processes, and times that result in greater network penetration, greater connectivity, higher quality, lower costs, and more affordable prices for consumers. A substantial issue to address in public policy is the definition of rules that promote investment in digital infrastructure. It is not only about the installation of new radio interfaces but also investing in the network infrastructure that is necessary to achieve territorial coverage with quality of services. As such infrastructure is very expensive and its construction is complex, since it is necessary to deal with federal, state, and municipal authorities, operators must look for new cost-sharing schemes that allow them to financially face the necessary investments. It is also important to negotiate public–private agreements that facilitate the execution of works.

For the deployment of fifth-generation networks, a competitive environment must be preserved and the participation of different actors in the 5G ecosystem must be promoted. For this, an effective spectrum policy is required that encourages the deployment of different services in a convivial environment, free of interferences between services, and that favors efficient spectrum management. A great effort must be made to train young people to adopt and assimilate the set of technologies related to 5G (artificial intelligence, Internet of Things, machine learning, Big Data, cybersecurity, etc.). This is essential for the development and adoption of solutions to problems in the fields of education, e-health, mobility and manufacturing, which is a key component for Mexico's recovery after COVID-19.

The Mexico, United States, and Canada Agreement (USMCA) has at least two new chapters, telecommunications, and digital commerce, which should be used to "pull" Mexico toward greater and better digitization. But that cannot arise spontaneously, so a specific policy must be designed, and resources allocated for its implementation. There is no time to wait, as the evolution of this technology is taking place at great speed. Mexico can be left at the level of complete technological dependency if it limits itself to being a passive buyer of technologies, applications, and solutions related to 5G.

The transition to 5G must be active, with a long-term vision, and differentiated in terms of the segments and regions where it will be applied, since the requirements of specific industries are different from those of digital government or end-users. If Mexico can develop the applications for each segment through the collaboration of the actors of its digital ecosystem, it will be able to take full advantage of the technology. It will be necessary to create digital skills and invest in research and development. Mexico should urgently generate the necessary public policies to adopt 5G in an orderly and planned manner, and that the benefits are seen in the different areas of application and not only in the one with the highest payment capacity and economic rate of return.

Acknowledgements This chapter is a partial result of a study sponsored by Huawei Technologies de México. The authors wish to thank the company's economic and technical support for this piece of research.

References

Bravo, J. (2021, July 16). *Altán la red compartida a reestructurar deuda* [Altán shared network to restructure debt]. El Economista. https://www.eleconomista.com.mx/opinion/Altan-la-Red-Compartida-a-reestructurar-deuda-20210716-0042.html

Cámara de Diputados del H. Congreso de la Unión (1917, February 5). *Constitución Política de los Estados Unidos Mexicanos* [Political Constitution of the United Mexican states]. Article 60, added paragraph, June 11, 2013. Mexico. http://www.diputados.gob.mx/LeyesBiblio/pdf_mov/Constitucion_Politica.pdf

Ericsson. (2021, June). *Ericsson mobility report*. https://www.ericsson.com/en/mobility-report/reports/june-2021

GSMA. (2019). *Manual de políticas públicas de comunicaciones móviles* [Mobile communications public policy manual]. https://www.gsma.com/latinamerica/wp-content/uploads/2019/03/GSMA_Mobile-Policy-Handbook_2019_ESP.pdf

Huawei. (2021). *5G unlocks a world of opportunities. Top ten 5G use cases.* X Labs Wireless. https://www-file.huawei.com/-/media/corporate/pdf/mbb/5g-unlocks-a-world-of-opportunities-v5.pdf?la=en

IFT. (2019). *Análisis de impacto regulatorio* [Regulatory impact analysis]. http://www.ift.org.mx/sites/default/files/industria/temasrelevantes/9135/documentos/airdtift-007-2019opb4mod20191104limpiobis.pdf

ITU. (2020). *5G, human exposure to electromagnetic fields (EMF) and health.* International Telecommunication Union. https://www.itu.int/es/mediacentre/backgrounders/Pages/5G-EMF-health.aspx

ITU. (2019). *5G-Fifth generation of mobile technologies.* https://www.itu.int/en/mediacentre/backgrounders/Pages/5G-fifth-generation-of-mobile-technologies.aspx

JHU. (2021). *Estadísticas. Nuevos casos y muertes* [Statistics. New cases and deaths]. Johns Hopkins University. The Center for Systems Science and Engineering [CSSE]. https://github.com/CSSEGISandData/COVID-19

Muñoz, D., Rodrigo, L., & Rodrigo, I. (2018). La tecnología 5G y su papel en la conversión de las ciudades en Smart Cities: el caso de Segovia [5G technology and its role in the conversion of cities into Smart Cities: The case of Segovia]. *Revista Ibérica de Sistemas y Tecnologías de la Información, 16,* 15–27.

Saldaña, J., San Juan, G., & Ruiz, J. (2021, May 11). *Seminario Diálogos para el desarrollo. De la revolución industrial a la revolución digital, Mesa 2: Educación, tecnología y revolución digital* [Seminar dialogues for development. From the industrial revolution to the digital revolution, Roundtable 2: Education, technology and digital revolution. Conference session]. Hacia una agenda digital para México. IIE-UNAM. https://idic.mx/2021/05/11/educacion-tecnologia-y-revolucion-digital-dialogosparaeldesarrollo/

Swain, W., Lopes, A., & Agnese, S. (2020). *Why 5G in Latin America? A call to action for Latin American operators and policymakers.* Omdia–Nokia. https://news.america-digital.com/wp-content/uploads/2020/08/Nokia_Why_5G_in_Latin_America__Report_ES.pdf

Siriwardhana, Y., Gür, G., Ylianttila, M., & Liyanage, M. (2021). The role of 5G for digital healthcare against COVID-19 pandemic: Opportunities and challenges. *ICT Express, 7*(2), 244–252. https://www.sciencedirect.com/science/article/pii/S2405959520304744

Wiley. (2021). *5G and government: A regulatory roadmap.* Washington, DC: Wiley Rein LLP.

WEF. (2020). *The impact of 5G: Creating new value across industries and society.* World Economic Forum. http://www3.weforum.org/docs/WEF_The_Impact_of_5G_Report.pdf

CHAPTER 5

The Structural Impact of COVID-19 on Employment: The Role of Skills and Gender in an Industrialized Local Economy

Cecilia Y. Cuellar and Jorge O. Moreno

INTRODUCTION

The year 2020 represented a significant challenge for global economies, as in March of the same year, the World Health Organization (WHO) declared COVID-19 a pandemic. More than two-thirds of the world's countries were economically paralyzed as a result of this health crisis, with tourism being one of the leading sectors affected. For Mexico, this

C. Y. Cuellar · J. O. Moreno (✉)
Universidad Autónoma de Nuevo León, San Nicolás de los Garza, Mexico
e-mail: jorge.morenotr@uanl.edu.mx

C. Y. Cuellar
e-mail: cecilia.cuellartp@uanl.edu.mx

© The Author(s), under exclusive license to Springer Nature Switzerland AG 2022
A. M. López-Fernández and A. Terán-Bustamante (eds.), *Business Recovery in Emerging Markets*, Palgrave Studies in Democracy, Innovation, and Entrepreneurship for Growth,
https://doi.org/10.1007/978-3-030-91532-2_5

scenario was not favorable since the tourism sector represents one of the country's primary sources of income (Esquivel, 2020). This situation caused economic uncertainty, accumulating, at the beginning of the pandemic, more than half a million losses in the formal employment for the country (INEGI, 2020). Nonetheless, for the state of Nuevo Leon, the opposite happened; in August 2020, this state ranked second in terms of formal job recovery in Mexico, only surpassed by the state of Jalisco (Coparmex Nuevo Leon, 2020; ENOE, 2020).

According to the Population and Housing Census conducted by the National Institute of Statistics, Geography, and Informatics (INEGI) in 2020, Nuevo Leon was one of the seven most populated states in the country, with the Monterrey metropolitan area standing out as the second most populated urban area in Mexico. Hence, understanding the labor market structure in this state and its different segments will allow us to have a broader perspective on regional employment dynamics and their relationship with unexpected situations, such as those that occurred due to the COVID-19 economic crisis.

This paper analyzes the dynamics and persistence in the regional labor market of the state of Nuevo Leon as a consequence of the COVID-19 economic shock. We accomplish this study by segmenting the labor market by workers' skills and gender, allowing us to identify heterogeneous effects and changes across market structures. Defining heterogeneity between groups, particularly between genders, allows us to recover the market structure, changes in these trends, and analyze long-term differentiated dynamics by labor market segment (Cuellar, 2019; Moreno & Cuellar, 2021). We construct micro-founded formal employment time series, which retrieves consistent and homologous regional aggregate data over time. These series are obtained directly from micro-data from employment surveys in Mexico. The aggregate data are quarterly from 1987:Q1 to 2020:Q1, focusing on the urban areas of Nuevo Leon. The urban areas represent more than 90% of the total employment of this dynamic region, the second largest after Mexico City, according to the 2020 Mexican Census by INEGI.

Employment is segmented as mentioned above (skill and gender-skill). With it, we define and estimate two VAR models that link each segment of formal employment with the state economic activity (defined by the ITAEE NL) to identify the depth and persistence of the first COVID-19 pandemic shock (defined as *I-shock* COVID-19). Once the models are estimated, we use the impulse-response function methodology to perform an impact analysis, introducing the first shock observed in the economic activity of Nuevo Leon. With this, we recover the employment growth trends if the pandemic had not occurred and the trend with the I-shock COVID-19. Once these trends are estimated, they are compared with the observed employment to identify the structural changes and the potential recovery period of formal employment for each segment.

This chapter contributes to the economic literature in four aspects. First, it uses several homologous and consistent time series constructed from micro-data provided in all employment surveys for Mexico. Second, it is the first regional study that analyzes the particular dynamics of the *high-skill* and *low-skill* employment segments for the state of Nuevo Leon. Third, we estimate dynamic employment models for gender-skills, identify heterogeneous impacts across segments, and estimate impulse-response functions to compare the observed employment structure with the employment trend originated by the I-shock COVID-19. Finally, this study estimates potential recovery periods for each segment of the regional labor market.

This chapter is divided into five sections, including this introduction. The second section briefly analyzes previous findings related to the theoretical framework, regional labor market, and the COVID-19 crisis. The third section presents the data and methodology proposed to study regional employment dynamics divided by skills and gender. The fourth section presents the results obtained from the study. And the fifth section presents the conclusions and implications of the analysis.

COVID-19, Mexican Labor Market and Formal Regional Employment

A Theoretical Framework of Labor Market

The relationship between the labor market, economic growth, and productivity has been a recurring topic of study since the last century (Becker, 1965; Mincer, 1975; Schumpeter, 1934). Different theories show the complex interrelationships and sources of endogeneity in the labor market, including the connection between unemployment and economic growth (Okun, 1962). For this study, a neoclassical theoretical framework proposed by Arrow et al. (1961) is used as a reference, in which elasticities of substitution are proposed to identify causal effects of productivity in the labor market.

Moreno and Cuellar (2021) use a neoclassical model approach. This framework assumes perfectly competitive markets, and where the production function is of CES-type, and there are factors of production, which are capital (K) and labor (L); also, this function presents returns to scale (s) and ρ is a positive parameter that measures the elasticity of substitution, expressed in Eq. 5.1. From the optimality conditions, it can be observed that the marginal productivity of both factors equals their market price, r, and w (Eq. 5.2). Furthermore, following the mathematical notation of Akkemik (2007), taking logarithms from the labor's first-order condition, we obtain Eq. 5.3.

$$Q = f(K, L) = \theta\left[\beta L^{-\rho} + (1-\beta)K^{-\rho}\right]^{\frac{s}{\rho}} \tag{5.1}$$

$$f'(K, L) = f_k = r, \ f'(K, L) = f_L = w \tag{5.2}$$

$$\ln L = \alpha_0 + \alpha_1 \ln Q + \alpha_2 \ln w \tag{5.3}$$

The parameters of the last equation (α_1 and α_2) show the expected effect on the labor market derived from economic activity and wages. This neoclassical theoretical framework allows us to recover the causal structural effects caused by the exogenous shocks "ε_t" derived from COVID-19 on the different segments of the labor market in the state of Nuevo Leon. The following section presents the data and methodology used to capture the expected effects on the labor market as mentioned above.

Regional Employment and the COVID-Crisis

The COVID-19 pandemic caused one of the world's worst economic crises, causing short-term losses and predicted long-term effects. According to the International Monetary Fund (2020), the global economy fell by around 3%, with a recovery forecast until mid-2021. These unfavorable economic scenarios result in negative impacts, especially in lagging economies like Latin America, which also project losses between 3 and 4% (CEPAL, 2020). In Mexico, despite being a leader in these economies, recovery will depend on its capacity to react to the shocks that the effects of the COVID-19 pandemic may cause.

One of the first exogenous productivity shocks derived from the pandemic in Mexico was observed in the tourism sector (Esquivel,

2020) due to the implementation the social distancing policy. Given this first exogenous shock, structural effects began to be observed. Structural effects in economics are caused by the interrelationships between economic agents, which produce complex relationships, and these relationships cause different effects in the market (Sampedro & Cortiña, 1969). In Mexico, three ways of structural effects were observed: supply, demand, and financial. Identifying these sources will allow us to understand the repercussions of these effects on the market, especially labor.

As Mexico is a labor-intensive country, understanding its dynamics and structure is fundamental to reactivate the Mexican economy. Some authors predicted employment losses for the country that fluctuate between 5 and 20% (Altamirano et al., 2020; Jimenez-Bandala et al., 2020; Maldonado & Ruiz, 2020; Nunez, 2020), each work with its respective study methodology, but all agree on the slow recovery of employment in the country, some of them predicting recovery by mid-2021 (Banco de Mexico, 2020; Mexico Como Vamos, 2020; Moreno & Cuellar, 2021). For the state of Nuevo Leon, the panorama was very different from the national one, since right in the middle of the pandemic, it reported formal employment recoveries, placing it among the first states to achieve an early job recovery (Coparmex Nuevo Leon, 2020; ENOE, 2020).

There is little literature studying the employment dynamics of Nuevo Leon related to the COVID-19 pandemic for this state. Sanchez (2020) makes projections of employment recovery for the northern border states, including Nuevo Leon; these projections observe recovery starting in the last quarter of 2020 and finally normalizing in the second quarter of 2021. On the other hand, the Centro de Investigaciones Economicas (CIE) forecasts an employment recovery in Nuevo Leon of 4.90% by the end of 2021 (Flores, 2021).

Accordingly, conducting a regional study for the state of Nuevo Leon contributes not only to the literature but also to understanding the dynamics and structure of the labor market in a state considered one of the country's leading economies. Therefore, the main contribution of our work is to allow for regional heterogeneity in the labor market, differentiating employment by gender and skills. This segmentation will allow us to analyze the impact of COVID-19 on formal employment in the state of Nuevo Leon and, thereby, estimate potential employment recoveries in the different segments of the market.

Data and Methodology
Data

For the estimations, we construct micro-founded time series from all existing employment surveys for Mexico: Encuesta Nacional de Empleo Urbano (ENEU), Encuesta Nacional de Empleo (ENE), and Encuesta Nacional de Ocupacion y Empleo (ENOE). This methodology of construction and homologation based on micro-foundations has been employed in previous works studying employment, and gender gap for the country are also analyzed (Cuellar & Moreno, 2021; Moreno & Cuellar, 2021). The construction of this long-run database makes it possible to control both inclusion and exclusion biases that may exist due to the data structure and other structural changes. Moreover, with this approach and model choice, micro-founded time series are recovered, allowing us to study them in a consistent time macro-time series perspective.

The ENEU, ENE, and ENOE are published by INEGI and capture data on employment and sociodemographic characteristics of a representative sample of individuals in this country. Employment micro-data is public for all surveys, and the publication periods are quarterly. For the ENEU, the available periods are from 1987 to 2004, for the ENE 1988 to 2004, and the ENOE from 2005 to date. These surveys are a dynamic panel; they include the same individual for five quarters and alternate each quarter to 20% of the sample.

For this research, we take advantage of the characteristics of cross-sectional data to construct quarterly aggregate data for Nuevo Leon from 1987:Q1 to 2020:Q1, that is, quarterly employment time series, because we are interested in obtaining the behavior in the aggregate of these series. To estimate the implied pre-COVID-19 forecasted trend in employment, we decided to use ENOE before the pandemic and later apply the parameter estimation of long-run trends to compare the actual values of the ENOE post-COVID-19 to the implied estimation. This choice was to have a pre-pandemic structural model to build a counterfactual trend and then identify the structural change due to the pandemics by comparing this trend to the actual observed values.

In this study, we are interested in recovering the structure of the labor market segmented by skills and gender. Therefore, the following time series are constructed: *low-skill* employment, and *high-skill* employment.

And then, we construct time series by skill-gender: *low-skill* male employment and *low-skill* female employment, *high-skill* male employment, and *high-skill* female employment.

According to the above, the terms *high-skill* and *low-skill* must be defined; for this study, the ability is measured through the level of schooling achieved by the worker (Werner et al., 2021). Therefore, individuals with basic education (primary, secondary) or less are classified as *low-skill* employment. In contrast, individuals with technical, high school, undergraduate, or graduate education are considered *high-skill* employment. Since we will link employment and regional economy, we use the Quarterly Indicator of State Economic Activity (ITAEE) for Nuevo Leon. This series is obtained directly from INEGI. Furthermore, the last series to be constructed is the real average hourly wages from employment surveys.

Based on the facts described above, the construction of the time series of employment and wages is limited to employment growth rates for this research. The final sample consists of individuals between the ages of 16 and 65 working and receiving a monetary payment greater than zero, excluding individuals who work informally and without receiving any payment or remuneration. Formal employment is that individual who has social security. In employers, subcontractors, and self-employed workers, it is decided to reference the number of workers employed and whether the company name is registered (Cuellar & Moreno, 2021; Moreno & Cuellar, 2021). For the analysis, six time series are constructed at the regional level (Nuevo Leon) and removing the seasonal factor and are presented as growth rates. Finally, all rural areas of Nuevo Leon are excluded from homologating both databases since the ENEU only includes urban areas of Mexico.

Empirical Strategy

Since we want to analyze the relationship between economic activity and employment, this study takes as a reference a dynamic neoclassical model of labor market equilibrium, which allows us to study the relationships among production, productivity, employment, and wages (Akkemik, 2007; Arrow et al., 1961).

This model allows us to estimate the causal impact of the economy on employment, so this theory will allow us to propose an empirical model with simultaneous interactions between these variables. The econometric methodology proposed is Vectors Auto-Regressive (VAR) in reduced and unrestricted form. This method allows us simultaneity between variables and helps us find persistence between the same series, in the long run, with the correct specification of the lags. Moreover, since the technique does not impose restrictions on the model, it avoids specification errors (Sims, 1980).

Two models are estimated for this study. The first model studies the dynamics of formal employment by skills and economic activity in Nuevo Leon (Model 1). The time series of interest are represented in growth rates, where y_{1t} is *low-skill* employment, y_{2t} is *high-skill* employment, y_{3t} is the ITAEE NL, and y_{4t} is the real hourly wage. For the second model (Model 2), skill employment is segmented by gender, so this model contains six variables, where y_{1t} is *low-skill* male formal employment, y_{2t} is *low-skill* female formal employment, y_{3t} is formal employment *high-skill* men, y_{4t} is *high-skill* female formal employment, y_{5t} is the ITAEE NL, and finally, y_{6t} the real hourly wage.

Each vector has its respective autoregressive component $(t-p)$, and a component associated with the white noise process, ε_t. The reduced VAR model can be represented in terms of its characteristic polynomials defined over the number of "L" lags, $a(L, \phi)$ and $b(L, \theta)$, as follows:

$$y_t = a(L, \phi) y_{t-p} + b(L, \theta) \varepsilon_t \tag{5.4}$$

$$a'(L, \phi) y_t = b(L, \theta) \varepsilon_t \tag{5.5}$$

Given the time stability of the series distribution, we could represent it in terms of the Gaussian white noise process, as Eq. 5.6. The new characteristic polynomial $c(L, \phi, \theta)$ is unique for each VAR process defined over the number of lags (L), and we used the maximum likelihood method through the properties of the Gaussian process to recover the parameters associated with the original model, $\{\phi, \theta\}$.

$$y_t = \frac{b(L, \theta)}{a'(L, \phi)} \varepsilon_t = c(L, \phi, \theta) \varepsilon_t \tag{5.6}$$

In addition to this model, since the objective is to analyze the impact derived by the COVID-19 I-shock, each respective model's Impulse-Response Functions (IRF) is estimated. The IRFs allow capturing the reaction of the model variables to an unanticipated "shock" in the error component of the model (ε_t). Information is obtained from the variance decomposition of the orthogonal error term on the random innovations of each endogenous variable belonging to each model. Once the IRFs are obtained, where the impulse is in economic activity (ITAEE NL) and the response is in employment, everything is retrieved regarding employment levels to compare pre-COVID-19 trends, *I-shock* COVID-19 trends, and observed employment structure.

Estimation and Results

The study's objective is to analyze and recover long-term employment trends in Nuevo Leon. Once these estimates are obtained, they are compared with the employment structure observed up to the most recent data (2020:Q4). To study the dynamics and structure of employment, we divide the analysis into three time series:

- *Pre-COVID-19 trend*: These time series forecast employment levels using the long-run estimates without any shock; namely, this would give us the expected level of employment if COVID-19 crises had not happened.
- *I-shock COVID-19* + *Pre-COVID-19* trend: These time series forecast employment levels given the first shock due to the crises (ITAEE NL) and the respective trend from this impact.
- Actual employment: Theses series show us the employment levels observed for the Nuevo Leon state on each market segment.

With these forecasted time series, we can recover the *counterfactual gaps* on long-term employment by market segments as follows:

- Pre-COVID-19 vs. post-COVID employment long-run trend.
- Pre-COVID-19 vs. observed employment trend.
- Post-COVID-19 vs. observed employment trend.

To estimate trends and gap impact, we introduce a negative shock equivalent to the observed impact of COVID-19 crises over ITAEE NL through the IRFs. Moreover, the VAR model will allow us to estimate the pre-COVID-19 trend, differentiating what would have been without the pandemic. Finally, the observed employment captures the magnitude of the structural effects. With this, we can project scenarios of potential recovery in the different employment segments in the state of Nuevo Leon. First, unit root tests and optimal lag tests are performed to confirm the statistical validity and stability of the VAR models. Then, the employment impact analysis is presented, in which the Impulse-Response Functions are presented. With them, the trends, pre-COVID-19, and I-shock COVID-19 are estimated for each model (Model 1 and 2) and compared with the structural effects of observed employment.

Unit Root Test and Selection Criterion Optimal Lags

The time series are presented in growth rates, so two types of unit root tests were performed: Augmented Dickey-Fuller (ADF) and Phillips-Perron unit root test, to test the series's stability in the long-term. Table 5.1 presents the stationarity tests for the ITAEE, the employment segments, and the real hourly wage. It is observed that all series are stationary in both tests, so these series are consistent with order-one I(1) data. Once the statistical validity of the time series is confirmed, a model fitting must be performed to perform the impact analysis. This study uses an unrestricted VAR model, so a critical point is the order of the variables and the optimal number of lags to be used in the models. For this analysis, we take the basis of the theoretical model to order the variables as follows: employment-ITAEE NL-real wages.

According to the order of variables implemented, we proceed to estimate five optimal lag criteria, from which we must choose which criterion we are going to keep. Table 5.1 presents the statistics associated with the selection of the optimal lag for both models. Table 5.1 shows that two groups (LL, LR, FPE, AIC, HQIC) propose that one lag and (SBIC) propose that it should be 0 lag. According to the literature, it will be proposed that the model should have one lag, given the size and periodicity of the series (Ivanov & Kilian, 2005). This criterion is applied in both models, and once the criterion is selected, we perform the employment impact analysis.

Employment Impact Analysis:
The I-shock COVID-29 and Structural Effect

Given the nature of the models and the high multicollinearity among the variables, it is not recommended to make individual inferences of the estimators (Akkemik, 2007), so the model is reported in the Annex

Table 5.1 VAR model: tests and selection criteria

Z-statistics for hypothesis testing unit roots		
Growth rates	Augmented Dickey-Fuller (ADF)	Phillips-Perron Test (PP)
PIB	−7.93***	−78.05***
ITAEE	−8.94***	−95.33***
Low-skill employment	−11.709***	−140.22***
High-skill employment	−11.206***	−125.24***
Real wage per hour	−17.63***	−172.41***
Men		
Low-skill employment	−11.45***	−132.42***
High-skill employment	−12.65***	−141.45***
Women		
Low-skill employment	−14.05***	−159.39***
High-skill employment	−11.82***	−124.58***

Selection criterion for optimal lags in VAR models

Model 1: Employment skills

Lag	LL	LR	FPE	AIC	HQIC	SBIC
0	868.161		1.60E-11	−13.5025	−13.4663	**−13.4134***
1	895.379	**54.435***	**1.3E-11 ***	**−13.6778***	**−13.4967***	−13.2322
2	907.724	24.691	1.40E-11	−13.6207	−13.2948	−12.8186
3	918.474	21.499	1.60E-11	−13.5387	−13.0679	−12.38
4	930.731	24.515	1.70E-11	−13.4802	−12.8646	−11.965

Model 2: Employment gender-skills

Lag	LL	LR	FPE	AIC	HQIC	SBIC
0	1187.34		3.90E-16	−18.4584	**−18.4041***	**−18.3247***
1	1232.79	90.904	**3.3E-16 ***	**−18.6061***	−18.2258	−17.6702
2	1263.62	**61.662***	3.60E-16	−18.5253	−17.8192	−16.7874
3	1286.99	46.745	4.50E-16	−18.328	−17.296	−15.7879
4	1310.05	46.106	5.60E-16	−18.1257	−16.7677	−14.7835

p-value: 0.01***, 0.05**, 0.10
Source Own estimations with time series constructed and homologized of employment surveys (ENEU-ENE-ENOE). Seasonally adjusted series presented by growth rates
Notes Sample 128 observations. LL: log-likelihood, LR: likelihood ratio, FPE: final prediction error, AIC: Akaike's information criterion, HQIC: Hannan and Quinn information criterion, SBIC: Schwarz's Bayesian information criterion

(Fig. 5.3). Focusing on the dependent variables of interest will help us analyze the behavior after introducing the I-shock COVID-19. This section presents the main contribution of our research, which is to recover and quantify the impact of the I-shock COVID-19 on the employment of skills in Nuevo Leon.

Once the structure of skills employment (*low-skill* and *high-skill* employment) is analyzed, we segment the labor market by gender to understand the labor market dynamics. To estimate the impact, we rely on Impulse-Response Functions, using economic activity (ITAEE NL) as the impulse variable, and the response variables are the different segments of the labor market. For Model 1, the response variables are Nuevo Leon's *low-skill* and *high-skill* formal employment. For Model 2, these skill segments are divided by gender, so the response variables are *low-skill* male and female employment and *high-skill* male and female; all segments belong to formal employment.

For both models, we introduce as *I-shock* COVID-19 the observed change in economic activity (ITAEE NL) of Nuevo Leon for the second quarter of 2020, which was −21% (INEGI, 2020). The magnitude of the impulses in the IRFs is introduced in one standard deviation, so a 21% drop had to be converted in standard deviations for the models, a magnitude of −2.14 standard deviation (s.d.). Figure 5.3 (Annex) presents the Impulse-Response Functions of each model differentiated by skill-employment structure (Model 1) and gender-skills (Model 2).

It can be seen in Figure 5.3 that both formal employment structures in Nuevo Leon decline in the face of the negative impact of the COVID-19 I-shock in the short-run (period $t + 1$), as estimated in several sources for IMSS registered workers (Banco de Mexico, 2020). On the other hand, our estimation shows that, if we segment by skills, employment loss is differentiated, with *high-skill* employment being more reactive (15% drop) relative to *low-skill* employment (1.6% drop), but with greater adjustment capacity, i.e., *high-skill* employment recovers faster from the *I-shock*. As for Fig. 5.2, both genders show independent dynamics, with women being more inelastic to the COVID-19 I-shock, while men are more reactive to it. The shock for men was more profound for the *low-skill* employment (2.1%), while *high-skill* employment presents potential rapid recovery (2020:Q4).

Female employment presents a different dynamic to male employment since *high-skill* employment is observed more significantly. In contrast, *low-skill* employment seems to be inelastic to this COVID-19 I-shock. While for the *low-skill* represented a decrease of 0.2%, for *high-skill* it was 1%. These impulse-response functions allow us to recover the trend with the *I-shock* COVID-19 in employment in Nuevo Leon, and with the support of the models, we estimate the pre-COVID-19 trends. Once these trends are estimated, in the next section, we append the employment observed in the four quarters of 2020. We can differentiate between the employment losses derived from the I-shock and the losses derived from the structural effects triggered by the COVID-19 shock.

Formal Employment by Skills

As other authors have previously analyzed (Altamirano et al., 2020; Esquivel, 2020; Moreno & Cuellar, 2021), formal employment tends to be more elastic to economic shocks. This study introduces a negative I-shock derived from the COVID-19 shock through the economic activity indicator for Nuevo Leon (ITAEE) and recovers skill employment losses by comparing the observed employment level and the different trends (pre-COVID-19 trend and *I-shock* COVID-19 trend).

Figures 5.1 shows the cumulative loss of skills employment in Nuevo Leon, compared to employment trends, respectively (one without COVID-19 shock and the other including it). Three series can be identified in the figure; in black with dots, the first represents observed employment obtained from the ENOE for the sample. Only the second quarter of 2020 was calculated from the Encuesta Telefonica de Ocupacion y Empleo (ETOE), this being an extension of the previous survey due to the months of confinement. The red dotted line estimates the long-run employment growth trend (pre-COVID-19 non-crisis situation); this was estimated from the VAR Model 1. Finally, the gray line is the trend recovered from introducing the negative I-shock COVID-19 in the impulse-response function and adding the long-run growth trend to it.

The most profound employment loss for the state of Nuevo Leon was in 2020:Q2, which is somewhat different from the dynamics presented for the country, as by 2020:Q3 Mexican formal employment reported its lowest levels (Moreno & Cuellar, 2021). In percentage terms, the drop in *low-skill* employment in 2020:Q2 represented a loss of 23%, while *high-skill* employment fell by only 9% in the same period. Figure 5.1 shows that the I-shock COVID-19 created a long-term employment gap of 2%. According to the latest 2020:Q4 *low-skill* employment observation, there are still permanent job losses for the state. In levels, these losses represent almost 9 thousand *low-skill* jobs.

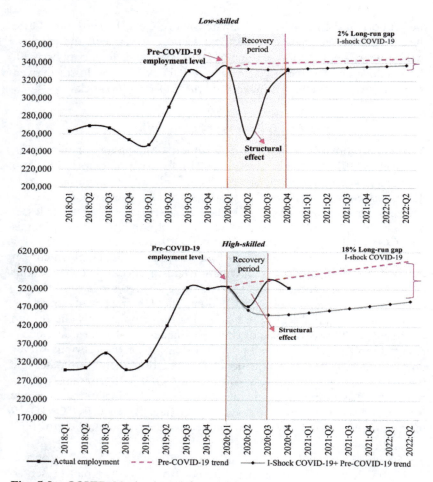

Fig. 5.1 COVID-19 shock and formal labor employment in Nuevo Leon, by skill level (*Notes* Trend estimation uses VAR Model 1. The data of employment observed of 2020:Q2 was calculated of ETOE. *Source* Own estimations with time series constructed and homologized of employment surveys [ENEU-ENE-ENOE])

5 THE STRUCTURAL IMPACT OF COVID-19 ON EMPLOYMENT ... 75

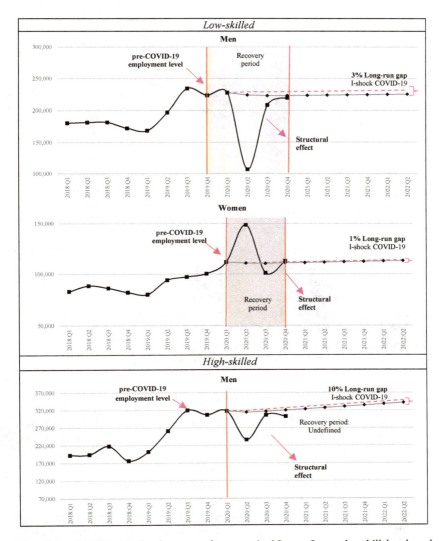

Fig. 5.2 COVID-19 shock on employment in Nuevo Leon, by skill level and gender (*Notes* Trend estimation uses a VAR model. The data of employment observed of second 2020 quarterly was calculated of ETOE. *Source* Own estimations with time series constructed and homologized of employment surveys [ENEU-ENE-ENOE])

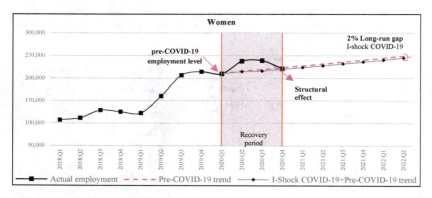

Fig. 5.2 (continued)

Regarding the *high-skill* labor market (Fig. 5.1), the COVID-19 I-shock originated an 18% gap in long-term employment. However, given that this employment segment is more dynamic and adjusts more rapidly, the gap is reduced to only 5% concerning the last observation. Two effects are observed in *high-skill* employment levels, one of the gains and one of the losses. Almost 72 thousand *high-skill* jobs were gained compared to the I-shock COVID-19 trend, while for the pre-COVID-19 trend, there are still losses of about 28 thousand *high-skill* jobs in the long run.

Formal Employment by Gender-Skills

Employment in Nuevo Leon represents one of the main strengths since, in mid-2020 when employment seemed to have collapsed in the country, this state was one of the best entities in terms of employment recovery, only behind Jalisco (Coparmex Nuevo Leon, 2020). For this reason, understanding the dynamics of employment will lead us to a better understanding of the market, so segmenting employment by skills and gender could provide us with some structure of the labor market in the region. For the case of Latin America, the International Monetary Fund (2020) found that *low-skill* employment was the most adversely affected during the second quarter of 2020, presenting decreases, mainly in female employment. On the other hand, *high-skill* employment also shows losses, but the recovery is faster than *low-skill* employment.

The following section is divided into two parts; the first presents the structure of the *low-skill* market and its gender differences, and the second, the *high-skill* market for men and women. Figure 5.2 shows the dynamics of *low-skill* employment for men and women in Nuevo Leon; the first thing to note is the peculiar behavior of both structures. Men in 2020:Q2 show a 53% drop, while in female employment, the opposite is observed since, for this same period, the observed employment increased by 33%. In the literature, this behavior of the labor market between genders is known as the "substitution effect," which responds to the hypothesis that in times of economic crisis, the female labor market functions as a driver of employment, i.e., it increases, as opposed to male employment, which decreases (Gomez & Mosino, 2019; Humphries, 1988; Skoufias & Parker, 2006).

The COVID-19 I-shock was also differentiated between genders, while it originated a 3% gap for men. For women, it represented a 1% gap for the pre-COVID-19 employment trend. This phenomenon could be translated in terms of elasticity, i.e., female employment was more inelastic relative to male employment in the face of this first economic shock.

In terms of employment levels, this crisis represented an increase in female employment as it reports a gain of just over 1 thousand *low-skill* jobs over the pre-COVID-19 trend, while men still show permanent job losses of almost 10 thousand over the same trend. Finally, it is worth noting the speed in the adjustment dynamics while for women, two quarters was enough to adjust and overcome the long-term growth trend in employment (pre-COVID-19 trend). For men, two quarters was not enough. According to the latest available observation, they continue to present permanent losses of *low-skill* employment (2020:Q4).

Figure 5.2 also shows the structure of *high-skill* employment by gender. This employment segment is very similar to the *low-skill* segment, where the gender effect is a proxy. In 2020:Q2 male employment presented a drop of about 26%, and female employment increased 13% for this same period. Regarding the COVID-19 I-shock, both the male and female segments are more reactive to shocks than the *low-skilled*. For *high-skill* male employment, this first shock represented a 10% gap compared to the pre-COVID-19 gap. This gap was relatively minor for women, representing only a 2% gap compared to the non-pandemic employment growth gap. The employment levels presented for both groups are in negative figures, with men reporting a loss of *high-skill* employment of a little more than 24 thousand jobs compared to the pre-COVID-19 trend. In comparison, women only lost around 2 thousand jobs compared to the same trend. In *high-skill* employment, the recovery dynamics for men represent a problem since, despite being a dynamic employment structure, there are still permanent losses concerning their last observation, so a recovery period cannot be defined. As for female employment, the recovery is observed in 2020:Q4 in Fig. 5.2.

Finally, the above results show decreases in the gender employment gap for the state of Nuevo Leon as a result of structural employment dynamics. The COVID-19 pandemic represented an opportunity in favor of labor market integration for Nuevo Leon women. The crisis decreased the relative gender employment gap observed in the state by 7% points for *high-skill* employment and by 2% points for women's *low-skill* employment. In 2020:Q1 (pre-COVID-19), the relative *high-skill* employment gap between genders was 34%, while in 2020:Q4, the gap was 27%. For the same period, the relative employment gap between gender for the *low-skill* market was 51%, while in the end, it was 49%. The main relative gains associated with the gender gap are integrating women in the high-skill segment and job substitution favoring women in low-skill due to the estimated dynamics in the first segment.

Concluding Remarks

In this study, we analyze the depth and persistence of employment losses by skill and gender-skill for the state of Nuevo Leon, trying to identify structural changes during the COVID-19 pandemic. We use quarterly data from 1987–2020 and construct a consistent, micro-founded employment time series for each labor market segment from employment surveys for Mexico. Two VAR models are defined, linking each labor market segment (skills and gender-skills) and the state's economic activity (ITAEE NL) by gender. This method allows recovery trends (pre-COVID-19 and I-shock COVID-19) to analyze observed employment losses compared to both trends.

The main results show differentiated impacts on employment; according to the different segments analyzed, *high-skill* employment is more reactive than *low-skill* employment, so employment recovers faster. Recovery takes about six months for the *high-skill*, while it takes about one year for the *low-skill*. On the other hand, if we segment skill employment by gender, we observe gains in observed employment, resulting in decreased relative employment gaps and a more significant proportion for *high-skill* employment; these gender employment gaps represented about seven and 2% points *high-skill* and *low-skill*, respectively. The limitation of this study is that the analysis only focuses on the formal labor market in urban areas of Nuevo Leon, as this allows us to identify the long-term impacts on these market segments more accurately.

The implications of this analysis allow us to understand the regional employment dynamics derived from the COVID-19 crisis, highlighting the importance of designing public policies in favor of investment in human capital, as proposed by classic economic theories (Becker, 1965; Heckman, 2012; Schultz, 1961). On the other hand, for gender public policies, more significant opportunities in the state translate into greater female labor participation. One important feature is that the women labor market shows an impressive counterintuitive structural dynamic behavior. In particular, women's employment for both high-skilled and low-skilled segments shows the creation of employment during the COVID-19 pandemic for the state.

These findings present an interesting additional fact: access to internet and technological infrastructure that predominate in Nuevo Leon might have played a fundamental role in the insertion and transition of women in the labor market, as we observed for the case of the high-skilled segment. Thus, employment gender gaps are reduced naturally by each of their market dynamics. Adjustments are given human capital levels without implementing policies that distort market prices (*enforced minimum wages*) or impose gender quotas (*affirmative actions and contracts*). Therefore, investment in technology and infrastructure permits better employment levels and dynamics, integrating women into the formal sector and in particular in the high-skilled and higher wages sector.

Allowing for heterogeneity among human capital at the regional level permitted us to identify the differentiated behaviors among segmented labor market groups and analyze the existing structural changes derived from the current COVID-19 pandemic. In conclusion, this study allows us to understand the dynamics of employment in the state of Nuevo Leon, mainly the dynamics between the different employment segments and gender, so that more and greater access to employment opportunities for women would allow an accelerated recovery of the labor market in the state. Even so, one of our primary concerns is to understand the dynamics of employment by skills across the different states of Mexico. For future analyses, we propose extending the study of employment dynamics across the country's different states.

Annex

See Fig. 5.3.

VAR Models and Impulse-Response Function to negative shock in ITAEE
Time set: quarters after I-shock COVID-19 related to the economic crisis

Model 1: Structure and dynamic of employment by skill levels in Nuevo Leon

Employment

Variable	Low-skilled employment	High-skilled employment
L1.lsemp	−0.094	0.0603
L1.hsemp	0.135 *	0.0246
L1.itaee	0.480	0.416
L1.rwhr	−0.0335	−0.112
Constant	−0.0034	0.0094
N	131	131
RMSE	0.04913	0.064806
Chi2(prob)	0.1136	0.3503

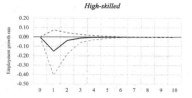

Model 2: structure and dynamic of employment by gender-skills in Nuevo Leon

	Men		Women	
Variable	Low-skilled employment	High-skilled employment	Low-skilled employment	High-skilled employment
L1.lsemp.m	−0.176	0.0849	0.127	0.0666
L1.lsemp.w	0.0822	−0.0191	−0.243 *	0.0107
L1.hsemp.m	0.0862	−0.198	0.205	0.287 *
L1.hsemp.w	0.0536	0.125	−0.0519	−0.114
L1.itaee	0.648 *	0.467	0.0468	0.294
L1.rwhr	0.0121	−0.0524	−0.0707	−0.0159
Constant	−0.00587	0.00687	0.00261	0.0144
N	131	131	131	131
RMSE	0.046642	0.068579	0.084761	0.089594
Chi2(prob)	0.0591	0.3093	0.1276	0.4166

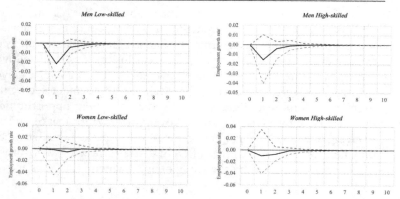

Fig. 5.3 VAR model: estimation and Impulse-Response Functions (IRLs) (p-value: 0.001***, 0.01**, 0.05*. *Source:* Own estimations with time series constructed and homologized of employment surveys (ENEU-ENE-ENOE). Seasonally adjusted series presented by growth rates)

References

Akkemik, K. (2007). The response of employment to GDP growth in Turkey: An econometric estimation. *Applied Econometrics and International Development, 7*(1), 65–74.

Altamirano, A., Azuara, O., & Gonzalez, S. (2020). ¿Cómo impactará la COVID-19 al empleo? *Posibles escenarios para America Latina y el Caribe.* Banco Interamericano de Desarrollo.

Arrow, K., Chenery, H., Minhas, B., & Solow, R. (1961). Capital-labor substitution and economic efficiency. *The Review of Economics and Statistics, 43*(3), 225. https://doi.org/10.2307/1927286

Banco de Mexico (2020). *Banco de Mexico: Resumen Ejecutivo del Informe Trimestral enero-marzo 2020.*

Becker, G. (1965). A theory of allocation of time. *The Economic Journal, 75*, 493–517.

CEPAL, N. (2020). *América Latina y el Caribe ante la pandemia del COVID-19: efectos economicos y sociales.*

Coparmex Nuevo Leon. (2020). *Lidera Nuevo Leon en empleos formales recuperados.* https://coparmexnl.org.mx/2020/11/18/lidera-nl-en-empleo-formales-recuperados/

Cuellar, C. (2019). *Evolucion de la brecha salarial en Mexico: Un enfoque de genero y capital humano para el sector formal asalariado* [Tesis de maestría no publicada]. Universidad Autonoma de Nuevo Leon.

Cuellar, C., & Moreno, J. (2021). *Employment, wages, and the gender gap in Mexico: evidence of three decades of the urban labor market.* Article submitted for publication.

Encuesta Nacional de Empleo Urbano (ENEU), años de 1987 a 2000, INEGI. www.inegi.gob.mx

Encuesta Nacional de Empleo (ENE), años de 2001 a 2004, INEGI. www.inegi.gob.mx

Encuesta Nacional de Ocupación y Empleo (ENOE), años de 2005 a 2020, INEGI. www.inegi.gob.mx

Encuesta Nacional Telefonica de Ocupacion y Empleo (ENOE), años de 2020, INEGI. www.inegi.gob.mx

Esquivel, G. (2020). Los impactos economicos de la pandemia en Mexico. *Economia UNAM, 17*(51), 28–44. https://doi.org/10.22201/fe.24488143e.2020.51.543

Flores, L. (2021, April 21). *Nuevo Leon podria crecer 6.4% en el 2021: CIE.* El Economista. https://www.eleconomista.com.mx/estados/Nuevo-Leon-podria-crecer-6.4-en-el-2021-CIE-20210421-0108.html

Gomez, C., & Mosino, A. (2019). El genero del empleo en America Latina. *Formacion de problemas de desarrollo*, pp. 249–271.

Heckman, J. (2012, December). *Invest in early childhood development: Reduce deficits, strengthen the economy*. The Heckman Equation, University of Chicago.

Humphries, J. (1988). Women's employment in restructuring America: The changing experience of women in three recessions. In J. Rubery (Ed.), *Women and recession* (pp. 20–47). Routledge and Kegan Paul.

INEGI (2020). *Indicadores de ocupacion y empleo*. Cifras oportunas durante marzo de 2020. Instituto Nacional de estadistica y Geografia.

International Monetary Fund. (2020). *World economic outlook: The great lockdown*. International Monetary Fund.

Ivanov, V., & Kilian, L. (2005). A practitioner's guide to lag order selection for VAR impulse response analysis. *Studies in Nonlinear Dynamics & Econometrics, 9*(1).

Jimenez-Bandala, C., Peralta, J., Sanchez, E., Olvera, I., & Aceves, D. (2020). La situacion del mercado laboral en Mexico antes y durante la COVID-19. *Revista Internacional de Salarios Dignos, 2*(2), 1–14.

Maldonado, D., & Ruiz, J. (2020). La crisis ocasionada por la COVID-19 y sus efectos en el empleo y la pobreza en Mexico. *Revista Internacional de Salarios Dignos, 2*(3), 23–38.

Mexico Como Vamos. (2020). *El impacto del COVID-19 sobre el empleo formal en los estados*. https://mexicocomovamos.mx/new/md-multimedia/1597177275-38.pdf

Mincer, J. (1975). Education, experience, and the distribution of earnings and employment: An overview. In T. Juster, *Education, Income, and Human Behavior* (pp. 71–94). National Bureau of Economic Research, Inc.

Moreno, J., & Cuellar, C. (2021). Informality, gender employment gap, and COVID-19 in Mexico: Identifying persistence and dynamic structural effects. *Revista Mexicana de Economía y Finanzas Nueva Época REMEF, 16*(3), 636. https://doi.org/10.21919/remef.v16i3.636

Nunez, R. (2020). *Impacto del COVID-19 en el empleo en Mexico: posibles escenarios y algunas recomendaciones de politica economica*.

Okun, A. (1962). Potential GNP: Its measurement and significance. In *Proceedings of the Business and economic statistics section of the American statistical association* (pp. 89–104). American Statistical Association.

Sampedro, J., & Cortiña, R. (1969). *Estructura economica: theoria basica y estructura mundial*. Ediciones Ariel.

Sanchez, I. (2020). *Empleo en la frontera norte de Mexico ante el COVID-19*. Instituto de Ciencias Sociales y Administración.

Schultz, T. (1961). Investment in human capital. *The American Economic Review, 51*(1), 1–17.

Schumpeter, J. (1934). *Theory of economic development*. Oxford University Press.

Sims, C. (1980). Macroeconomics and reality. *Econometrica: Journal of the Econometric Society, 48*(1), 1–48.

Skoufias, E., & Parker, S. W. (2006). Job loss and family adjustments in work and schooling during the Mexican peso crisis. *Journal of Population Economics, 19*(1), 163–181.

Werner, A., Komatsuzaki, T., & Pizzinelli, C. (2021). IMF Blog. [Blog]. https://blogs.imf.org/2021/04/15/short-term-shot-and-long-term-healing-for-latin-america-and-the-caribbean/

CHAPTER 6

Finally Back to Campus? Motivations for Facemask Adoption in the Higher Education Sector

Paolo Morganti, Antonia Terán-Bustamante, and Enrique Murillo

INTRODUCTION

The COVID-19 pandemic has forced Higher Education Institutions (HEI) and governments around the world to restrict campus attendance by students and instructors in order to limit the spread of the disease. Some countries, including Mexico, have opted for complete campus lockdown with practically all classes imparted through online platforms (Rodriguez-Abitia, 2021); other countries, such as Spain and

---

P. Morganti · A. Terán-Bustamante · E. Murillo (✉)
Facultad de Ciencias Económicas y Empresariales, Universidad Panamericana, Mexico City, Mexico
e-mail: emurillo@up.edu.mx

P. Morganti
e-mail: pmorganti@up.edu.mx

© The Author(s), under exclusive license to Springer Nature Switzerland AG 2022
A. M. López-Fernández and A. Terán-Bustamante (eds.), *Business Recovery in Emerging Markets*, Palgrave Studies in Democracy, Innovation, and Entrepreneurship for Growth,
https://doi.org/10.1007/978-3-030-91532-2_6

USA, have permitted limited campus attendance with various protective measures required of students, such as prior COVID-19 testing, staggered attendance, and facemask wearing (Walke et al., 2020).

In Mexico City, public and private HEI's campuses were closed around the middle of March of 2020, with all instruction moving to online platforms (El Financiero, 2020; Rodriguez-Abitia, 2021). The local city government decreed a lockdown of non-essential businesses and services starting on March 30 and ending until June 29, when the saturated occupation level of hospitals finally abated (Hernández, 2020). Local regulations prescribe the use of facemasks in public spaces, although no penalty is attached to individuals for failing to do so. However, people cannot board public transportation without a facemask, and businesses can be fined or closed for failing to enforce facemask use among patrons.

Since the start of the pandemic, the use of facemasks has been recommended by the World Health Organization as an effective protective measure for both the individual and the people around him or her (World Health Organization, 2020). Months later, when national vaccination campaigns got underway, the organization recommended that people who had received a COVID-19 vaccine should keep using a facemask when in public spaces (World Health Organization, 2021). However, facemask wearing relies, to a considerable extent, on voluntary adoption by the individual, and it became a polarizing issue in many countries from the start of the pandemic (Clements, 2020).

When campus attendance is again permitted, it will very likely be under a mandatory policy that all persons wear a facemask while on-campus, a situation that has as little precedent as the pandemic itself. Therefore, researching the factors that contribute to the voluntary adoption of facemasks among university students, in the various social contexts they will face when they begin in-person instruction, becomes a worthy research objective. To this end, it is necessary to increase our understanding of students' behavior in situations where individual actions are personally costly (such as facemask wearing) but can bring about social benefits. An extensive literature in Social Psychology (Van Lange et al., 1998, 2013; Murphy & Ackermann, 2014; Pletzer et al., 2018) has studied specific conducts under social dilemmas, emphasizing the role of Social

---

A. Terán-Bustamante
e-mail: ateran@up.edu.mx

Value Orientation (SVO) in explaining pro-social behavior (Van Lange, 1999). Defined as the individual predisposition "for particular patterns of outcomes for self and others" (McClintock, 1972), SVO is positively related to the adoption of cooperative behavior (Balliet et al., 2009; Pletzer et al., 2018).

To explore this important issue, survey data was collected from a large convenience sample of students enrolled in Mexico City HEIs during the Fall semester of 2020. Our most important contribution to knowledge is that facemask wearing among students is a complex behavior, formed by different types of conducts, each one with different significant antecedents. In particular, our results show that SVO and Trust affect certain conducts but not others. It follows that, if facemask wearing is viewed as a single, general conduct, the understanding of the problem can become obfuscated. As a practical implication, any kind of public health communication promoting adoption of facemasks should avoid general messages, and instead target specific desired outcomes by leveraging conduct-specific variables.

Literature Review

This research analyzes the willingness to engage in cooperative behavior of students from HEIs in Mexico City during the COVID-19 pandemic. While this is not a representative sample of the general population, it does afford the opportunity to focus on one of the demographic groups that is becoming most critical in shaping the dynamics of diffusion of the COVID-19 disease. In Europe, a few months after the re-opening of the economy, the average age of infected patients dropped, and several commentators pointed to the responsibility of young people in spreading the disease (Euronews, 2020). A very similar dynamic played out in residential campuses in the USA that reopened for the Fall 2020 semester (Wilson et al., 2020). By contrast, Mexico was one of the countries where HEIs' installations remained closed during the entire Fall semester.

The ease with which COVID-19 infects people and the saturation it causes in health systems forced governments to take unprecedented actions to convince their citizens to adopt burdensome precautionary measures in an attempt to limit the spread of the virus. This requires strong behavioral changes among the general population. To achieve this, governments around the world released extensive communication campaigns to convince people to adopt precautionary conducts. The precautionary behavior that is needed to prevent the spread of a pandemic requires social distancing and wearing of masks, among others.

In order to make such policies and targeted messages as effective as possible, it is important to understand people's behavior in situations where individual actions are personally costly (such as facemask wearing) but can produce social benefits by protecting others from contagion. While the standard economics paradigm prescribes that people act regarding exclusively one's own interest, laboratory evidence in economic games (Murphy & Ackermann, 2014) shows that a substantial amount of individuals also values social dimensions. This dichotomy suggests that public messages emphasizing consequences on the community might be more effective than messages focusing on personal consequences.

The nature of the problem forces the individual decision maker to sustain all of the costs of the action, while receiving only a fraction of its benefits which are rather spread over society. In particular, face covering benefits others more than it does oneself (van Der Westhuizen et al., 2020). Following Van Lange et al. (1998), we define a Social Dilemma as a situation in which there is a conflict between individual and collective interests. If individuals do not follow the cooperative option, in an attempt to gain a temporary benefit, everybody will be worse off (Hamburger, 1979; Messick & Brewer, 1983; Van Lange & Messick, 1996). In this research, we analyze the social dilemma created by the prescription to wear protective masks for the containment of the COVID-19 pandemic, and attempt to predict the behavior of HEI students, a critical demographic group within the general population.

Previous literature has shown that SVO is positively related to the adoption of cooperative behavior (Balliet et al., 2009; Pletzer et al., 2018). There are four types of social orientations but, for the purpose of this study, we only focus on pro-social and pro-self orientations: as the outcomes of the dilemma are binary, the categories of competitive and egalitarian do not apply. Pro-social individuals tend to assign a significant weight to the outcome received by others; on the other hand, pro-selfs, assign a low weight to the outcome received by others, and are predominantly concerned with their own outcome.

Recent articles that examine the public's reaction to government messages about protective measures have examined the effect of prosociality on cooperative behavior during the pandemic (e.g. Campos-Mercade et al., 2021; Capraro & Barcelo, 2020; Jordan et al., 2020).

In particular, Leder et al. (2020) examined whether protective behaviors, such as social distancing and facemask use, were more frequently adopted when perceived to increase self-protection versus protection to the public, and used SVO as the measure of prosociality. In general, these studies have found that in the context of the present crisis, and even in samples with high prosociality, people are concerned first and foremost with their own safety over the safety of the public. Moreover, no significant effects were detected between SVO and the adoption of protective measures (Leder et al., 2020). In line with studies that have explored the effect of prosociality on the adoption of measures to reduce the spread of the disease, the following hypothesis is advanced:

Hypothesis 1: SVO is positively associated with the use of facemasks

As Joireman et al. (1997) argue in a study on commuting decisions, SVO is unlikely to be the only determinant of cooperative behavior. Even prosocial orientation can fail to produce a cooperative behavior if a decision maker expects other people to not comply with the same costly measure, which calls forth the issue of trust in others.

The literature shows some ambiguity around the notion of Trust. Yamagishi and Yamagishi (1994) discuss Trust in two settings: as a cognitive bias that describes overconfidence about others' benevolent behavior given the available information (General Trust), and as assurance in another's behavior because of the presence of a binding implicit social contract and independently of the presence of goodwill (Knowledge-Based Trust). Barber (1983) distinguishes between expectations about a partner's competence (reframed as Confidence) and expectations about a partner's benign intent. Most research uses Trust as the expectation about others' benevolent motives during social interaction, i.e. general trust.

In their study of commuting preferences, Van Lange et al. (1998) theorize that high Trust leads pro-social individuals to commit to costly cooperative actions; however, high Trust also leads pro-self decision makers to free ride, and to adopt selfish courses of action. On the other hand, low Trust demotivates even pro-social individuals to cooperate, as the perceived efficacy (Kerr, 1989) of their action appears null (see also Boone et al., 2010). In other words, an interaction effect was posited between SVO and Trust (Van Lange et al., 1998), whereby individuals high in SVO and in Trust would be the most likely to commit to cooperative behavior. The empirical results of that study confirmed both a significant direct effect of generalized Trust on cooperative behavior, as well as a significant interaction effect of SVO and Trust (Van Lange et al., 1998). In addition, other studies show evidence that there are no significant differences in Trust between pro-socials and pro-selfs (Joireman et al., 1997; Parks, 1994). Based on these previous studies, the following hypotheses are posited:

Hypothesis 2: Trust is positively associated with the use of facemasks

Hypothesis 3: There will be a significant interaction between SVO and Trust, such that individuals with high SVO and high Trust will be more likely to use facemasks

Methods

The current research was launched at the start of the Fall semester in August 2020, when there was still some hope among students and faculty that at least a partial reopening of HEIs would take place during the semester. In point of fact, the pandemic did not abate during the Fall, and Mexico City's government was forced to decree a second lockdown that lasted from December 18 to February 14, 2021 (Ordaz Díaz, 2021). Accordingly, HEIs remained closed at the start of the Spring 2021 semester, although by April, students in some universities, mostly from the Health Sciences group, were allowed to attend campus for laboratory instruction but following strict protective measures.

To measure university students' perceptions and attitudes toward facemask use, we undertook a large survey among students enrolled in Mexico City HEIs during the Fall semester of 2020. Specifically, our target population was college-age students (between 17 and 25) enrolled in Mexico City HEIs and, thus, subject to the local government's public health communications and regulations. In common with most of the survey studies conducted during the emergency lockdowns detonated by COVID-19 (e.g. Abdelhafiz et al., 2020; Alzoubi et al., 2020; Azlan et al., 2020; Bates et al., 2020; Reuben et al., 2021), we relied on a non-probabilistic sample, albeit a large one, collected through social media contacts.

We used snowball sampling (Heckathorn & Cameron, 2017), whereby students enrolled in introductory business research courses taught by two of the authors invited their social media contacts to participate in the study, with class credit awarded for collected surveys. We carefully explained to students our research aim and the population we wanted to reach; hence, they shared the survey link with friends and acquaintances who were also university students. Because our snowball seeds were all students enrolled in a private university, we expected our sample would be biased toward students from private universities, with an under-representation of students from public universities. However, we found no theoretical argument to suggest that the variables of interest would be affected by the type of institution students attended. In particular, previous research of prosociality behaviors among students have documented significant differences by chosen university major (e.g. Frank et al., 1993; Tepe & Vanhuysse, 2017), but not by type of university attended (e.g. Weber et al., 2019). The survey instrument was assembled and hosted in a professional online platform (Surveygizmo.com), thus, ensuring that the questions displayed correctly in both PC and mobile phone screens, which we expected most respondents to use.

Measurement

Whenever possible, we used published scales to measure study constructs. For Trust, we used the Spanish adaptation of the Yamagishi scale (Montoro et al., 2014). For SVO, we used the slider measure developed by Murphy et al. (2011). In addition to controlling for age, gender, and university of enrollment (to confirm residency in Mexico City), we included a number of control variables in the survey, which had been used previously in international studies of attitudes and behaviors toward the pandemic (e.g. Bates et al., 2020; Clements, 2020). First, the level of knowledge about the COVID-19 disease (e.g. Abdelhafiz et al., 2020; Azlan et al., 2020; Reuben et al., 2021), for which we developed a seven question True-Not Sure-False instrument focused mostly on Coronavirus contagion behaviors, with correct answers obtained from the WHO and Centers for Disease Control and Prevention (CDC) Web sites. In a related vein, a specific question controlled whether respondents were enrolled in any undergraduate major from the Health Sciences group, such as Medicine, Nursing, Dentistry, etc. (Alzoubi et al., 2020).

To control for individual resistance toward wearing a facemask in social contexts, we included five items from the multidimensional scale by Howard (2020). In addition, the survey controlled whether respondents had personally contracted COVID-19 in the previous six months, and in a separate question whether a person who was close to the respondent had contracted the disease in the previous six months (the survey took place in September 2020).

To measure facemask wearing conducts, we reviewed a number of studies but could not find an appropriate scale. Hence, from our reading of the international literature and local Mexico City regulations, we developed seven questions (see Appendix) framed around common situations for college-age students, where they would face an increased risk of COVID-19 contagion, and what facemask conduct they would likely follow in that situation. We rejected a question about facemask wearing while using public transportation because a local ordinance already prohibited boarding buses or the subway without a mask, making this question moot.

Data Collection

The instrument was tested through a pilot run using the students attending the authors' courses. A total of 48 complete surveys were collected during the pilot. Multi-item scales were all evaluated with a 7-point Likert scale. Analysis of pilot responses detected that two of the seven questions depicting facemask wearing (Conducts 2 and 3) were highly skewed toward "very strongly agree" and displayed minimal variance; these were discarded from the final instrument. Other multi-item scales, including Trust, SVO and COVID-19 knowledge displayed a reasonable distribution of responses. The pilot results also suggested other minor corrections on question wording, and the instructions preceding the SVO scale. Final scales are available in the Appendix.

The revised survey was released to students on the 24th of September, and they shared the link with their social media contacts. The survey remained open until October 4, 2020, a total of 11 days, with 2486 surveys turned in. Since we were unable to fully control the sharing of the survey link, we received a substantial number of surveys from respondents not matching our target demographic (i.e. younger than 17 or older than 25), and also from students not currently enrolled in a Mexico City university and, hence, not subject to the local government health regulations and public messaging. In all, we discarded 19 incomplete surveys, 225 surveys not meeting the age criteria, and 178 surveys that either did not list a university or listed a university not located in Mexico City. The final valid sample comprised 2064 complete surveys.

Descriptive statistics of the sample are displayed in Table 6.1(A and B). In Table 6.1A we compare sociodemographic characteristics of the sample with available official statistics, namely same-age population statistics for Mexico City 2019–2020 HEI enrollment published by the National Association of Higher Education Institutions (ANUIES, 2020). The age and gender distribution of our sample are roughly similar to the Mexico City student population; not so with the public versus private university proportion which, as expected, is heavily skewed toward private institutions. Because our sample, albeit large, is nevertheless a convenience sample, we follow the guidelines of Hirschauer et al. (2020) and refrain from reporting p-values, as they can only be meaningfully interpreted in the context of a probabilistic sample. Table 6.1B reports additional sample characteristics for which there is no official data for comparison purposes.

Table 6.1A Sample descriptives: sociodemographic variables versus comparable official data

Sample characteristic	n	%	ANUIES	%
Age				
17	10	0.48	7591	1.71
18	83	4.02	42,280	9.50
19	371	17.97	71,531	16.07
20	483	23.40	76,519	17.19
21	426	20.64	73,163	16.44
22	400	19.38	63,216	14.20
23	203	9.84	46,894	10.54
24	56	2.71	38,209	8.59
25	32	1.55	25,652	5.76
Total	2064	100	445,055	100
Gender				
Female	1244	60.27	225,557	50.68
Male	820	39.73	219,498	49.31
Total	2064	100	445,055	100
Type of university				
Private	1804	87.4	149,604	33.61
Public	260	12.6	295,451	66.39
Total	2064	100	445,055	100

Table 6.1B Sample variables that lack an official data comparison

Sample characteristic	n	%
Undergraduate major		
Health Sciences	321	15.55
Other majors	1743	84.45
Total	2064	100
Respondent has contracted COVID-19		
Yes	158	7.66
No	1906	92.34
Total	2064	100
Close person has contracted COVID-19		
Yes	967	46.85
No	1097	53.15
Total	2064	100
COVID-19 quiz number of correct answers		
0	22	1.07
1	19	0.92
2	55	2.66
3	113	5.47
4	345	16.72
5	583	28.25
6	586	28.39
7	341	16.52
Total	2064	100

Results

Based on the literature review, our study focuses on SVO and Trust as the main predictors for voluntary adoption of facemasks in Social Dilemmas. Joireman et al. (1997), and Parks (1994) show evidence that there are no significant differences in Trust between pro-socials and pro-selfs. On the other hand, Kuhlman et al. (1986) and Kanagaretnam et al. (2009) find that pro-selfs exhibit lower levels of Trust relative to pro-socials. Our sample conforms to the latter study as we find a significant positive relationship between pro-social orientation and the level of Trust (see Table 6.2; the asterisk denotes significance at the 95% level). Moreover, we find that women tend to be more pro-social than men. A separate test reveals no correlation between Gender and the level of Trust.

This preliminary exploration sheds light on prosociality attitudes among the students in our survey, and it allows us to compare our sample

Table 6.2 Regression of SVO over trust and gender

SVO	Coefficients
Trust	0.838*
	(0.232)
Gender	4.352*
	(0.594)

with others used in similar studies. From a technical point of view, it also reveals that SVO and Trust are going to be collinear in our regressions. As a consequence, we should expect standard errors to be inflated relative to the real model and, therefore, some variables that are significant may not appear to be so. In our work, we take a conservative stance and focus only on significant results. We proceeded to estimate five separate multivariate regressions to explain each of the different facemask wearing conducts. While our main concerns with these regressions are SVO, Trust and their interaction, per our hypotheses, we also report on the significance of the various control variables.

Despite the fact that we control for different explanatory variables, we detect the inevitable presence of substantial unobservable ones. Unobservable variables represent dimensions or characteristics that the researchers cannot measure (Riegg, 2008). Unobservable variables can cause, in worst-case scenarios, problems of endogeneity. Endogeneity occurs when unobservable variables contained within the error term end up being correlated with some of the observed variables, leading to biased estimates. Even in best-case scenarios, unobservable variables reduce the significance of the estimates and the R^2. This creates a practical challenge to any researcher.

As a fortunate byproduct of studying multiple conducts at the same time, we obtain a technical advantage that allows us to address the problem. Because the conducts are correlated and are affected by similar sets of unobservable variables, one can use them as proxies in each other's regressions. By construction, a proxy variable captures some of the variation generated by the unobservable variables, removing it from the error terms (Stahlecker & Trenkler, 1993). As a result, proxies reduce the noise of the model without affecting its identification. As we picked any of the five conducts as dependent variable, and used the remaining four as independent variables, we were able to dramatically improve the quality of our model without altering any of the estimates. Removing the proxies from the regressions did not affect the estimate but reduced the precision of the analysis (Riegg, 2008).

Another problem was that in each of the five models, the residuals presented strong signs of heteroskedasticity, and they were not normally distributed. While these two failures of the classic assumptions of the regression model do not affect the consistency of the estimates, they seriously hamper their precision and any test of significance. For this reason, we discarded the standard Normal-based confidence intervals and p-values, and computed Bootstrapped standard errors. In particular, we use the Bias-Corrected and Accelerated (BCA) option to correct for bias and skewness in the procedure (Efron, 1987). In Table 6.3, we report a selected subset of results where we focus on the relevant explanatory variables and omit most control variables. The coefficients are standardized for ease of comparison. We also report the Adjusted R^2 for each model.

As it is possible to see from our analysis, different conducts possess different explanations. In particular, SVO and Trust explain only some behaviors, but not others.

Conduct 1: "When I leave my house I always wear the mask"

The model has a poor explanation, due to the low variability in the dependent variable. In fact, the vast majority of the students responded "Strongly Agree". Even so, variability in knowledge about the disease is positively and significantly associated to variability in the cooperative behavior. In addition, it is possible to see that the Conducts, used as proxies, help to improve the model.

Conduct 4: "When I travel in any car I always wear the mask"

Starting from this survey question, responses become more evenly distributed across the different options. With this facemask-use conduct, SVO emerges as a significant predictor, consistently with the literature. SVO has a positive impact on facemask wearing. However, contrary to the literature (Van Lange et al., 1998) this behavior is not affected by Trust, nor we observe an interaction between Trust and SVO. Therefore, within this type of conduct, we do not find support for Hypothesis 2 and 3. We also observe that students who had been sick in the past tend to wear masks more than students who had never been sick. Finally, we detect a positive relation between a student's knowledge about the disease and the use of facemasks.

Table 6.3 Regressions of facemask wearing conducts

Variables	Conduct 1	Conduct 4	Conduct 5	Conduct 6	Conduct 7
Trust	−0.003	0.252	0.389*	0.041	0.291*
	(0.071)	(0.139)	(0.119)	(0.108)	(0.136)
SVO	0.001	0.483*	0.091*	0.312*	0.019
	(0.019)	(0.138)	(0.047)	(0.110)	(0.041)
SVO*Trust	0.022	−0.064	−0.332*	−0.083	−0.133
	(0.065)	(0.144)	(0.121)	(0.109)	(0.136)
Conduct 1	–	0.227*	0.286*	−0.011	0.062**
		(0.044)	(0.037)	(0.037)	(0.041)
Conduct 4	0.088*	–	0.411*	−0.068	−0.083**
	(0.016)		(0.041)	(0.038)	(0.042)
Conduct 5	0.134*	0.492*	–	−0.099*	−0.601*
	(0.022)	(0.049)		(0.040)	(0.043)
Conduct 6	−0.007	−0.097	−0.120*	–	0.896*
	(0.02)	(0.053)	(0.048)		(0.044)
Conduct 7	0.036	−0.122	−0.738*	0.930*	–
	(0.024)	(0.062)	(0.052)	(0.050)	
KnowledgeCovid	0.056*	0.196*	−0.006	0.265*	−0.077*
	(0.021)	(0.091)	(0.042)	(0.077)	(0.037)
Health Sciences	−0.029	0.048	0.346*	−0.159	0.123
	(0.043)	(0.123)	(0.108)	(0.105)	(0.104)
dummySick	−0.009	0.362*	−0.015	0.039	0.068
	(0.069)	(0.164)	(0.149)	(0.133)	(0.136)
dummySickClose	0.026	−0.089	−0.151*	−0.011	−0.036
	(0.032)	(0.086)	(0.077)	(0.072)	(0.070)
Gender	0.040	−0.139	0.079	0.040	−0.142*
	(0.038)	(0.089)	(0.079)	(0.073)	(0.070)
Adjusted R^2 (%)	8.91	15.30	29.20	34.29	41.76
N. Observations	2064	2064	2064	2064	2064

Conduct 5: "When I go to a meeting or party I keep the mask on"

In the social context of a meeting or party, not only SVO, but also Trust is positively associated with facemask wearing, supporting both Hypothesis 1 and 2 for this conduct. Interestingly, we find a significantly negative interaction between SVO and Trust. While our Hypothesis 3 predicted a significant interaction between the two constructs, what we expected was a positive sign of the effect. Contrary to Van Lange et al. (1998), rather than *complementing* each other, SVO and Trust act as *substitutes* for this particular type of behavior. Pro-social students who score low in Trust are more likely to keep wearing the facemask during social gatherings with their peers, while those who score high on Trust are more likely to take it off.

This result highlights the difference between cooperative behaviors associated with standard Social Dilemmas and those associated with the COVID-19 pandemic crisis that is hitting the world. It is likely that the sense of danger perceived during the pandemic twists the interaction between the two social constructs.

Finally, and unexpectedly, we discover that having a close relative who successfully recovered from the virus leads students to feel less pressure to wear masks during gatherings with friends. Although these students perceive a lower risk of exposing their own families to COVID-19, thanks to temporary immunization, they should still be concerned for the potential externality they impose on the rest of society. In addition to that, because it is possible to get infected more than once after the temporary immunization has disappeared, this behavior can lead such families to be proportionally more at risk than others. This result uncovers a so-called *Peltzman effect* (Peltzman, 1975), which postulates that individuals adapt their behavior toward less careful measures in response to a decrease in perceived risk. Iyengar et al. (2021) and Trogen and Caplan (2021) warn about the dangers of a Peltzman effect following COVID-19 vaccinations. Such a finding highlights a potentially critical risk that needs to be addressed with specific messages.

Conduct 6: "When I am visiting relatives whom I trust, I take off my mask"

SVO appears as a significant variable for this conduct; however we do not detect any impact of Trust. Therefore, for this specific conduct, we reject Hypothesis 2 and 3.

Conduct 7: "When I meet friends whom I know well, I take off my mask"

Similar to Conduct 5, Trust has a significant and positive impact on the precautionary behavior, providing support to Hypothesis 2. However, SVO is not significant in the regression, nor is the interaction between SVO and Trust, forcing us to reject Hypothesis 1 and 3.

Interestingly, only under this conduct the role of gender emerges as significant with women less likely to wear facemasks than men, in the context of interactions with close friends. This result contrasts with previous findings that women are more likely to wear a facemask (Capraro & Barcelo, 2020; Galasso et al., 2020), but we attribute our different result to the particular context posed by this survey question, i.e. interactions with close friends, which is not examined as such in previous studies.

Following the suggestion of an anonymous referee, we ran a Principal Component Analysis on the five Conducts to attempt to extract a more parsimonious model. In the preliminary analysis, we found that the eigenvalues are close to each other, suggesting that the use of a single component might not suffice to improve model fit. Nevertheless, we estimated the regressions with this the most prominent component as predictor; as anticipated, the fit was poor. This exercise was however helpful in reinforcing the confidence in our strategy of separating the analysis by conducts.

One final note is that the means for the questions measuring facemask resistance revealed that our large student sample exhibited relatively low resistance to the use of this precautionary measure. This will come as good news for HEI authorities contemplating a campus reopening with a mandate for facemask use. In the regression models, the path coefficient for these control variables was non-significant in all Conducts, except for Conduct 5, where it was significant and positive (i.e. it contributed toward the use of the facemask).

Discussion and Implications

As the 2021 Spring semester got underway, vaccination campaigns had started in many countries, including Mexico. However, these campaigns prioritized at-risk and older populations; college-age students are scheduled to be the last to be vaccinated in Mexico, not before June 2021 (El Economista, 2020). In the meanwhile, experts have warned that the use of facemasks will be required into 2022 (Goodnough, 2021) and that, even after receiving a COVID-19 vaccine, the use of facemasks is still strongly recommended (Cleveland Clinic, 2021; World Health Organization, 2021). While HEI authorities are anxious to reopen their installations and return to in-person instruction, they may be required by governments to set limits to the number of people allowed in situ, and may have to mandate that both faculty and students wear facemasks at all times while on-campus. Accordingly, the results of this exploratory study will be of interest.

The main contributions of our work to the Social Psychology literature are methodological. First, as mentioned above, we found that facemask wearing is a complex behavior, reflecting distinct conducts. This implies that separate analyses should be run for each of its different dimensions. While it is common practice to merge such different dimensions into a single dependent variable, doing so blurs the explanatory power of important factors, which might affect only some conducts, but not others. For this reason, we recommend future works to identify as many different conducts as possible from surveys or field analysis.

More interestingly, we were able to leverage the previous observation to identify a novel empirical strategy in order to reduce issues of endogeneity. Social studies are often affected by the presence of significant unobservable variables that could plague empirical results. By keeping the different conducts separate, we were able to use them as proxies in each other's regressions. The rationale is that all conducts are likely explained by similar sets of unobservable variables. Moreover, each behavior is only imperfectly correlated with the others. The combined effect of the last two points permitted the creation of powerful proxies that significantly impacted the explanatory power of the model without distorting other estimated coefficients. In fact, often times they allowed important variables to emerge as significant antecedents after part of the noise was removed.

As a final contribution, we extend the breadth of variables employed in the analysis and identify some unexpected effects on facemask adoption during the COVID-19 pandemic. First, we detect that having a close relative recently infected by the virus leads to a riskier behavior in gatherings with friends. Second, although women have consistently been associated with higher levels of prosociality, our analysis shows they are less prone to wear facemasks but only in the context of meeting with close friends. Third, we find that prosociality and trust are important to explain facemask adoption by students in some social contexts, but not in all, which opens avenues for future research. Finally, our findings confirm previous results in the literature to the effect that knowledge about the COVID-19 disease promotes facemask wearing in any situation.

While more research is needed to learn how to design an effective language, this study already highlights the fact that general messages are not likely to be successful in inducing university students to wear facemasks in certain situations. Hence, a key implication stemming from our results is that public health communications should craft nuanced messages targeting specific social situations.

First, a frequent behavior among young adults, and which arguably has been the greatest concern for HEI authorities in countries that went forward with campus reopenings, is social gatherings and/or parties (e.g. Wilson et al., 2020). Regarding this conduct, our results show that students perceive a significant difference between large parties and small gatherings. In both cases, Trust plays a significant role in facemask wearing. Messages reinforcing the responsibility accompanied with receiving trust from one's friends are recommended to prevent the spread of the disease. On the other hand, messages highlighting SVO (care about someone else's health) will only have a minor effect, and only when the context is that of larger gatherings. Moreover, SVO might substitute from the stronger effect brought by Trust. For this reason, we recommend to avoid SVO-related messages when targeting these particular contexts.

Second, our results suggest that female students are more prone to take off their facemasks when meeting with close friends. Targeted messages are recommended to counteract the effects of gender-related social pressure. Finally, SVO plays a significant role when students meet some of their relatives. As the most vulnerable people are likely to belong to the extended family, it is important to sensitize students about the use of facemasks in their presence. Messages emphasizing care about other people will have the strongest effect.

In acknowledging study limitations, the use of a convenience sample should be pointed out, which precludes making generalizations about the student population. Another limitation is the small number of facemask conducts that were modeled. Given the strong likelihood of on-campus facemask mandates in the coming months, we suggest that future research could replicate and extend our results by examining specific facemask conducts in the context of reopened university campuses. Some relevant questions could be: "When I go to campus I keep the mask on all the time", "When I am on campus, and I sit down to chat with friends, I keep the mask on", or "When I am on campus I prefer to eat alone than to sit with others". The results of such a study could help HEI authorities craft nuanced and targeted communications to promote campus safety.

Appendix—Multi-item Scales in the Survey

Facemask Wearing Conducts

Conduct 1. When I leave my house, I always wear a mask
Conduct 4. When I travel in any car, I always wear a mask
Conduct 5. When I go to a meeting or party, I keep the mask on
Conduct 6. When I am visiting relatives whom I trust, I take off my mask (R)
Conduct 7. When I meet friends whom I know well, I take off my mask (R)

Resistance Toward Facemask Use

It is difficult to breathe when wearing a facemask
Wearing a face mask is too much of a hassle
I do not like feeling forced to wear a facemask
I do not like what other people think, when they see me wearing a facemask
I do not like how I look when I wear a facemask

Knowledge About COVID-19 (Correct Answer)

To prevent the spread of Coronavirus facemasks are more effective than face shields (True)
It is possible to be sick with COVID-19 and not show any symptoms (True)
People with COVID-19 can spread it to others simply by talking, even if they do not sneeze (True)
Shaking hands with a person infected with Coronavirus is a cause of contagion because the virus can penetrate the skin (False)
Children have a lower risk of contracting Coronavirus than adults (False)
Coronavirus is spread by respiratory droplets that infected people breathe out when they speak or cough (True)
People infected with Coronavirus cannot infect others if they do not have a fever (False)

Generalized Trust

Most people are basically honest
Most people are trustworthy
I am generally trustful
Most people are basically good and kind
Most people are trustful of others

REFERENCES

Abdelhafiz, A. S., Mohammed, Z., Ibrahim, M. E., Ziady, H. H., Alorabi, M., Ayyad, M., & Sultan, E. A. (2020). Knowledge, perceptions, and attitude of Egyptians towards the novel coronavirus disease (COVID-19). *Journal of Community Health, 45*, 881–890. https://doi.org/10.1007/s10900-020-00827-7

Alzoubi, H., Alnawaiseh, N., Al-Mnayyis, A., Lubad, M. A., Aqel, A., & Al-Shagahin, H. (2020). COVID-19-knowledge, attitude and practice among medical and non-medical University Students in Jordan. *Journal of Pure and Applied Microbiology, 14*(1), 17–24. https://doi.org/10.22207/JPAM.14.1.04

ANUIES (Asociación Nacional de Universidades e Instituciones de Educación Superior). (2020). *Anuario educación superior 2019–2020*. Ciudad de México: ANUIES. http://www.anuies.mx/informacion-y-servicios/informacion-estadistica-de-educacion-superior/anuario-estadistico-de-educacion-superior

Azlan, A. A., Hamzah, M. R., Sern, T. J., Ayub, S. H., & Mohamad, E. (2020). Public knowledge, attitudes and practices towards COVID-19: A cross-sectional study in Malaysia. *PLoS ONE, 15*(5), e0233668. https://doi.org/10.1371/journal.pone.0233668

Balliet, D., Parks, C., & Joireman, J. (2009). Social value orientation and cooperation in social dilemmas: A meta-analysis. *Group Processes & Intergroup Relations, 12*(4), 533–547.

Barber, B. (1983). *The logic and limits of trust*. Rutgers University Press.

Bates, B. R., Moncayo, A. L., Costales, J. A., Herrera-Cespedes, C. A., & Grijalva, M. J. (2020). Knowledge, attitudes, and practices towards COVID-19 among Ecuadorians during the outbreak: An online cross-sectional survey. *Journal of Community Health, 45*(6), 1158–1167.

Boone, C., Declerck, C., & Kiyonari, T. (2010). Inducing cooperative behavior among proselfs versus prosocials: The moderating role of incentives and trust. *Journal of Conflict Resolution, 54*(5), 799–824.

Campos-Mercade, P., Meier, A. N., Schneider, F. H., & Wengström, E. (2021). Prosociality predicts health behaviors during the COVID-19 pandemic. *Journal of Public Economics, 195*, 104367. https://doi.org/10.1016/j.jpubeco.2021.104367

Capraro, V., & Barcelo, H. (2020). The effect of messaging and gender on intentions to wear a face covering to slow down COVID-19 transmission. *Journal of Behavioral Economics for Policy, 4*(S2), 45–55. https://sabeconomics.org/journal/RePEc/beh/JBEPv1/articles/JBEP-4-S2-5.pdf

Clements, J. M. (2020). Knowledge and behaviors toward COVID-19 among US residents during the early days of the pandemic: cross-sectional online questionnaire. *JMIR Public Health and Surveillance, 6*(2), e19161. https://doi.org/10.2196/19161

Cleveland Clinic (2021, February 2). *Already vaccinated? Here's why you shouldn't stop wearing your face mask yet.* https://health.clevelandclinic.org/already-vaccinated-heres-why-you-shouldnt-stop-wearing-your-face-mask-yet

Efron, B. (1987). Better bootstrap confidence intervals. *Journal of the American Statistical Association, 82*(397), 171–185.

El Economista. (2020, December 8). Esquema de vacunación Covid-19 en México: etapas de aplicación. https://www.eleconomista.com.mx/politica/Esquema-de-vacunacion-Covid-19-en-Mexico-etapas-de-aplicacion-20201208-0081.html

El Financiero. (2020, March 16). UNAM suspenderá clases a partir de mañana de forma paulatina por coronavirus. https://www.elfinanciero.com.mx/salud/unam-suspendera-clases-a-partir-de-manana-de-forma-paulatina-por-coronavirus

Euronews. (2020). Coronavirus: Could young people spreading COVID-19 amongst themselves lead to more deaths? *RetrEuronews*. Retrieved September 11, 2020, from https://www.euronews.com/2020/09/11/coronavirus-what-s-the-problem-with-young-people-testing-positive-for-covid-19-

Frank, R. H., Gilovich, T., & Regan, D. T. (1993). Does studying economics inhibit cooperation? *Journal of Economic Perspectives, 7*(2), 159–171.

Galasso, V., Pons, V., Profeta, P., Becher, M., Brouard, S., & Foucault, M. (2020). Gender differences in COVID-19 attitudes and behavior: Panel evidence from eight countries (H. G. Hamburger, Ed.). *Proceedings of the National Academy of Sciences of the United States of America, 117*(44), 27285–27291.

Goodnough, A. (2021, February 21). Fauci expects Americans could still need to wear face masks in 2022. *The New York Times*. https://www.nytimes.com/2021/02/21/world/fauci-face-masks-2022.html

Hamburger, H. (1979). *Games as models of social phenomena*. W.H. Freeman.

Hernández, E. (2020, June 26). CDMX pasa a semáforo naranja; así serán las reaperturas. *El Universal.* https://www.eluniversal.com.mx/metropoli/cdmx/coronavirus-cdmx-pasa-semaforo-naranja

Heckathorn, D. D., & Cameron, C. J. (2017). Network sampling: From snowball and multiplicity to respondent-driven sampling. *Annual Review of Sociology, 43,* 101–119. https://doi.org/10.1146/annurev-soc-060116-053556

Hirschauer, N., Grüner, S., Mußhoff, O., Becker, C., & Jantsch, A. (2020). Can p-values be meaningfully interpreted without random sampling? *Statistics Surveys, 14,* 71–91.

Howard, M. C. (2020). Understanding face mask use to prevent coronavirus and other illnesses: Development of a multidimensional face mask perceptions scale. *British Journal of Health Psychology, 25*(4), 912–924.

Iyengar, K. P., Ish, P., Botchu, R., Jain, V. K., & Vaishya, R. (2021). Influence of the Peltzman effect on the recurrent COVID-19 waves in Europe. *Postgrad Medical Journal.* Published Online First: 29 April 2021. https://doi.org/10.1136/postgradmedj-2021-140234

Joireman, J. A., Van Lange, P. A. M., Kuhlman, D. M., Van Vugt, M., & Shelley, G. P. (1997). An interdependence analysis of commuting decisions. *European Journal of Social Psychology, 21,* 441–463.

Jordan, J., Yoeli, E., & Rand, D. (2020). Don't get it or don't spread it? Comparing self-interested versus prosocially framed COVID-19 prevention messaging. *PsyArXiv, 10.* https://doi.org/10.31234/osf.io/yuq7x

Kerr, N. L. (1989). Illusions of efficacy: The effects of group size on perceived efficacy in social dilemmas. *Journal of Experimental Social Psychology, 25,* 287–313.

Kanagaretnam, K., Mestelman, S., Nainar, K., & Shehata, M. (2009). The impact of social value orientation and risk attitudes on trust and reciprocity. *Journal of Economic Psychology, 30*(3), 368–380.

Kuhlman, D. M., Camac, C., & Cunha, D. A. (1986). Individual differences in social orientation. *Experimental Social Dilemmas, 3,* 151–176.

Leder, J., Pastukhov, A., & Schütz, A. (2020). Social value orientation, subjective effectiveness, perceived cost, and the use of protective measures during the COVID-19 pandemic in Germany. *Comprehensive Results in Social Psychology, 7,* 1–23.

McClintock, C. G. (1972). Social motivation-a set of propositions. *Behavioral Science, 17,* 438–454.

Messick, D. M., & Brewer, M. B. (1983). Solving social dilemmas: A review. In L. Wheeler & P. Shaver (Eds.), *Review of personality and social psychology* (pp. 11–44). Sage.

Montoro, A., Shih, P. C., Román, M., & Martínez-Molina, A. (2014). Spanish adaptation of Yamagishi general trust scale. *Anales de Psicología/Annals of Psychology, 30*(1), 302–307.

Murphy, R. O., Ackermann, K. A., & Handgraaf, M. J. (2011). Measuring social value orientation. *Judgment and Decision Making, 6*(8), 771–781.

Murphy, R. O., & Ackermann, K. A. (2014). Social value orientation: Theoretical and measurement issues in the study of social preferences. *Personality and Social Psychology Review, 18*(1), 13–41.

Ordaz Díaz, A. (2021, February 12). CDMX y Edomex pasan a semáforo naranja; Sheinbaum pide no bajar la guardia. *Forbes México.* https://www.forbes.com.mx/noticias-cdmx-edomex-semaforo-naranja/

Parks, C. D. (1994). The predictive ability of social values in resource dilemmas and public goods games. *Personality and Social Psychology Bulletin, 20,* 431–438.

Peltzman, S. (1975). The effects of automobile safety regulation. *Journal of Political Economy, 83*(4), 677–725.

Pletzer, J. L., Balliet, D., Joireman, J., Kuhlman, D. M., Voelpel, S. C., Van Lange, P. A., & Back, M. (2018). Social value orientation, expectations, and cooperation in social dilemmas: A meta–analysis. *European Journal of Personality, 32*(1), 62–83.

Reuben, R. C., Danladi, M. M., Saleh, D. A., & Ejembi, P. E. (2021). Knowledge, attitudes and practices towards COVID-19: An epidemiological survey in North-Central Nigeria. *Journal of Community Health, 46,* 457–470. https://doi.org/10.1007/s10900-020-00881-1

Riegg, S. K. (2008). Causal inference and omitted variable bias in financial aid research: Assessing solutions. *The Review of Higher Education, 31*(3), 329–354.

Rodriguez-Abitia, G. (2021). Coping with COVID-19 in Mexico: Actions for educational inclusion. *Communications of the Association for Information Systems, 48*(1), 11.

Stahlecker, P., & Trenkler, G. (1993). Some further results on the use of proxy variables in prediction. *The Review of Economics and Statistics, 75*(4), 707–711.

Tepe, M., & Vanhuysse, P. (2017). Are future bureaucrats more prosocial? *Public Administration, 95*(4), 957–975. https://doi.org/10.1111/padm.12359

Trogen, B., & Caplan, A. (2021). Risk compensation and COVID-19 vaccines. *Annals of Internal Medicine, 74,* 858–859.

van Der Westhuizen, H. M., Kotze, K., Tonkin-Crine, S., Gobat, N., & Greenhalgh, T. (2020). Face coverings for covid-19: From medical intervention to social practice. *The BMJ, 19,* 370.

Van Lange, P. A., Joireman, J., Parks, C. D., & Van Dijk, E. (2013). The psychology of social dilemmas: A review. *Organizational Behavior and Human Decision Processes, 120*(2), 125–141.

Van Lange, P. A., & Messick, D. M. (1996). Psychological processes underlying cooperation in social dilemmas. In M. M. W. Gasparski (Ed.), *Social agency: Dilemmas and educational praxiology* (Vol. 4, pp. 93–112). Transaction.

Van Lange, P. A., Vugt, M. V., Meertens, R. M., & Ruiter, R. A. (1998). A social dilemma analysis of commuting preferences: The roles of social value orientation and trust. *Journal of Applied Social Psychology, 28*(9), 796–820.

Van Lange, P. A. (1999). The pursuit of joint outcomes and equality in outcomes: An integrative model of social value orientation. *Journal of Personality and Social Psychology, 77*(2), 337–349. https://doi.org/10.1037/0022-3514.77.2.337

Walke, H. T., Honein, M. A., & Redfield, R. R. (2020). Preventing and responding to COVID-19 on college campuses. *JAMA, 324*(17), 1727–1728.

Weber, J., Loewenstein, J., Lewellyn, P., Elm, D. R., Hill, V., & Warnell, J. M. (2019). Toward discovering a national identity for millennials: Examining their personal value orientations for regional, institutional, and demographic similarities or variations. *Business and Society Review, 124*(3), 301–323. https://doi.org/10.1111/basr.12177

Wilson, E., Donovan, C. V., Campbell, M., Chai, T., Pittman, K., Seña, A. C., ..., & Moore, Z. (2020). Multiple COVID-19 clusters on a university campus—North Carolina, August 2020. *Morbidity and Mortality Weekly Report, 69*(39), 1416.

World Health Organization. (2020). *Coronavirus disease (COVID-19) advice for the public: When and how to use masks.* https://www.who.int/emergencies/diseases/novel-coronavirus-2019/advice-for-public/when-and-how-to-use-masks

World Health Organization. (2021). *Coronavirus disease (COVID-19): Vaccines.* https://www.who.int/emergencies/diseases/novel-coronavirus-2019/question-and-answers-hub/q-a-detail/coronavirus-disease-(covid-19)-vaccines

Yamagishi, T., & Yamagishi, M. (1994). Trust and commitment in the United States and Japan. *Motivation and Emotion, 18*(2), 129–166. https://doi.org/10.1007/BF02249397

CHAPTER 7

The K-shape Economic Recovery and a New Company Classification

Salvador Rivas-Aceves and Mauricio Maawad Morales

INTRODUCTION

By the end of May 2021, new cases of COVID-19 continue to grow due to the third wave; the rhythm of vaccination is yet to improve worldwide and, nevertheless, people are eager to get back to normal. Most governments are applying as many policies as possible to start the economic recovery while the pandemic is controlled. Until now, there are still several regions with low levels of vaccinated people which are causing new cases and an increase of deaths increase. Europe and the American continent have been the regions with more cases since the beginning;

S. Rivas-Aceves (✉) · M. M. Morales
Facultad de Ciencias Económicas y Empresariales, Universidad Panamericana, Mexico City, Mexico
e-mail: srivasa@up.edu.mx

M. M. Morales
e-mail: 0206227@up.edu.mx

© The Author(s), under exclusive license to Springer Nature Switzerland AG 2022
A. M. López-Fernández and A. Terán-Bustamante (eds.), *Business Recovery in Emerging Markets*, Palgrave Studies in Democracy, Innovation, and Entrepreneurship for Growth,
https://doi.org/10.1007/978-3-030-91532-2_7

the highest number of new cases in a single week was reported in India with 2,738,957 cases, and worldwide the number of cases is around 157 million according to the newly reported and cumulative COVID-19 cases and deaths (WHO, 2021). By region, the cumulative cases are in America have reached 63,554,005 cases, in Europe 52,871,662 cases, South-East Asia 25,552,640 cases, East Mediterranean with 9,428,375 cases, Africa with 3,357,846 and Western Pacific with 2,597,134 cases (WHO, 2021).

One of the main consequences the pandemic has brought is the economic recession, since governments have had to employ lockdowns in order to diminish the contagion rate. Therefore, economic activities have been affected and, as a final result, several companies have declared themselves bankrupt and people have lost their jobs. After the South Asian region was infected, Europe suffered next from this virus. Several studies have already analyzed the consequences of it, for instance, Nehrebecka (2021) argues that the economic consequences of the COVID-19 pandemic will be profound and serious in Europe. In particular, the Polish economy is already under a real stress test, but most relevant is that the resumption of economic activities is not generating a rapid recovery. In fact, most of the economic activity in Poland is still frozen because of the COVID-19 wave that started in June.

According to Nehrebecka (2021), the pandemic crisis and the associated massive lockdowns hit all economic sectors in Europe hard; therefore, bankruptcy of large companies is appearing, and some other micro, small and medium-sized enterprises are taking longer to resume work even after quarantine measures have already been canceled. Within Poland, the highest probability of going bankrupt corresponds to companies dealing in: accommodation and catering, motor vehicle trade, entertainment and recreation, business services, retail and other services related to culture. One of the main characteristics of these activities is high face-to-face interaction with clients. Dávila-Aragón et al. (2021) define face-to-face interaction as the physical collaboration between economic agents and analyze the economic implications of it during the current pandemic. This is the starting point of the present research; because of the pandemic, physical interaction among people is creating new conditions to carry out economic activities which are generating a new classification, besides the economic sector a company belongs to. So far, most companies that have gone bankrupt have an economic activity that strongly depends on the physical interaction with economic agents. Traditional real sectors are suffering this scenario as never before, since the Great

Depression. Nonetheless, Bieszk-Stolorz and Dmytrów (2021) show that negative impacts are reaching other markets too; for example, several stock exchanges reacted almost simultaneously to the spread of the virus. The greatest risk of declining is on American stock exchanges, since around 87% of indexes lost 20% of their value, at the same time European exchanges are having the highest intensity of decline.

Lockdowns and other non-pharmaceutical interventions were also implemented around the globe; for example, closures of schools, workplaces, public transport, cancelations of public events, restrictions of internal movement and tracing infected persons, etcetera. All intending to flatten the virus transmission, but economic impacts are enormous as Castex et al. (2020) point out. The effectiveness of these interventions and their economic consequences are also analyzed by Askitas et al. (2020), Chen and Qiu (2020), Jinjarak et al. (2020), Kucharski et al. (2020), Friedson et al. (2020), Fang et al. (2020), Cho (2020), Ullah and Ajala (2020), U.S. Chamber Staff (2021), Willem and Ben-Haim (2020) and Hartl et al. (2020). In particular, the analysis of the pandemic's impact on some specific sectors is needed to understand the current situation in a deeper way. For instance, Sheridan et al. (2020) analyzed the consumption response due to shutdowns across groups with different risk infection levels and concluded that shutdowns reduce the expenditure in low health risk households and, at the same time, showed that the effects are greater for high social proximity activities such as personal care and social spending. On the other hand, shutdowns raise high health risk household expenditures. Therefore, health risk is related to consumption movements during the pandemic.

Murray (2020) proved that economic variables were affected because of COVID-19 by applying epidemiology models under time pressure to determine the key relation. Gehringer and Mayer (2021) showed that the global economy, during 2019, was negatively impacted by the pandemic in specific traditional economic sectors. On the other hand, Hoseini and Valizadeh (2021) estimated a 41% reduction in the annual growth rate of transactions in Europe, especially while lockdowns were the longest. Estimations are closer between Portugal, Spain and the United Kingdom (Carvalho et al., 2020a, 2020b; Hacioglu et al., 2020).

The economic recession is getting deeper, and employment and income have been decreasing worldwide. According to Mamgain (2020), India lost 123.8 million jobs in April 2020 which affects over 30% of the total workforce. The most affected were small traders, daily wage labor, self-employed, migrant workers, youth, women and the less educated, who work mostly in the informal sector. In consequence, economic activities related to consumption, production and investment have decreased continuously in India. But the effects are not exclusively for India or the household sector. Kumar and Babu (2021) and Ravi and Chandra (2020) argue that COVID-19 is having enormous implications for the agriculture sector, as well as in food and agriculture value chains, around the globe.

In order to diminish the negative impacts on the economy, cross-governmental policy making has been carried out to support the macro-meso-micro-interaction during the pandemic. The main objective is to mobilize cross-sector business activity, promoting industrial strategies and increasing investment and innovation. Policy strategies of governments in Europe and North America are based on enhancing aggregate demand, rising infrastructure investment, preserving jobs and business activities as well as controlling uncertainty (see Van den End & Ben-Haim, 2021).

Nowadays, the net U.S. GDP losses from COVID-19 are estimated at USD 3.2 trillion, employment has declined by 23.8% only during 2020 and, despite the economic stimulus of almost 4 trillion USD applied during the first quarter of 2021, employment and economic growth have are not fully recovered (see Walmsley et al., 2020). The pandemic has created scenarios in which uncertainty is intense, where there is a fear in stock investors so creating a pessimistic analysis is normal. Most of the stock market's results revealed an unprecedented sensitivity of connectedness with the rapid spread of the COVID-19 pandemic, see Youssef et al. (2021) and Koundouri and Sachs (2021). The latter shows a connection between economic uncertainty and the pandemic within financial markets. In this sense, different authorities, central banks, commercial banks, companies and even households have to implement efficient strategies/policies to avoid negative effects from the COVID-19 crisis.

The scenario described above has generated company bankruptcy in every region worldwide. Furthermore, negative impacts are specific according to the economic activity type a company carries out, creating a new type of classification; mainly due to face-to-face interaction intensity with economic agents, or because of the company's adjustability to endure during the pandemic. This complements the basic idea the present research is relying on: companies that were able to innovate, adjust or improve the way economic activities were conducted, not only resisted the pandemic but also grew because of it; companies that were not able to innovate stopped growing or, even worse, shrunk or went bankrupt. Therefore, the objective of this research is to show that both economic recession and recovery alike are creating a broader two-sector classification based on the physical interaction intensity of economic activities. In order to do so, the possible link between the economic recovery and the causes of company bankruptcy is analyzed by economic activity. This exploration is carried out by two main world regions: Europe and North America, in particular: 14 European countries, Canada, The United States and Mexico were the studied economies. Findings show that face-to-face interaction is one of the main factors for some economic activities to decline; hence, business bankruptcy is related to that interaction and, therefore, creating the K-shape economic recovery. Consequently, the pandemic could be generating a new classification for companies.

Economic Recovery Types

According to economic theory, an economic cycle is made up of 4 stages: expansion, peak, contraction and trough. During the expansion phase, an economy experiences high growth rates, low interest rate levels, small inflationary pressures and growing employment. Then, peak is achieved when economic growth rates are at the maximum rhythm and inflation is usually high due to the market dynamics, so the economy tends to be corrected by adjustments on demand and rises on interest rates; thus, contracting production at the same time inflation stagnates. When contractions are regular and employment starts to fall, the economy slows down and faces the trough stage. In this last phase, the economy reaches the lowest level in economic activities, unemployment is high, interest rates tend to decrease to promote activities, and inflation declines. At the very end of the trough stage, economic recovery shows up when economic activities begin to surge, interest rates are at the minimum possible level and inflation increases at a low pace. When economic recovery is constant, expansion takes place, and a new cycle begins. Several conditions need to be present for recovery to start, the most common ones are an increase in investment and public spending, low interest rates, a growing demand, stagnation on prices and low employment levels. These conditions could be combined with complementary economic elements such as taxation, economic stimulus and credit, etcetera; consequently, the economic recovery shape depends on this combination. Because of past economic and financial crises, economic theory has developed scenarios for understanding different ways in which economic recovery has occurred.

The first one is the L-type recovery characterized by a very slow and gradual increase in economic activities when the economy does not get back to its original trend line since it is permanently damaged. Then, there is the U-shaped recovery which is based on a pessimistic perspective due to a prolonged stagnation between the trough and expansion stages. But, if recovery is based on optimistic dynamics, a V-shaped recovery can be observed and it usually tends to be quick and proportional to the decrease. During a V-shaped recovery, a second downward movement in economic activities might appear, so the economy could fall to the same previous level, now this second decrease is usually less resilient and then the economy starts to recover once more. This economic recovery is known as W-shape. At the end of 2020, the World Economic Forum presented an economic analysis based on a new form of economic recovery, the K-type. This new perspective, created by J.P. Morgan, states that the world's economy is experiencing "a forked road with two directions" in which rapid growth, consolidation or recovery for a large transnational and technological group of companies can be seen; while micro, small and medium-sized manufacturing, seasonal or labor-intensive types of enterprises are going bankrupt.

According to Clark (2020) and Yarrow (2021), on the upward side, there could be tech, education and health companies, as well as some retail industry segments, basically, the ones that support daily life. Companies that are adapting and expanding during the pandemic are characterized by economic activities that do not rely on physical interaction with economic agents or are supporting remote work or learning, or have changed the method in which products and services are supplied. In particular, those that participate in stock markets have created spillovers and are estimated to drive a higher economic growth rate. On the downward side, travel, entertainment, leisure, hospitality, some food services and other nonessential service companies are identified. These companies are experiencing diminished revenue since they have not been able to adjust economic activities to maintain social distancing and public health restrictions; or, if the change was created, then a market share loss appeared because of movements in household preferences. Another reason why these companies are having economic problems is that they need physical interaction with clients, think of a gym, for example.

Economic activity is not the only variable where negative effects can be observed, unemployment is another variable that reflects economic crises. Within industries, it is natural to expect employment to behave according to economic activities' rhythm. In this sense, employment in tech, education, health and financial sectors is rising while the travel, entertainment, leisure and hospitality sectors are recovering slowly, if not going down, see Jones (2020). For instance, in the United States, the financial sector had recovered around 94% from its pre-pandemic employment level by the end of 2020; meanwhile, leisure and entertainment sectors had brought back only 74% of the workforce, according to the U.S. Chamber of Commerce data. Figure 7.1 summarizes all types of economic recovery that have been analyzed so far.

Based on the K-shape economic recovery, it is easy to infer that travel, entertainment, hospitality and food services are growing less than technology, retail and software service activities due to face-to-face interaction intensity. The number of physical interactions with people is more likely to be higher in the first type of economic activities than in the second. If the contagion risk is a concern for economic agents, then, it is very easy to understand that avoiding these activities becomes natural. When economic agents avoid activities, trade, sales and revenue decrease, therefore, companies' economic performance decreases, and so does the sectoral economic growth. Having these conditions constantly present,

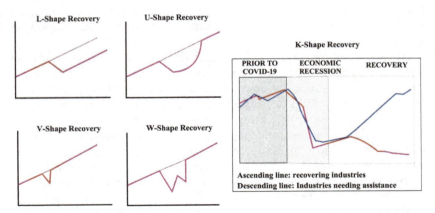

Fig. 7.1 Economic recovery shapes (*Source* Own elaboration based on Hansen [2020], Clark [2020], and 1X. Exchange Staff [2020] information)

leads to capital decumulation, and eventually bankruptcy. The decrease in economic units leads to a decrease in income, rise in unemployment rates and a fall in the economic growth rate. On the contrary, economic activities that involve low physical interaction with people are at least normally carried out or, as until now, more often conducted since they can be done without breaking social distance; hence, trade, sales and revenues are growing, as with sectoral growth. Consequently, economic performance, from the microeconomic perspective, is being affected by the pandemic and, as a result, economic growth from the macroeconomic point of view.

Bankruptcy in Europe and North America

In order to show if the K-shape economic recovery is indeed happening, a statistics set related to company bankruptcy in Europe and North America is analyzed. It is important to highlight the fact that there is a large number of companies that are dying due to the pandemic and the economic crisis generated as a result, especially because those companies were related to economic activities with high face-to-face interaction. Regarding Europe, Fig. 7.2 shows the bankruptcy percentage of change compared with the previous quarter, for a set of 14 European countries. During 2020, bankrupt companies increased in a significant manner, especially from April to September, a time interval in which the first COVID-19 wave hit countries like Belgium, Germany, Estonia, Spain, France, Italy, Lithuania, Netherlands and Portugal, which were the most affected. This information shows the negative effects on the economy, in general.

At the same time, Fig. 7.2 shows that transportation, accommodation and food services, education, health and social activities were the most affected sectors, especially after the first two quarters of 2020. From 2015Q1 to 2020Q2, a decreasing tendency in the business bankruptcy index can be seen, which means companies were dying less and less; from 2020Q2 onwards, the bankruptcy index increased in the same sectors. Furthermore, bankruptcy went down really fast during 2019Q4 and 2020Q2 because pretty much everything was locked, that represents 9 months of closure, too much time to sustain a company without economic activity. Then, the index rapidly increases since companies went bankrupt due to the prolonged closure. When combining all the information, it can be inferred that the pandemic is affecting companies in high

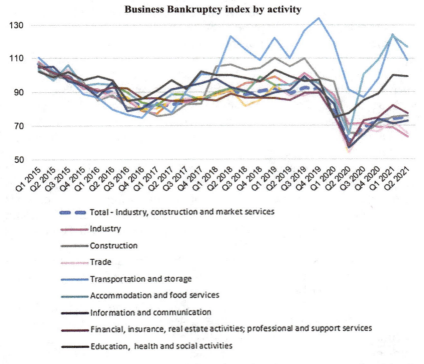

Fig. 7.2 Bankruptcy business declarations % change compared with the previous quarter and business bankruptcy index by activity, seasonally adjusted of the Europe Union, available countries (2015–2021) (*Source* Own elaboration based on Eurostat [2021] information)

face-to-face interaction economic sectors. As a counter example, the information and communication sector was the least affected, so the number of bankrupt companies must be low and the reason should be because of the low physical interaction within the industry.

Regarding North America, Table 7.1 shows business bankruptcy by each economic sector in Canada during 2019–2020, where the worldwide decreasing tendency in the economic activities to be present also in Canada can be observed. Businesses and corporations are the most affected sectors since both account for the highest number of bankrupt companies; other sectors like construction, accommodation and food services also were negatively impacted. In other words, the decrease in the economic growth rate is reflected in the data.

When the year 2020 is analyzed, it is easy to infer that the decreasing tendency in the economic growth rate continues since a high number of bankrupt companies is still present, especially in sectors like corporations, construction, retail trade, transportation and warehousing, real estate, rental and leasing, accommodation and food services, manufacturing, professional, scientific and technical services, among other similar sectors when the high intensity in face-to-face interaction with people is considered. Meanwhile, low face-to-face interaction sectors scored really few bankrupt companies, see agriculture, forestry, fishing and hunting, mining and oil and gas extraction, educational services, finance and insurance, among other similar sectors, for instance.

Besides Europe, Canada is another example of the K-shape economic recovery. As a reminder, for this economic recovery to be present two main conditions are necessary: economic agents being concerned about the contagion risk so economic activities are affected by it, and having sectoral growth rates going up in low face-to-face interaction industries while going down in high face-to-face interaction industries. Therefore, there are two types of companies: with high face-to-face interaction being placed in the lower branch of the K, and the low face-to-face interaction placed in the upper branch.

Concerning the United States, the scenario is not much different. Industries with the highest number of bankrupt companies are real estate, restaurant, retail, entertainment, and oil and gas. Specifically, the entertainment sector was the most affected with an increase of 296% bankrupt companies in 2020, followed by the oil and gas sector with a growth of 232%, restaurants with 65%, real estate sector with 62.8% and retail with a 54.92% increase in bankruptcies. Once more, the main affectations were

Table 7.1 Business bankruptcy by economic sector in Canada, 2019–2020

CANADA economic sectors	Q1 2019	Q2 2019	Q3 2019	Q4 2019	Q1 2020	Q2 2020	Q3 2020	Q4 2020
Business	753	726	617	650	630	451	503	524
Corporations	558	541	441	472	483	385	408	418
Agriculture, Forestry, Fishing and Hunting	18	8	7	13	11	11	13	9
Mining and Oil and Gas Extraction	9	6	6	4	5	2	5	13
Construction	143	130	121	105	98	45	51	64
Manufacturing	54	71	54	64	49	43	38	35
Wholesale Trade	38	34	28	32	32	24	29	25
Retail Trade	77	70	61	85	84	59	72	55
Transportation and Warehousing	53	36	28	47	47	15	29	32
Information and Cultural Industries	20	16	9	15	18	4	3	11
Finance and Insurance	16	16	9	11	9	3	5	11
Real Estate and Rental and Leasing	33	31	26	29	19	24	20	39
Professional, Scientific and Technical Services	54	66	62	42	40	20	31	51
Management of Companies and Enterprises	17	18	17	16	17	19	20	12
Administrative and Remediation Services	28	39	27	30	18	12	30	24
Educational Services	6	5	7	5	7	8	7	10
Health Care and Social Assistance	18	15	11	14	10	14	10	19
Arts, Entertainment and Recreation	16	14	20	12	21	31	25	16
Accommodation and Food Services	122	110	85	83	109	92	84	72
Other Services (except Public Administration)	31	40	36	43	34	24	28	25

Source Own elaboration with data from the Office of the Superintendent of Bankruptcy (2021a, 2021b)

Table 7.2 Number of bankruptcies in the U.S. by industry and bankrupt companies by sector as a percentage of total companies for Mexico

Bankruptcies in the U.S.			Bankruptcies in Mexico		
Industry	2019	2020	Economic activity	Formal (%)	Informal (%)
Real state	605	985	Manufacturing	8.8	12.2
Restaurant	400	660	Commerce	41.3	38.0
Retail	284	440	Non-financial services	32.1	28.1
Oil and gas	236	785			
Entertainment	132	524			

Source Own elaboration based on O'Connell and Narayanswamy (2021) and INEGI (2021) information

in sectors whose economic activities rely on the interaction with economic agents, see Table 7.2.

Mexico presents the same pattern. At the end of March 2021, the National Institute of Statistics and Geography, known as INEGI, presented a study of business demography identified as END in which information on micro, small and medium-sized companies in Mexico was provided. In particular, the information is about companies that are dedicated to economic activities related to manufacturing, commerce and all non-financial services. In other words, it is an analysis of the real economy that supports around 75% of economic activities at a national level. The objective of this study was to measure the impact of the pandemic in the aforementioned sectors.

Among the main results, the following stand out: the 2019 Economic Census reported 4.9 million micro, small and medium establishments from which it is estimated that around 3.9 million are still open, which is approximately 79.2% of the total. This implies that around 1,010,857 establishments went bankrupt in just 17 months, a time interval between which the Economic Census and the END were lifted. On the aggregate side, economic units in Mexico fell 8.1% in the same period. During 2020, micro, small and medium establishments averaged 2 employed persons when in 2018, the average was 3 persons. This last data is consistent with the loss of jobs of around 1.2 million during 2020 reported by the INEGI in January 2021. The study also shows that the largest drop in employment occurred during the second quarter of 2020 at around 27%. Inside

México, the highest proportion of establishments that went bankrupt is in the state of Quintana Roo with 28.9% followed by the state of Campeche with 24.9%, both relying on touristic activities.

As expected, the absence of an economic policy aimed to contain the economic crisis derived from the pandemic generated great losses. While several countries such as the United States, Brazil, Germany, China, Japan, among others, managed to mitigate the economic effects through an expansive fiscal policy, in Mexico, the negative effects were greater than expected, by the absence of it. To explore this, let us remember that the World Bank estimated that Brazil would fall by 8% in terms of economic growth, while Mexico would do so by 7.5%, this at the end of June 2020. Based on economic incentives for around 7.1% of GDP, Brazil contained its fall to just 4.1%. For its part, with the Mexican stimulus policy of around 1.1% of GDP, the economy fell by 8.5%. Such economic impact created losses even in the Mexican informal economy. From the entire business population measured by the 2019 Economic Census, around 20.8% went bankrupt and 12.8% were informal businesses, while 7.2% were formal. Table 7.2 also shows the proportion of companies by main economic activity that went bankrupt during those 17 months, for Mexico.

From the 4.9 million establishments in the private and parastatal sectors registered in the 2019 Economic Censuses, nearly 99.8% belong to the set of micro, small and medium establishments. From this universe, besides the 1,010,857 establishments that went bankrupt, another 1,873,564 businesses had an economic impact due to the pandemic, which is 86.6% of total companies. A decrease in revenue was the main economic problem reported by 85.1% of affected companies.

When analyzing companies by size, from the total number of bankrupt companies, around 21.2% were small and medium, meanwhile, 20.8% were micro. Within micro, small and medium companies, the rates of bankruptcy by main economic sector was 24.92% for non-financial service businesses, 18.98% retail and commerce entrepreneurs and 15% manufacturing companies.

Discussion

There is an undoubtedly negative effect of lockdowns on economic activity worldwide. When governments declared the closure of non-essential activities, several companies were put at risk and eventually could or indeed suffer bankruptcy if they are not able to adjust economic activities to avoid face-to-face interaction with economic agents. In that sense, the findings of this research are consistent with Nehrebecka (2021) and Bieszk-Stolorz and Dmytrów (2021), since the relation of lockdowns and economic activities is inverse. Lockdowns are mandatory public policies for controlling the pandemic, but when they are no longer mandatory, most people continue to the lockdown in order to prevent infections. In this sense, the contagion risk directly affects the economic performance of a company.

Consequently, if the economic activity of a business relies on a high face-to-face interaction, the probability of surviving is low, especially if the company does not adjust its activities. This is the main reason why, for example, digital companies are in the upper side of the K-shape economic recovery, and as we saw during the present research, the highest level of bankrupt companies are in traditional sectors. This idea is consistent as well with the studies performed by Castex et al. (2020), Askitas et al. (2020), Chen and Qiu (2020), Jinjarak et al. (2020), Kucharski et al. (2020), Friedson et al. (2020), Fang et al. (2020), Cho (2020), Ullah and Ajala (2020), and Hartl et al. (2020).

During the research, the analyzed statistics verify the relation between the type of economic activities, based on the physical interactions between economic agents, and the effects by sector. For instance, construction, retail commerce and trade, transportation and warehousing, real estate, rental and leasing, accommodation and food services, entertainment, tourism, and manufacturing are the most affected sectors of an economy. These are economic activities with a high dependency on physical interaction with people. So, the notion of a company not adjusting the economic activities when facing a pandemic is related to the effects, either because of the activity's nature or because of lockdowns. For traditional sectors, the results are according to Sheridan et al. (2020), Kumar and Babu (2021), Van den End and Ben-Haim (2021) and Youssef et al. (2021).

As Gehringer and Mayer (2021) and Hoseini and Valizadeh (2021) state, the above described economic sectors that are considered as traditional are the most affected because of the pandemic. A sectoral analysis related to traditional as well as non-traditional sectors was performed through the European Union, Canada, the United States and Mexico. Findings show that, for selected countries, the relation between lockdowns, economic activity type and face-to-face interaction is present. Therefore, the research corroborates Carvalho et al. (2020a, 2020b),

Hacioglu et al. (2020) and Mamgain (2020) results when regarding effects by country.

The main implication is that COVID-19 has increased the concern of contagion risk, so for controlling the infection rhythm, governments used lockdowns, social distancing and suspension of non-essential activities. Because of that, most economic activities are being negatively affected since aggregate demand and supply have decreased, creating falls in trade, sales and revenues for most companies; thus, conditioning economic performance on economic units, and some enduring the economic crises but mostly going bankrupt due to the unavailability to adjust or because of the unsustainability of the losses or both. Therefore, the K-Shape economic recovery provides a new company classification based on face-to-face interaction for economic agents. This phenomenon has been exacerbated by the second and third infection waves during 2021. Any company not able to adjust to the pandemic's scenario concerning production, distribution and commerce processes is very likely to die.

Conclusions

The economic recovery is appearing in several regions and, for the first time, it is not in a conventional way. Usually, few companies can grow during an economic or financial crisis, and it is normal to find bankrupt companies across all sectors and countries. But nowadays, this is not the case; during the COVID-19 pandemic and subsequent economic crisis, some companies grow due to two possibilities: the activity's nature or ability to adjust the business model, to avoid bankruptcy. In this sense, it is really easy to identify that digital companies are an example of those that are taking advantage of the pandemic. Therefore, the economic recovery has taken a K-shape in which digital companies are placed on the upper side, while traditional companies are on the lower side.

This economic recovery type exists due to face-to-face interaction among economic agents across economic activities. Because of the spread of the virus, economic activities have suffered partial and total lockdowns when governments have tried to control the pandemic. Therefore, companies have been facing bankruptcy risk since decreases in trade, sales, and income continue to show. Most affected industries show high physical interaction with people, like construction, retail commerce and trade, transportation and warehousing, real estate, rental and leasing, accommodation and food services, entertainment, tourism, and manufacturing, among others. This behavior is present worldwide, and more specifically in Europe and North America.

As a consequence, the pandemic has brought a new company classification: on one side high face-to-face interaction companies and the other side low face-to-face interaction companies. That is the reason why the K-shape economic recovery is in place. Now, due to the pandemic, a company needs to create business plans to tackle lockdowns and avoid bankruptcy. Furthermore, the business model needs to be flexible enough to adjust production and distribution for goods and services, from the supply side of the market. Evidently, the first issue they need to understand is the face-to-face interaction intensity inherent to economic activities that are performed. In other words, to define the type of company based on this new company classification.

References

1X. Exchange Staff. (2020). *What the "K-Shaped" economic recovery means for you, 1X Exchange report.* Retrieved May 18, 2021 from https://www.1x.exchange/insights-what-k-shaped-economic-recovery-means/

Askitas, N., Konstantinos, T., & Verheyden, B. (2020). *Lockdown strategies, mobility patterns and covid-19* (IZA Discussion Paper No. 13293).

Bieszk-Stolorz, B., & Dmytrów, K. (2021). A survival analysis in the assessment of the influence of the SARS-CoV-2 pandemic on the probability and intensity of decline in the value of stock indices. *Eurasian Economic Review,* 1–17. https://doi.org/10.1007/s40822-021-00172-7

Carvalho, B. P., Peralta, S., & Pereira, J. (2020a, June). What and how did people buy during the great lockdown? Evidence from electronic payments. *Covid Economics, 28,* 119–158.

Carvalho, V. M., Hansen, S., Ortiz, Á., García, J. R., Rodrigo, T., Mora, S. R., & Ruiz, J. (2020b). *Tracking the COVID-19 crisis with high-resolution transaction data* (Working paper). Centre for Economic Policy Research.

Castex, G., Dechter, E., & Lorca, M. (2020). Covid-19: The impact of social distancing policies, cross-country analysis. *Economics of Disaster and Climate Change, 5,* 135–159. https://doi.org/10.1007/s41885-020-00076-x

Chen, X., & Qiu, Z. (2020). *Scenario analysis of non-pharmaceutical interventions on global Covid-19 transmissions* (Covid Economics: Vetted and Real-Time Papers, 7).

Cho, S. (2020). *Quantifying the impact of non-pharmaceutical interventions (NPI) during the COVID-19 Outbreak - The Case of Sweden* (COVID Economics: Vetted and Real-time Papers, 35).

Clark, S. (2020). *What is the K-shaped recovery?* Retrieved May 17, 2021 from U.S. Chamber of Commerce: https://www.uschamber.com/series/above-the-fold/what-the-k-shaped-recovery

Dávila-Aragón, G., Rivas-Aceves, S., & Ramírez-Pérez, H. (2021). Survival likelihood of micro and small businesses facing a catastrophe. In *The future of companies in the face of a new reality* (pp. 17–36). Springer.

Eurostat. (2021). *Quarterly registrations of new businesses and declarations of bankruptcies–statistics.* Retrieved May 26, 2021 from https://ec.europa.eu/eurostat/web/experimental-statistics/quarterly-registrations-and-bankruptcies

Fang, H., Wang, L., & Yang, Y. (2020). *Human mobility restrictions and the spread of the novel coronavirus (2019-nCoV) in China* (NBER Working Paper No. 26906).

Friedson, A., McNicols, D., Sabia, J., & Dhaval, D. (2020). *Did California's shelter in place order work? Early Coronavirus-Related public health effects* (IZA DP No. 13160).

Gehringer, A., & Mayer, T. (2021). Measuring the business cycle chronology with a novel business cycle indicator for Germany. *Journal of Business Cycle Research*, 1–19. https://doi.org/10.1007/s41549-021-00054-6

Hacioglu, S., Känzig, D., & Surico, P. (2020). *Consumption in the time of Covid 19: Evidence from U.K. transaction data* (CEPR Discussion Paper 14733).

Hansen, S. (2020). *U-Shape? V-Shape? Recovery shapes explained and what they mean for America's Economy.* Retrieved May 17, 2021 from *Forbes*: https://www.forbes.com/sites/sarahhansen/2020/06/03/u-shape-v-shape-recovery-shapes-explained-and-what-they-mean-for-americas-economy/?sh=40f52f7225a5

Hartl, T., Walde., K, & Weber, E. (2020). *Measuring the impact of the German public shutdown on the spread of COVID19, Covid economics* (Vetted and real-time papers. CEPR Press, 1, pp. 25–32).

Hoseini, M., & Valizadeh, A. (2021). The effect of COVID-19 Lockdown and the Subsequent Reopening on Consumption in Iran. *Review of Economics Household, 19*, 373–397. https://doi.org/10.1007/s11150-021-09557-8

INEGI. (2021). *Estudio Demográfico de Negocios.* Retrieved April 10, 2021 from: https://inegi.org.mx/app/saladeprensa/noticia.html?id=6425

Jinjarak, Y., Ahmed. R., Nair-Desai, S., Xin, W., & Aizenman, J. (2020). *Accounting for global COVID-19 diffusion patterns, January-April 2020* (NBER Working Paper No. 27185).

Jones, C. (2020). *Three charts show a K-Shaped recovery.* Retrieved May 17, 2021 from *Forbes*: https://www.forbes.com/sites/chuckjones/2020/10/24/three-charts-show-a-k-shaped-recovery/?sh=27584bd4305f

Koundouri, P., & Sachs, J. (2021). The role of patient finance and fiscal policy in the European COVID recovery. *Sustainable Development Solutions Network*, pp. 1–9. https://www.jstor.org/stable/resrep29196.8

Kucharski, A. J., Russell, T. W., Diamond, C., Liu, Y., Edmunds, J., Funk, S., Eggo, R. M., Sun, F., Jit, M., Munday, J. D., Davies, N., Gimma, A., van Zandvoort, K., Gibbs, H., Hellewell, J., Jarvis, C. I., Clifford, S., Quilty, B. J., Bosse, N. I., Abbott, S., Klepac, P., & Flasche, S. (2020). Early dynamics of transmission and control of COVID-19: A mathematical modelling study. *The Lancet Infectious Diseases*.

Kumar, N., & Babu, S. (2021). Value chain management under COVID-19: Responses and lessons from grape production in India. *Journal of Social and Economic Development*, 1–23. https://doi.org/10.1007/s40847-020-00138-6

Mamgain, R. P. (2020). Understanding labour market disruptions and job losses amidst COVID-19. *Journal of Social and Economic Development*, 1–25. https://doi.org/10.1007/s40847-020-00125-x

Murray, E. J. (2020). Epidemiology's time of need: COVID-19 calls for epidemic-related economics. *The Journal of Economic Perspectives, 34*(4), 105–120. https://www.jstor.org/stable/10.2307/26940892

Nehrebecka, N. (2021). COVID-19: Stress-testing non-financial Companies: A macroprudential perspective, the experience of Poland. *Eurasian Economic Review*, 1–37. https://doi.org/10.1007/s40822-020-00163-0

O'Connell, J., & Narayanswamy, A. (2021). The wave of Covid bankruptcies has begun. Retrieved March 23, 2021 from *The Washington Post*: https://www.washingtonpost.com/business/2021/02/26/pandemic-economy-bankruptcies

Office of the Superintendent of Bankruptcy Canada. (2021a, February). *Insolvency statistics in Canada by North American Industry Classification System (NAICS)*. Retrieved April 10, 2021 from https://www.ic.gc.ca/eic/site/bsf-osb.nsf/eng/home

Office of the Superintendent of Bankruptcy Canada. (2021b, February). *Insolvency statistics in Canada by Forward Sortation Area (FSA)*. Retrieved April 10, 2021 from https://www.ic.gc.ca/eic/site/bsf-osb.nsf/eng/home

Ravi, K. N., & Chandra, S. (2020). Value chain management under COVID-19: Responses and lessons from grape production in India. *Journal of Social and Economic Development*, 1–23. https://doi.org/10.1007/s40847-020-00138-6

Sheridan, A., Andersen, A. L., Hansen, E. T., & Johannesen, N. (2020) *Pandemic, shutdown and consumer spending: Lessons from Scandinavian policy responses to COVID-19*. Proceedings of the National Academy of Sciences (p. 202010068). https://doi.org/10.1073/pnas.2010068117

Ullah, A., & Ajala, O. A. (2020). Do lockdown and testing help in curbing Covid-19 transmission? *Covid Economics, 13*, 138156.

U.S. Chamber Staff. (2021). *Nearly 400 businesses make rally for recovery commitment to help defeat pandemic*. Retrieved May 17, 2021 from U.S. Chamber of Commerce: https://www.uschamber.com/series/above-the-fold/nearly-400-businesses-make-rally-recovery-commitment-help-defeat-pandemic

Van den End, J., & Ben-Haim, Y. (2021). Robust policy in times of pandemic. *Robust Policy Strategies*, 1–5. https://doi.org/10.1007/s10272-021-0961-1

Walmsley, T., Rose, A., & Wei, D. (2020). The impacts of the coronavirus on the economy of the United States. *Economics of Disasters and Climate Change., 5*, 1–52. https://doi.org/10.1007/s41885-020-00080-1

Willem, J., & Ben-Haim, Y. (2020). *Robust policy in times of pandemic*, pp. 1–5. Leibniz Information Centre for Economics. https://doi.org/10.1007/s10272-021-0961-1

WHO. (2021). *COVID-19 weekly epidemiological update*. Retrieved May 28, 2021 from https://www.who.int/emergencies/diseases/novel-coronavirus-2019/situation-reports

Yarrow, R. (2021). Snap AV: Another K-shaped indicator. *Financial Times*. Retrieved May 17, 2021 from https://www.ft.com/content/006cb742-0483-4d57-a384-ce73c8a94436

Youssef, M., Mokni, K., & Noomen, A. (2021). Dynamic connectedness between stock markets in the presence of the COVID-19 pandemic: Does economic policy uncertainty matter? *Financial Innovation, 7*(13), 1–27. https://doi.org/10.1186/s40854-021-00227-3

CHAPTER 8

Business Model Innovation and Decision-Making for the Productive Sector in Times of Crisis

Antonieta Martínez-Velasco and Antonia Terán-Bustamante

INTRODUCTION

Nowadays, markets have changed and business models must change in parallel to remain competitive. The pandemic, related to SARS-COV-19, presented enterprises with a nonstop sequence of events that have put them at high risk in relation to their subsistence. Even though the nature of a company is to adapt and evolve, this is a completely different

---

A. Martínez-Velasco (✉)
Facultad de Ingeniería, Universidad Panamericana, Mexico City, Mexico
e-mail: amartinezv@up.edu.mx

A. Terán-Bustamante
Facultad de Ciencias Económicas y Empresariales, Universidad Panamericana, Mexico City, Mexico
e-mail: ateran@up.edu.mx

© The Author(s), under exclusive license to Springer Nature Switzerland AG 2022
A. M. López-Fernández and A. Terán-Bustamante (eds.), *Business Recovery in Emerging Markets*, Palgrave Studies in Democracy, Innovation, and Entrepreneurship for Growth, https://doi.org/10.1007/978-3-030-91532-2_8

situation that has forced them to become more agile, innovative, and creative. However, for most companies, it has been difficult to change their business model. Before the pandemic, businesses were already facing significant competitive pressure, derived from globalization, the deregulation of entire markets, the accelerated innovative projects and economic integration, among others. This is a challenge that has resulted in the market being more dynamic, competitive and, above all, complex (Wirtz, 2020). One strategy that companies could implement is Business Model Innovation.

For Lindgardt et al. (2009), Business Model Innovation is valuable in times of uncertainty and instability. Because the essence of the business model is how a company delivers value proposition to its customers, Business Model Innovation is identified as the way a company creates its value, and upgrades the interaction of the company with their customers, and the way they develop their projects and processes. This often happens when a set of elements is substantially altered or their interrelation that intervenes in the generation of value for the customer and subsequent profit-making is altered.

Kraus et al. (2020) identified the temporal innovation of BMI as a possible solution to recover from this crisis. Meaning, if a company's business model is innovated through a sequence of substantial changes to elements and/or configurations (Breier et al., 2021; Foss & Saebi, 2017; Saebi et al., 2017), new opportunities can be undertaken that improve the company's performance and can help it to recover. By doing so, BMI is the superior capacity to reinvent a BM, known as a business model, before the circumstances force the same company to do so (Breier et al., 2021; Zott & Amit, 2013). Therefore, BMI first allows companies to commercialize new ideas and technologies, second, to have a source of innovation (Eyring et al., 2011) and, third, to be a response to a crisis such as that caused by COVID-19 (Kraus et al., 2020), and as a source of competitive advantage, without losing sight of the fact that the development of new business models generally begins with the articulation of a new value proposition for the customer (Eyring et al., 2011).

According to Chesbrough (2003, 2010) and Bogers et al. (2019), by exploring new ideas and technologies, companies can obtain new investments and processes to analyze, although they do not have the capacity to innovate the commercial model through which inputs will pass. This is important because this idea or technology brought to market through two different models will produce two different economic results. Therefore, according to Byrnes and Wass (2021), when developing a highly profitable business model to attract target customers, the company has two basic options: I. To increase the value of its customer, namely, value proposition, or II. To reduce the cost of the product or service.

BMI is companies' single configuration related to their value proposal (which means, what a company offers and to whom?), the creation of value (which means, how this value proposition is created?), and the capture of value (which means, how the company generates profit, and from which approach?) (Breier et al., 2021; Clauss, 2017; Clauss et al., 2019). Due to the above, according to Byrnes and Wass (2021), by developing a high-profit business model, to attract their target customers, the company has two basic options: I. increase clients' value, or II. reduce the service cost (or develop both options), for which decisions must be made.

Decision-making is one of the key elements in an organization and for BMI. There are many decision problems which can be handled by built systems. One of the fields where a company can apply this decision-making process is known as Bayes Nets, which allows problem analysis to make a proper predictions (Terán-Bustamante et al., 2021). Based on the above, the main objective of this research is to analyze the Business Model Innovation (BMI) to develop a model that allows predicting which decisions must be made to generate a competitive advantage. For this, this research seeks to elucidate which are the most significant processes, factors, and generators of value that must be considered when a company decides with a BMI. This study is developed by using Bayesian Nets to obtain a predictive model according to the enterprise. The questions that guide this research are which are the elemental factors for an optimal management of BMI in an enterprise? How can an enterprise, based on BMI management, make adequate decisions in the innovation of a new product/service and new experiences for their clients? How can a company, based on the management of BMI, make better decisions in the proposal, creation, capture, and delivery of value?

LITERATURE REVIEW

Model and Business Model Innovation: Conceptualization

Nowadays, enterprises must maintain productivity and competitiveness to innovate. Innovation is a change based on the knowledge that creates value and is key for the enterprise's competitiveness. Therefore, innovation is not only a process that implies the generation of new tactics, but also the application of new forms of knowledge, skills, and competencies, which entails research, development, and commercialization (Rose et al., 2009; Terán-Bustamante & Colla-De-Robertis, 2018). To carry out these actions, enterprises rely on business plans, where the proposal, creation, and capture of value are a medullary point. Linked to a business plan is the concept of a business model and the innovation of a business model.

According to Hamel (2002), Chesbrough (2007, 2010), and Teece (1986, 2006, 2018), innovating a business model is a strong source of competitive advantage. To address BMI, first, we must conceptualize a business model. According to Amit and Zott (2001), a business model depicts the design of a transaction content, structure, and governance to create value through the exploitation of business opportunities. For Osterwalder and Pigneur (2010) and Osterwalder et al. (2020):

> A business model is a conceptual tool that, through a set of elements and relationships, allows the expression of a logic by which the company tries to earn money by generating and offering value to one or more customer's segments, the architecture of the firm, their net of allies that create, trade and deliver this value, and the relational capital to generate rentable and sustainable profit sources.

For Schallmo and Brecht (2010), a business model is a "description of an organization combined with a set of elements that create value for the client and the associates. The value maintains a relationship with the clients, supports the differentiation against the competition and its created with products and services" (Schallmo & Brecht, 2010, p. 3). Accordingly, an innovative business model basically consists of the integration of a new perspective about the market that identifies new problems with clients and a new target client, an innovative value proposition that can answer those problems, and innovative problems capable to materialize this value proposal.

Business Model Innovation is oriented to the future and the client, considering a macro and micro perspective that is valid at all the levels of the business model. This innovation can be realized for one or more elements of a business model. Its objective is oriented to know clients' future needs and to satisfy them in such a way that it can create value. As with other innovations in products, services, and processes, innovating the business model must be executed in a structured way. For Wirtz et al. (2016) and Wirtz (2020), BMI describes the design process as the creation of a new diverse business model for the market which is accompanied by an adjustment of the value proposal to generate or ensure a sustainable competitive advantage in the market.

According to the above, Business Model Innovation is a process of improving the creation of advantages and value during the realization of simultaneous changes, and mutual assistance, either in the value proposal or an organization for customers and in its operating model. This value proposal consists of various elements such as: the election of target segments, the offer of products or services, the operating model, profitability, among others. And the value proposal answers the question, what are we offering and how are our customers? (BCG, 2010; Young & Gerard, 2021; Young & Reeves, 2020).

Companies pursue their Business Model Innovation by exploring new ways to define value proposal by creating and capturing value for customers, vendors, and associates (Bock et al., 2012; Teece, 2010). Among these enterprises and value proposals, the pandemic era brought to light the transformation of a business model, supported by digital technology. Value proposals' main objective is to be the answer during disruptive changes; particularly, technology can help the company identify new commercial tactics. Saying this, digital technology has been the ideal answer to all changes produced by the pandemic of SARS-COV-19. The adjustment of this external stimulus must be done continually and not only as a single action (Priyono et al., 2020).

As can be seen, the core of BMI is value proposal; Andreini and Bettinelli (2017) recognized value as the main purpose of a business model and BMI; this value's component has been examined through different historic lenses: marketing (that is, value for the customer), economy (that is, profits and margins), strategy (that is, competitiveness), the organization (that is, organizational efficiency), entrepreneurship (that is, innovation), and an institutional lens (that is, the efficiency of the market's structure). Magretta (2002) highlights the business model as a structured management tool that helps a company achieve its objectives. For Serrat (2012), a business model is a central design that allows an organization to capture, create, and deliver value to satisfy explicit or latent needs.

This new value proposal requires considering customers as the process' means and ends; meaning, considering the customer before and during the process of generating a value proposal. A proposal dedicated to and consistent with BMI in one or more areas of the customer's value proposal can forge a theory of the company to improve, at least for a time, the business structure, organization, supply chain, products and services, customer service, customer experience, and the management of a large archetypal organization. A business model describes the architecture of a company that creates and delivers value to the clients and the employed mechanisms to capture a part of the value. It is a combined set of elements that span cost streams, profits, and earnings (see Fig. 8.1).

Considering that a business model constitutes a conceptual and comprehensive management tool for companies to differentiate themselves from their competitors (de Jong & van Dijk, 2015), it can be

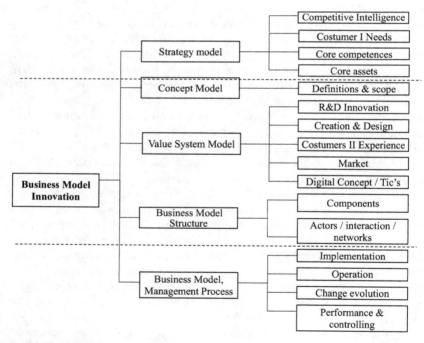

Fig. 8.1 Business model innovation (*Source* Own elaboration based on Wirtz et al. [2016], Wirtz and Daiser [2017, 2018], Wirtz (2020), Baden-Fuller and Mangematin [2013], Boons et al. [2013], Bocken et al. [2014], and DaSilva and Trkman [2014])

developed through various degrees of innovation. This is from an evolutionary process of continuous adjustment to a disruptive process of the existing model's substitution (Ramdani et al., 2019). Velu (2015, 2016) affirms that companies' survival depends on their model's degree of innovation. These degrees of innovation range from modifying a single element to altering several elements simultaneously and/or changing the interactions among their elements. However, these changes and interactions require research by the company to examine which element(s) of the business model are associated with Business Model Innovation. In addition to knowing the value proposition (Eyring et al., 2011), the value chain and potential customers should be analyzed because technology and innovation drive the market (Ramdani et al., 2019). According to the above, a business model is a set of key decisions, that is a holistic description of the logical concept from which a company generates value for its customers and itself.

Making Decisions by Machine Learning: Bayesian Approach to Data Analysis

Most decisions are currently made under uncertainty, relying on limited information. Bayesian analysis can constitute a systematic approach for dealing with uncertainties (Arnaldo et al., 2018). This approach provides a much more complete picture of the uncertainty surrounding the estimation of the unknown parameters, which is well suited for organizations' structure. The Bayesian approach treats parameters as random variables and allows a subjective interpretation of probability (Zoullouti et al., 2019). The frequentist or classical approach to measuring uncertainty requires information on many past instances of an event under identical conditions (repeated trials). The Bayesian approach is based on the existing body of knowledge. This can be based on subjective expert opinions on the parameter of interest (McNair, 2019).

Often, many events of uncertain interest do not have sufficient historical data to satisfy the condition of frequentist statistics. Therefore, the Bayesian approach is a feasible option to address many practical problems. Knowledge obtained from experts in some fields of study takes uncertainty into account. This can be included in data analysis performed using the Bayesian approach. Bayesian analysis provides a convenient setup for a wide range of models, including missing data problems and models, among others (Zhihua & Guanghui, 2018).

Inference problems involving only two variables are simple. However, the calculation becomes much more complex when several variables are involved with conditional dependencies between them. To address this, several graphical models have been developed for complex probabilistic inference. There are several graphical models, such as decision trees, Bayesian networks, and the influence diagram, which are used to represent, code, store, and manipulate probabilistic problems.

Decision trees (DTs) are graphic models that consist of random nodes that represent random variables and decision nodes that represent the decision to be made. The decision is a mutually exclusive set of actions, alternatives, or options that the decision-maker can make. Decision trees can be used to quantify action's potential risk about the possible costs or benefits in the face of uncertainties. They are useful in determining the most favorable outcome of various alternatives (Pearl & Russell, 2011). They have traditionally been used in decision-making to choose an optimal decision from a finite set of options. The value that is optimized is the utility function expressed for each result. DTs have some major drawbacks, such as the order of decision nodes in a tree is arbitrary regardless of the condition and information relationships that exist in the real world (causal knowledge), and the number of combinations of states increases exponentially as the number of decisions and outcomes increases. Consequently, many practical decision problems are addressed by a more refined decision framework, such as Bayesian networks.

Like DTs, Bayesian Networks (BNs) also provide a framework for reasoning, with graphical models, for problems involving uncertainty (López-Puga, 2009). The computational mechanism in BNs is based on Bayes' theorem, which is described below. Bayes' theorem shows how a conditional probability (such as the probability of a hypothesis given the observed evidence) depends on its inverse (the probability of evidence given the hypothesis). Formally, Bayes' theorem is stated as:

$$p(H|E) = \frac{p(H,E)}{p(E)} = \frac{p(E|H)p(H)}{p(E)}, p(E) \neq 0$$

The p(H) above represents the prior belief about the hypothesis before looking at any evidence. The probability of observing the evidence given the hypothesis p (E|H) is called the likelihood function. The numerator p(E) is called the marginal probability of evidence (E); this is the probability of witnessing new evidence E under all possible hypotheses. This computational mechanism calculates posterior distributions for unobserved variables given the observations on one or more observable variables. The beauty of a BN stems from its capacity for intuitive representation and effective calculation of the joint probability distribution over a set of random variables (Sucar, 2011).

A Bayesian Network is a model that consists of a qualitative and a quantitative part. The qualitative part is a directed acyclic graph with a set of nodes and edges. The nodes represent a random variable in the study domain and the edges are used to represent the relationship between the nodes. By convention, BNs' nodes are represented as circles labeled by the names of the variable they represent, while the edges between nodes are represented by connecting arrows. The direction of an edge is from parent to child. If there is an arc directed from node X_i to node X_j, then we say that X_i is a parent of X_j and the edge encodes the probabilistic dependencies between X_i and X_j. The inverse probability concept makes BNs versatile and capable of making bidirectional inferences. This makes BNs ideal for modeling decision-making problems where reasoning is sometimes from causes to effects; at other times, it could be backward reasoning from effects to causes.

Knowledge Representation in Bayes Networks

It is common to use expert knowledge to build a BN model. It is also possible to use existing data from the problem field to construct a BN. The role of experts in the field of work in which modeling occurs is to provide specialized knowledge in the domain. This helps synthesize and translate domain knowledge into BNs' components, such as nodes, causal relationships, and probabilities. The building process of a BN is carried out through the following steps: Selection of variables (qualitative part) and evaluation of conditional probabilities (quantitative part), which are accomplished using expert knowledge or historical data. To identify process variables, the following steps are suggested: (i) To identify the model objectives: prediction, explanation, exploration, among others; (ii) to identify the observations that may be relevant to the problem; (iii) to determine the subset of the observations identified as relevant, considering the complexity of the network; and (iv) to define a set of mutually exclusive and collectively exhaustive states for each node (Heckerman, 2008).

The variables defined in a node must adequately represent the level of detail required by the model. These can be discrete or continuous; the values of the discrete variables must be mutually exclusive and collectively exhaustive (Beltrán et al., 2014). Next, the relationships between the variables should be described. A common approach is causal relationship analysis based on the opinions of experts in the domain. The expert identifies the variables that make another variable have a value or those that prevent it from taking on a given value. The dependency structure of a BN can also be learned from historical data (Conrady & Jouffe, 2013). Next, the probability table is defined for each node. Probabilities quantify the strength of causal relationships; these can be discrete or continuous, depending on the nature of each node. The probabilities can be estimated subjectively using expert opinion or from historical data. The most common sources of information for probabilities come from literature and experts in the domain. If there is data paucity, the knowledge and experience of domain experts are the main sources of probabilistic information (Pearl & Russell, 2011). Among the formal methods to estimate probabilities, the most widely used is structured interviews with experts (van der Gaag et al., 2013).

Probabilistic Inference in Bayesian Networks

The main objective of a BN is to make inferences about unobserved variables given the observed variables. The BN inference algorithm calculates the posterior marginal distributions for all unobserved nodes given the evidence nodes. The computational complexity of the inference depends on the structure of the BN model. One of the most common inference algorithms is the junction tree algorithm, which was developed in the 1990s by Lauritzen and Spiegelhalter (1988).

The union tree algorithm (JTA) organizes the joint distribution so that the marginal distributions are calculated efficiently. Like BNs, a joining tree also has quantitative and qualitative parts. At a qualitative level, there are groups of variables that are often called cliques. A clique, in the crossing tree, is represented by a circle. Unlike the BN table, a connection between two cliques is established by their intersecting variables, often called "sepsets". A sepset is drawn as a rectangle on the junction tree. In a union tree, each variable must appear in at least one group that involves all its parents, and if a variable appears in any two groups, say V1 and

V2, then it must also appear in each group on a path between V1 and V2 (Ogunsanya, 2012).

At the quantitative level, each clique has a corresponding potential function (y). JTA controls the cliques' membership and assigns a variable to the clique that contains its parents. A BN's transformation into a joint tree follows a defined set of procedures, summarized in three steps: (i) Moralization: This is connecting pairs of nodes that have a common child and converting a directed graph to an undirected graph; (ii) Triangulation—The moral graph is triangulated so that there are no unconnected cycles on the graph; and (iii) The construction of a JT from the triangulated graph (Ogunsanya, 2012). In this work, the principles stated for JTA will be used to model the BMI. The Bayes Network was modeled by UnnBayes software (Tadlaoui et al., 2018).

Methodology

This research is mixed, qualitative (descriptive), and quantitative. A model is built to identify the main processes for innovation efficiency of a Business Model Innovation. For the model's design, the methodology of Bayesian Networks (BNs) was applied, which allows incorporating into the model the opinion of experts and the available statistics. Business experts, as external agents, participate in the innovation process and develop Business Model Innovation for organizations. They contribute their experience to make better decisions to improve processes in different companies. Based on expert knowledge from emerging markets in Latin America, the Bayes Network detailed below was developed. For the interaction model's construction, it is necessary to know in detail the variables that intervene in the Business Model Innovation and their causality (Fig. 8.2 and Table 8.1).

Business Model Innovation has two dimensions: theoretical and practical. The theoretical dimension allows the company a clear concept and structure of its own BMI. Namely, who is at the center of the decision and what the model needs to do. The practical dimension is where each of these variables is implemented to achieve an optimal BMI. The variables of the proposed model are described in Table 8.1. The process of implementing Business Model Innovation is interdisciplinary and transversal (Wirtz, 2020). To coordinate this process, it is necessary to classify the model's variables. This classification can be done in three dimensions: essential, triggering, and complementary (Table 8.2).

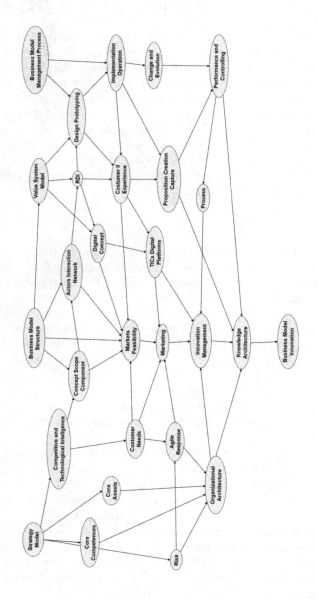

Fig. 8.2 Scheme of the Business model innovation: variables and nodes (*Source* Authors)

Table 8.1 Definition of variables and nodes

#	Variable	Concept	Dimension
1	Strategy Model	It is a plan of action designed to achieve a particular goal. It is the plan that presents the strategy, defined for the organization, as the guiding thread. It allows us to identify the products/services that a company can offer to respond to market needs	Yes/No
2	Competitive and technological intelligence	Those are activities that are carried out to monitor the technological environment of an organization	Optimum Regular Deficient
3	Customer I Needs. Whom? What? How? Analytics	Analysis customer needs	Optimum Regular Deficient
4	Organizational Core Competencies	It refers to the unique and differential knowledge or skill that a company has and that gives it a competitive advantage	Optimum Regular Deficient
5	Core Assets	An asset is a resource controlled by the enterprise as a result of past events and from which future economic benefits are expected to flow to the enterprise	Optimum Regular Deficient
6	Risk	A set of techniques and tools to support and help make the appropriate decisions, considering uncertainty, the possibility of future events, and the effects on the agreed objectives	Yes/No

(continued)

Table 8.1 (continued)

#	Variable	Concept	Dimension
7	Agile Response	The ability to respond to changes with flexibility and acuity, and structure. Agility is a multi-faceted concept that includes responsiveness, versatility, flexibility, resilience, innovativeness, and adaptability (Alberts, 2011, p. 204)	Optimum Regular Deficient
8	Organizational Architecture	It explains how the organization works and coordinates its work processes, people management, assignment of authority, the technologies to be developed and used, and decision-making. That is, how the firm develops its competencies	Optimum Regular Deficient
9	Business model structure	Design process to create a widely new business model in the market, which is accompanied by a value proposition that generates or ensures a sustainable competitive advantage	Yes/No
10	Concept & scope	The basic definition of the concept Ideation Components/dimensions Model characteristics	Optimum Regular Deficient
11	Digital Concept	Concept development based on technology	Optimum Regular Deficient

#	Variable	Concept	Dimension
12	Value system model	Structure of value proposition Value creation Value & delivery Value Capture Topology of value chain partners The value propositions. What are we offering to whom? Target Segment(s) Product or Service Offering Revenue Model	Optimum Regular Deficient
13	Actors, interactions & Networks	Analysis of the interactions and relationships of the different business model actors Analysis of the different interaction and relationship Social impacts	Optimum Regular Deficient
14	Design/Prototyping	Arrangement of the design process Graphical visualization s (ontologies)	Optimum Regular Deficient
15	Customers II Experience	Whom? How? Delivery and capture value proposal Here is the customer experience perceived by the customer The definition of the product or service I sell to clients. I and II are the most important detonators of the model	Optimum Regular Deficient
16	R + D*i	Research, Development & innovation	Optimum Regular Deficient
17	Market Feasibility	Identifiable group of consumers who are willing to pay for a product or service	Optimum Regular Deficient
18	Marketing	Seek, promote, serve, and adapt markets	Optimum Regular Deficient

(continued)

Table 8.1 (continued)

#	Variable	Concept	Dimension
19	Proposition Creation Capture	Value capture as the process of securing profits from value creation and the distribution of those profits among participating actors such as providers, customers, and partners (Chesbrough et al., 2018)	Optimum Regular Deficient
20	Business model management process	It is the management model of all the processes of the company's value chain	Optimum Regular Deficient
21	Implementation/Operation	Development plan Implementation process The operating model Arrangement of the operational process Value Chain Cost model	Optimum Regular Deficient
22	Change & evolution	Constant revision of the model to face the changes of the environment and evolve in the face of the demands of globalization Change of business models over time (evolution/revolution) Factors to adapt a business model	Yes No
23	Performance & controlling	Development of methods for testing the feasibility, sustainability, and profitability	Optimum Regular Deficient
24	Technological Platform	The conceptual model defines the structure, behavior, governance, and relationships between hardware, software, networks, data, human interaction, and the ecosystem that surrounds business processes	Optimum Regular Deficient
25	Process	A sequence of actions that are performed to achieve a particular goal	Optimum Regular Deficient

#	Variable	Concept	Dimension
26	Innovation Management Model Incremental Radical	Innovation is the conception and implementation of significant changes in the product, process, marketing, or organization of the firm to improve results. Innovative changes are made through the application of new knowledge and technology that can be developed internally, in external collaboration, or acquired through advisory services or by purchasing technology Entrepreneurship, socio-economic implications of business model Innovations (Terán & Colla, 2018). There are two types of innovations: radical ones, which completely change the way an activity is carried out, and gradual ones, which involve incredible changes to products and processes (Solleiro & Terán-Bustamante, 2012)	Optimum Regular Deficient
27	Knowledge Architecture	The conceptual model defines the structure of a systematic process of generation, documentation, dissemination, exchange, use, and improvement of individual and organizational knowledge	Optimum Regular Deficient
28	Business Model Innovation	A business model innovation describes the design process to create a new business model in the market, which implies that the (innovative) value proposition seeks to generate a sustainable competitive advantage (Wirtz, 2020; Wirtz & Daiser, 2018)	Optimum Regular Deficient

Source Authors

Table 8.2 Variables classification

Essential	Trigger	Complementary
1. Strategy Model	1. Competitive and technological intelligence	1. Technological Platform
2. Business Model Structure	2. Risk	2. Marketing
3. Business Model Management Process	3. Customer I Needs	
4. Core Competences	4. Who? What? How?	
5. Core Assets	5. Agile response	
6. Markets Feasibility	6. Consumer II experience	
7. Management Innovation Model Incremental Radical	7. Value system model	
	8. R + D*i Research, Development & innovation	
8. Business model innovation structure	9. Proposition, Creation/Delivery/Capture Value	
9. Concept & scope	10. Design Prototyping	
10. Organizational Architecture	11. Change & Evolution	
11. Knowledge Architecture	12. Digital concept	
12. Process		
13. Implementation /Operation		
14. Performance & controlling		

Source Authors

The development of the Bayesian Network is based on the scheme of the Business Model Innovation through the following steps: taking the BMI case, the Bayesian Network has five parent nodes named Strategy Model, Competitive and Technological Intelligence, Business Model Structure, Value System Model, Business Model Management Process. Each of these nodes is composed of child nodes. The value that measures the relative importance of each variable varies from 0 to 1. Those values are defined by the experts (Fig. 8.3). The Bayesian Network was designed according to the BMI scheme (Fig. 8.2).

A central characteristic of BN is its inference mechanism. Its goal is to find the conditional distribution of the variables' subset, conditional on known values for some other subset named evidence (Henze & Nejdl, 1999). In this work, we want to infer the values of the nodes corresponding to the dimensions of a BMI. The metrics used to measure

8 BUSINESS MODEL INNOVATION AND DECISION-MAKING ... 147

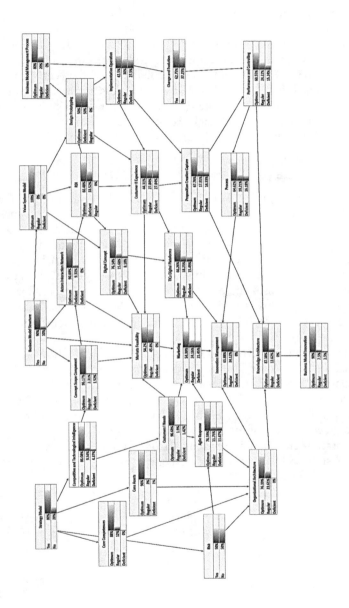

Fig. 8.3 BMI Bayesian Network (*Source* Authors)

the performance of the BMI model are (1) The global confusion matrix (GCM) computed for the selected target node and all the chosen evidence; (2) The Marginal improvement (MI) which is the probability of correct classification gained by adding the node, presented in the row, to the rest of nodes; (3) The Individual Probability of Correct Classification (IPCC) which is the probability of correct classification computed from the model considering only the evidence presented in the row; and (4) The Marginal Cost (MC) of each variable which indicates the total cost resulting from including it in the model.

Results and Discussion

There are four parent nodes for Business Model Innovation: Strategy Model, Business Model Structure, Value System Model, and Business Model Management Process, where Business Model Innovation is a target node and its parents are evidence nodes (Fig. 2). Some of the variables present in the model have a greater influence to reach the optimal value in BMI predictions. We found that adding evidence nodes in the evaluation of the target node increases the percentage of the Probability of Correct Classification (PCC). This is evaluated through the Marginal Improvement (MI) achieved by each one of the variables when generating data based on the proposed model.

The Global Confusion Matrix is a useful tool for evaluating how good a machine learning-based classification model is. It serves to explicitly show when one class is confused with another. The values achieved imply that the proposed model is suitable for classifying the target variable (BMI). The Global Confusion Matrix (GMM) shows that the Optimal state is correctly classified 99.05% of the time with the proposed model. Likewise, the Regular state is classified correctly in 61.64% of the occasions and for the Deficient state, 54.99% of correct classification was achieved (Table 8.3).

Table 8.3 Global confusion matrix for BMI model

	Optimum (%)	*Regular (%)*	*Deficient (%)*
Optimum	**99.05**	36.06	38.12
Regular	0.70	**61.64**	6.90
Deficient	0.25	2.30	**54.99**

Source Authors

In this work, we generated a data set of ten thousand instances to measure the influence that the variables that make up the Bayes Network have on the PCC. This amount of data allows us to evaluate the model and the influence that the variables have on the prediction of the target variable (BMI). Based on this data set, we measured the PCC for the target variable (BMI). We conducted several experiments to determine the highest value of PCC; after doing so, we found the best performance by reaching 80.2% PCC. Next, we selected the most influential variables for the BMI model based on their MI, which are Knowledge Architecture, Implementation Operation, Change and Evolution, and Agile Response. This was done to determine which variables should receive more attention to improve the PCC.

The Individual PCC (IPCC) is the probability of correct classification considering only the evidence presented in the row (Table 8.4). We found that the node that contributes individually the more is Knowledge

Table 8.4 Metrics for the model variables

Node	MI (%)	IPCC (%)	Marginal Cost (MC)
Knowledge Architecture	18.90	39.31	2.554
Implementation Operation	6.40	33.34	2.999
Change and Evolution	5.33	33.34	2.999
Agile Response	4.94	33.34	2.999
Innovation Management	4.54	33.33	2.999
Competitive and Technological Intelligence	3.97	33.34	2.999
Core Competences	3.97	33.35	2.999
Markets Feasibility	3.53	33.34	2.999
Organizational Architecture	3.46	33.34	2.999
TICs Digital Platforms	3.25	33.34	2.999
Customer Experience	3.05	33.35	2.999
Digital Concept	1.91	33.34	2.999
RDI	1.80	33.34	2.999
Core Assets	1.36	33.34	2.999
Customer Needs	0.34	33.34	2.999
Business Model Structure	0.25	33.34	2.999
Actors Interactions Networks	0.08	33.35	2.999
Value System Model	0.00	33.33	3.00

Source Authors

Architecture (IPCC = 39.31%). It is followed by Implementation Operation (IPCC = 33.34%), Change and Evolution (IPCC = 33.34%), Agile Response (IPCC = 33.34%), and Innovation Management (IPCC = 33.34%). The Marginal Cost (MC) of each variable indicates the total cost resulting from including the indicated variable in the model, which in this study are very similar among the most influential variables. It is important to note that in the case of the variables with the highest MI, they are also associated with the lowest MC of the whole set.

We applied the metrics mentioned in the previous paragraphs to evaluate the influence of each node on the entire Bayesian Network (Table 8.4). The data presented in this table indicates that it will be necessary to improve Knowledge Architecture more than any other variable to achieve the best results for BMI. This should be done without neglecting the care of the variables: Implementation Operation, Change and Evolution, Agile Response, Innovation Management, Competitive and Technological Intelligence, Core Competencies, Markets Feasibility, and the rest of the variables.

Conclusions

In this pandemic era of rapid and complex change, companies must respond quickly, lest they become obsolete or perish. Therefore, organizations must continually update their strategic decisions and approaches completely. Due to the pandemic, it became clear that many companies do not have enough experience to make new decisions in rapidly changing contexts. Therefore, organizations must bridge knowledge gaps between old and new; to achieve this, companies must create their business model for which they must adapt to market changes and improve operational performance.

This chapter proposes an innovation model for businesses by means of a quantitative analysis of the importance of each of the elements proposed by the experts in business models and innovation to achieve Business Model Innovation. In this model, the relationships between the mentioned elements are also considered. As a result of the analysis carried out, the variables with substantive importance for the generation of a BMI are determined. Thus, each company has a different business model, based on the skills and resources available, where the proposed BMI can provide a basis for generating its model. The aim is for organizations to generate a broader value proposal for their customers, considering new trends in the new normal, such as the use of technology platforms.

According to the model proposed in this work, it is a priority to focus on client's needs and their experience to generate value proposal. Next, the variables that need special care are Knowledge Architecture, Operational Implementation, Change and Evolution, and Agile Response, mainly. This model allows them to generate knowledge and have better value proposition that will allow them to be more profitable. The already difficult times have worsened with the COVID-19 pandemic, so organizations of any size must implement BMI as it is about creating an innovative value proposal for customers. It is important to consider that BMI is not static, and it is possible to adapt it to the particular characteristics of each company; therefore, this is the contribution to the knowledge of this research.

References

Alberts, D. (2011). *The agility advantage: A survival guide for complex enterprises and endeavors*. Office of the Assistant Secretary of Defense (Networks And Information Integration). Washington, DC.

Amit, R., & Zott, C. (2001). Value creation in e-business. *Strategic Management Journal, 22*(6–7), 493–520. https://doi.org/10.1002/smj.187

Andreini, D., & Bettinelli, C. (2017). Business model innovation. *Springer International Publishing AG*. https://doi.org/10.1007/978-3-319-53351-3

Arnaldo, R. M, Gómez, F., Rodríguez, A., & Sánchez, E. (2018). Bayesian networks for decision-making and causal analysis under uncertainty in aviation. In *Bayesian networks - Advances and novel applications* (p. 13). https://doi.org/10.5772/intechopen.79916

Baden-Fuller, C., & Mangematin, V. (2013). Business models: A challenging agenda. *Strategic Organization, 11*(4), 418–427. https://doi.org/10.1177/1476127013510112

Beltrán P. M., Muñoz Martínez, A., & Muñoz Alamillos, Á. (2014). Bayesian networks applied to credit scoring problems. A practical application. *Cuadernos de Economía (Spain), 37*(104), 73–86. https://doi.org/10.1016/j.cesjef.2013.07.001

BCG. (2010). *Innovation 2010. A return to prominence and the emergence of a new world order*. BCG

Breier, M., Kallmuenzer, A., Clauss, T., Gast, J., Kraus, S., & Tiberius, V. (2021). The role of business model innovation in the hospitality industry during the COVID-19 crisis. *International Journal of Hospitality Management, 92*, 102723. https://doi.org/10.1016/j.ijhm.2020.102723

Bogers, M., Chesbrough, H., Heaton, S., & Teece, D. J. (2019). Strategic management of open innovation: A dynamic capabilities perspective. *California Management Review*, 62(1), 77–94. https://doi.org/10.1177/000 8125619885150

Bock, A., Opsahl, T., George, G., & Gann, D. (2012). The effects of culture and structure on strategic flexibility during business model innovation. *Journal of Management Studies*, 49, 279–305. https://doi.org/10.1111/j.1467-6486. 2011.01030.x

Bocken, N. M., Short, S. W., Rana, P., & Evans, S. (2014). A literature and practice review to develop sustainable business model archetypes. *Journal of Cleaner Production*, 65, 42–56. https://doi.org/10.1016/j.jclepro.2013. 11.039

Byrnes, J., & Wass, J. (2021). How to create a winning post-pandemic business model. *Harvard Business Review*. https://hbr.org/2021/03/how-to-create-a-winning-post-pandemic-business-model.

Boons, F., Montalvo, C., Quist, J., & Wagner, M. (2013). Sustainable innovation, business models and economic performance: An overview. *Journal of Cleaner Production*, 45, 1–8.

Conrady, S., & Jouffe, L. (2013). *Introduction to Bayesian networks & BayesiaLab* (p. 30). https://www.researchgate.net/publication/268818712_ Introduction_to_Bayesian_Networks_BayesiaLab

Clauss, T. (2017). Measuring business model innovation: Conceptualization, scale development and proof of performance. *R&D Management*, 47, 385–403. https://doi.org/10.1111/radm.12186

Clauss, T., Abebe, M., Tangpong, C., & Hock, M. (2019). Strategic agility, business model innovation, and firm performance: An empirical investigation. *IEEE Transactions on Engineering Management*, 1–18. https://doi.org/10. 1109/TEM.2019.2910381

Chesbrough, H. (2003). *Open innovation: The new imperative for creating and profiting from technology*. Harvard Business School Press.

Chesbrough, H. (2010). Business model innovation: Opportunities and barriers. *Long Range Planning*, 43(2–3), 354–363.

Chesbrough, H. (2007). Business model innovation: It's not just about technology anymore. *Strategy & Leadership*. https://doi.org/10.1108/108785 70710833714

Chesbrough, H., Lettl, C., & Ritter, T. (2018). Value creation and value capture in open innovation. *Journal of Product Innovation Management*, 35(6), 930–938. https://doi.org/10.1111/jpim.12471

DaSilva, C. M., & Trkman, P. (2014). Business model: What it is and what it is not. *Long Range Planning*, 47(6), 379–389. https://doi.org/10.1016/j.lrp. 2013.08.004

de Jong, & van Dijk. (2015). Disrupting beliefs: A new approach to business-model innovation. *McKinsey Quarterly.*

Eyring, M., Johnson, M., & Nair, H. (2011). New business models in emerging markets. *Harvard Business Review, 89*(1/2), 88–95.

Foss, N. J., & Saebi, T. (2017). Fifteen years of research on business model innovation: How far have we come, and where should we go? *Journal of Management, 43*, 200–227. https://doi.org/10.1177/0149206316675927

Hamel, G. (2002). *Leading the revolution: How to thrive in turbulent times by Making innovation a way of life.* Harvard Business School Press.

Heckerman, D. (2008). A tutorial on learning with Bayesian networks. *Studies in Computational Intelligence, 156*, 33–82. https://doi.org/10.1007/978-3-540-85066-3_3

Henze, N., & Nejdl, W. (1999). *Student modeling in an active learning environment using bayesian networks.* In User Modeling.

Kraus, S., Filser, M., Puumalainen, K., Kailer, N., & Thurner, S. (2020). Business model innovation: A systematic literature review. *International Journal of Innovation and Technology Management, 17*(06). https://doi.org/10.1142/S0219877020500431

Lauritzen, S. L., & Spiegelhalter, D. J. (1988). Local computations with probabilities on graphical structures and their application to expert systems. *Journal of the Royal Statistical Society: Series B (methodological), 50*(2), 157–194. https://doi.org/10.1111/j.2517-6161.1988.tb01721.x

Lindgardt, Z., Reeves, M., Stalk, G., & Deimler, M. (2009). *Business model innovation. When the game gets tough, change the game.* BCG. The Boston Consulting Group.

López-Puga, J. (2009). *Modelos predictivos en actividades emprendedoras.* Universidad de Almeria.

Magretta, J. (2002). Why business models matter. *Harvard Business Review, 80*, 86–93.

McNair, D. S. (2019). Introductory chapter: Timeliness of advantages of Bayesian networks. In *Bayesian networks - Advances and novel applications.* https://doi.org/10.5772/intechopen.83607

Ogunsanya, O. V. (2012). *Decision support using Bayesian networks for clinical decision making* (Issue February).

Osterwalder, A., & Pigneur, Y. (2010). *Business model generation: A handbook for visionaries, game changers, and challengers.* Wiley.

Osterwalder, A., Pigneur, Y., Smith, A., & Etiemble, F. (2020). *The invincible company: How to constantly reinvent your organization with inspiration from the world's best business models* (Vol. 4). Wiley.

Pearl, J., & Russell, S. (2011). Department of Statistics, UCLA Department of Statistics Papers. *Statistics.* https://escholarship.org/uc/item/53n4f34m

Priyono, A., Moin, A., & Putri, V. N. A. O. (2020). Identifying digital transformation paths in the business model of SMEs during the COVID-19 pandemic. *Journal of Open Innovation: Technology, Market, and Complexity*, 6(4), 104. https://doi.org/10.3390/joitmc6040104

Ramdani, B., Binsaif, A., & Boukrami, E. (2019). Business model innovation: A review and research agenda. *New England Journal of Entrepreneurship*, 22(2), 89–108. https://doi.org/10.1108/NEJE-06-2019-0030

Rose, S., Shipp, S., Lal, B., & Stone, A. (2009). *Frameworks for measuring innovation: Initial approaches*. Athena Alliance, Science and Technology Policy Institute.

Saebi, T., Lien, L., & Foss, N. J. (2017). What drives business model adaptation? The impact of opportunities, threats and strategic orientation. *Long Range Planning*, 50, 567–581. https://doi.org/10.1016/j.lrp.2016.06.006

Schallmo, D., & Brecht, L. (2010, December 12–15). *Business model innovation in business-to-business markets. Procedure and examples*. In (Proceedings of the) 3rd ISPIM Innovation Symposium "Managing the Art of Innovation: Turning Concepts into Reality". Quebec City, Canada. ISBN 978-952-265-004-7

Serrat, O. (2012). Business model innovation. In *Knowledge solutions* (pp. 499–507). Springer.

Solleiro, J. L., & Terán-Bustamante, A. (2012). *Buenas prácticas de gestión de la innovación en centros de investigación tecnológica*. UNAM

Sucar, L. E. (2011). Introduction to Bayesian networks and influence diagrams. In *Decision Theory Models for Applications in Artificial Intelligence: Concepts and Solutions* (pp. 9–32). https://doi.org/10.4018/978-1-60960-165-2.ch002

Tadlaoui, M. A., Carvalho, R. N., & Khaldi, M. (2018). A learner model based on multi-entity Bayesian networks and artificial intelligence in adaptive hypermedia educational systems. *International Journal of Advanced Computer Research*, 8(37), 148–160. https://doi.org/10.19101/IJACR.2018.836020

Teece, D. J. (1986). Profiting from technological innovation: implications for integration, collaboration, licensing and public policy. *Research Policy*, 15(6), 285e305. https://doi.org/10.1016/0048-7333(86)90027-2

Teece, D. J. (2006). Reflections on profiting from technological innovation. *Research Policy*, 35(8), 1131e1146. https://doi.org/10.1016/j.respol.2006.09.009

Teece, D. J. (2010). Business models, business strategy and innovation. *Long Range Planning*, 43(2–3), 172–194. https://doi.org/10.1016/j.lrp.2009.07.003

Teece, D. J. (2018). Profiting from innovation in the digital economy: Enabling technologies, standards, and licensing models in the wireless world. *Research Policy*, 47(8), 1367–1387. https://doi.org/10.1016/j.respol.2017.01.015

Terán-Bustamante, A., & Colla-De-Robertis, E. (2018). Vinculando el talento de investigadores y emprendedores para la innovación. *Revista mexicana de economía y finanzas, 13*(4), 547–569. https://doi.org/10.21919/remef.v13i4.338

Terán-Bustamante, A., Martínez-Velasco, A., & Dávila-Aragón, G. (2021). Knowledge management for open innovation: Bayesian networks through machine learning. *Journal of Open Innovation: Technology, Market, and Complexity, 7*(1), 40. https://doi.org/10.3390/joitmc7010040

van der Gaag, L. C., Renooij, S., Witteman, C. L. M., Aleman, B. M. P., & Taal, B. G. (2013, January). How to elicit many probabilities. Proceedings of the Fifteenth Conference on Uncertainty in Artificial Intelligence (pp. 647–654). http://arxiv.org/abs/1301.6745

Velu, C. (2015). Business model innovation and third-party alliance on the survival of new firms. *Technovation, 35*(1), 1–11.

Velu, C. (2016). Evolutionary or revolutionary business model innovation through coopetition? The role of dominance in network markets. *Industrial Marketing Management, 53*(1), 124–135.

Wirtz, B. W. (2020). Business model innovation. In *Business model management* (pp. 159–185). Springer. https://doi.org/10.1007/978-3-030-48017-2_9

Wirtz, B., & Daiser, P. (2017). Business model innovation: An integrative conceptual framework. *Journal of Business Models, 5*(1). https://doi.org/10.5278/ojs.jbm.v5i1.1923

Wirtz, B., & Daiser, P. (2018). Business model innovation processes: A systematic literature review. *Journal of Business Models, 6*(1), 40–58. https://doi.org/10.5278/ojs.jbm.v6i1.2397

Wirtz, B. W., Pistoia, A., Ullrich, S., & Göttel, V. (2016). Business models: Origin, development and future research perspectives. *Long Range Planning, 49*(1), 36–54. https://doi.org/10.1016/j.lrp.2015.04.001

Young, D., & Gerard, M. (2021). *Four steps to sustainable business model innovation*. BCG Henderson Institute. https://www.bcg.com/publications/2021/four-strategies-for-sustainable-business-model-innovation

Young, D., & Reeves, M. (2020). *The quest for sustainable business model innovation*. BCG Henderson Institute. https://www.bcg.com/publications/2020/quest-sustainable-business-model-innovation.

Zhihua, M., & Guanghui, C. (2018). Bayesian methods for dealing with missing data problems. *Journal of the Korean Statistical Society, 47*(3), 297–313. https://doi.org/10.1016/j.jkss.2018.03.002

Zott, C., & Amit, R. (2013). The business model: A theoretically anchored robust construct for strategic analysis. *Strategic Organization, 11*(4), 403–411. https://doi.org/10.1177/1476127013510466

Zoullouti, B., Amghar, M., & Nawal, S. (2019). Using Bayesian networks for risk assessment in healthcare system. In *Bayesian networks - Advances and novel applications*. IntechOpen. https://doi.org/10.5772/intechopen.80464

CHAPTER 9

Innovation in Knowledge-Intensive Businesses: A Collaborative Approach for Post-pandemic Recovery

Ananya Rajagopal and José Anselmo Pérez Reyes

INTRODUCTION

Knowledge intensity within firms determines the speed of their growth and the ease in adoption of technology. Given the complexities in organizational and manufacturing processes, it is important to understand, manipulate, and disperse information in a structured manner. According to Bettencourt et al. (2002), knowledge-intensive organizations have

A. Rajagopal (✉)
Universidad Anáhuac México, Mexico City, Mexico
e-mail: ananya.rajagopal@anahuac.mx

J. A. P. Reyes
Tecnológico de Monterrey, Toluca, Mexico
e-mail: josea.perezre@tec.mx

© The Author(s), under exclusive license to Springer Nature Switzerland AG 2022
A. M. López-Fernández and A. Terán-Bustamante (eds.), *Business Recovery in Emerging Markets*, Palgrave Studies in Democracy, Innovation, and Entrepreneurship for Growth,
https://doi.org/10.1007/978-3-030-91532-2_9

been defined as firms that are reliant on knowledge management activities based on knowledge repositories in order to identify, gather, and disseminate knowledge with an aim to create value and offer improved product-related services to consumers. In many emerging economies, knowledge is considered as an organizational asset. Hence, in order to manage knowledge, it is vital to understand the origin, storage, organization, user-friendliness (easily accessible), and communicability of knowledge (Millar et al., 2016). Knowledge-intensive organizations (Millar et al., 2017; Swart & Kinnie, 2003) tend to overcome challenges in their organizational performance more easily as compared to traditional firms. This ease in overcoming challenges is mainly attributed to employee engagement, well-being of employees, and customer-centric value propositions leading to the overall growth of knowledge-intensive organizations (Jääskeläinen & Laihonen, 2013). Knowledge-intensive organizations tend to differ from traditional organizations due to high customization strategies, which make them high risk organizations. However, these organizations use such differentiation strategies to benefit the innovation-led market offering and develop customer value through organizational capabilities and competences (Javalgi et al., 2011). The success of these organizations is due to their dependence on highly qualified employees, flexibility in firms' processes, clarity in employee-oriented goals, and creativity-based motivation, which boost employee engagement and drive organizational performance.

Contemporary market practices are driven by innovation, circular economic systems, and development of sustainable and green business models. The synergetic interaction between innovation and ecologically sustainable business models has caught the eye of many emerging enterprises, as it provides them with a competitive market differentiation. Such synergetic interactions aid in developing shared values among customers and knowledge-intensive firms (Klewitz & Hansen, 2014). Knowledge-intensive firms not only drive stakeholder and customer engagement, but also try to communicate useful information in order to enhance customer experience through knowledge-sharing capabilities. Nonetheless, knowledge-sharing capabilities depend on social capital and social learning objectives of the organization, as they drive collective intelligence among stakeholders and customers. Knowledge-intensive firms co-evolve in the marketplace by identifying the critical factors of organizational management through key knowledge practices and key performance indicators of the employees as a result of their knowledge-intensive work practices (Razzaq et al., 2019).

Innovation-led firms in emerging markets face capital and human resource constraints during the product-introduction stage in the marketplace. In such circumstances, knowledge and learning play a pivotal role in the success of these innovation-led enterprises. The business model of knowledge-intensive firms is mainly based on knowledge dissemination through crowdsourcing initiatives leading to co-designing and co-creation of products and services. The competitive advantage of knowledge-intensive business models depends on co-creation, marketplace adaptation, and commercialization of innovative products and services. Such business models encompass product innovation and commercialization efforts based on the openness of the organizational structure, newness in the market offerings, and advancements in technological performance applied in the new product development (Siahtiri et al., 2020).

The question here is: how will knowledge-intensive services perform in the wake of the health crisis caused by SARS-COV-2 (COVID-19)? This study discusses that knowledge-intensive services were interrupted due to the social measures designed to reduce contagion. At the same time, the study explains that there was a high demand for IT services (remote work and cloud-based services) which represented a valuable opportunity for the development of new processes, capabilities, and new ways of working. This led to the development of many new solutions in emerging markets in reference to economic recovery based on the strength and opportunities of the internal capabilities of firms.

In previous studies, the concept of knowledge-intensive organizations in reference to co-creation and coevolution, aimed at boosting economic recovery in the post-pandemic era, has not been discussed. Therefore, this study presents a conceptual approach based on the evolution in the theory of organizations, theory of knowledge, entrepreneurial value-creation theory, and Schumpeter's theory of economic development to understand the effectiveness of knowledge-intensive firms in the commercialization of innovative products and services. Hence, this study significantly contributes to the existing literature by linking organizational knowledge and learning-foundations with resource management to accelerate the commercialization of innovation during the post-pandemic economic recovery process in emerging economies.

Economic Framework and Its Implication in the Context of Post-pandemic Recovery

As mentioned previously, knowledge-intensive business services have been interrupted abruptly due to social distancing and travel restrictions measures designed to reduce contagion caused by the pandemic. This implies that personal contact, face-to-face interaction, and teamwork, which can be considered as the most important characteristics of these services, have been interrupted. Hence, such services needed to adapt to the new practices associated with the health measures and reinvent themselves to continue to serve with the same degree of effectiveness to overcome the difficulties of the business processes in the context of the pandemic. According to Miles et al. (2021), the interaction and co-production with clients in knowledge-intensive businesses may involve a lot of exchange of documents, and the work is organized in terms of projects in which members of teams need to coordinate face-to-face activities. Sometimes, these teams involve collaborators in other firms where the main activities need to be exchanged between junior and senior staff. This implies that face-to-face activities are an important part of this paradigm.

However, the pandemic has caused an inevitable reduction of the traditional contact and intensive use of information technology. Therefore, professionals of business processes and managers need to conceive new tools to communicate effectively. In this context, the most important issue is improving the quality of the relationships necessary to break down the barriers for a genuine collaboration in the disruptive process. Hence, the challenges are even greater: first, the joint creation of value through interaction between the parties and, second, adapting to the new ways of communication and transmission of ideas in the context of an informal exchange through online communications—an innovative way to communicate for generating innovation. It is important to mention that everything that points to the pandemic will have long-lasting impacts on social interactions. Thus, the expert support based on professional knowledge of the business processes will have to design new work processes and capabilities to produce highly customized solutions for growth of the economic activity.

Literature Review and Framework of Propositions

Learning is a critical and adaptable process that allows people to fit in their social environment. The foundation of learning is based on the rate of acquiring and rate of dissemination of knowledge on various open and closed social ambiences. The cognitive process among stakeholders can take place through direct or indirect observation, rewards, and punishment. Such process is based on the principles of social learning theory (Bandura, 1971), which explains that most people learn through observation (influenced by motivation, emotional, and intellectual drive), imitation (influenced by reinforcement or punishment), and modeling (influenced by attention, retention, reproduction, and motivation) (Smith, 2021). Consequently, the process of social learning develops cognitive abilities in reference to knowledge retention, knowledge management, problem-solving skills, and rational interpretation leading to flexibility in behavioral attributes of the people. Such cognitive abilities increase the intellectual capacity not only of the stakeholders of the organization but also of consumers (Street & Laland, 2016). Social learning is used as an analytical tool for developing co-creative planning strategies. A case of Open Lab Ebbinge based in Groningen, Netherlands, is a clear example of synergy between social learning and co-creation in urban development planning (Bergevoet & van Tuijl, 2013). Open Lab Ebbinge developed spaces such as restaurants, exhibition venues, escape rooms, collective workspace, among others, for promoting social interaction using shipping containers in an abandoned redevelopment site. These spaces were then used to create jobs, societal upliftment, and in involving the local community in the creative development process of these spaces (von Schönfeld et al., 2019). Such application of social learning and co-creation has affected public policy development, changes in the mindset of society, and closer involvement of government entities toward societal improvements.

The process of social learning leading to the development of cognitive capabilities and intellectual capacity gives rise to the process of co-creation. The role of learning in the co-creation process can be analyzed through collective-intelligence and knowledge-sharing dynamics among the organization, stakeholders, and consumers. Therefore, through the paradigm of collective intelligence and co-creation, organizations intend to generate customer value much ahead of the introduction of innovative products and services in the marketplace (Wise et al., 2012). The strategic outlook for sharing knowledge among shareholders and consumers not only avoids loss of talent, skills, and expertise among the competition, but also promotes co-creation opportunities for the organization. Such strategies facilitate innovation and enhance the economic growth of emerging economies, which is much needed in the post-pandemic era, where the economic recession has adversely affected big corporations and restricted growth opportunities of emerging enterprises (Bonomi et al., 2015). Hence, in view of the above discussion, the following proposition has been framed:

P_1: Social learning and professional intelligence contribute to co-creation through extensive knowledge sharing.

Collective intelligence is a shared form of intelligence, which is based on the collaboration among stakeholders and consumers, knowledge-sharing attributes, and collective decision-making process. The aim of collective intelligence is to stimulate a peer review process facilitating the co-creation of innovative products and services. Such a process not only involves consumers from the ideation and designing stage of the product/service, but also diminishes the impact of market barriers on the organization. Co-creation through collective intelligence acts as a bubble that absorbs the impact of market competition, consumer criticism, and financial risk in order to invigorate the local economy (Woolley et al., 2010). The most important aspect of such coevolution is based on the integration of strategic alliance and adaptation to the latent and incipient consumer needs and provides a multifunctional platform.

The entrepreneurial alliances and consumer needs act as push-and-pull forces driving resource management, knowledge sharing, leadership qualities, and technology management process in inter-and intra-firm ecosystems (Nie et al., 2011). These forces cater to the economic growth of the emerging market through technological advancement, inter-firm collaboration, and intensity of innovation. The absorptive capacity of the shared knowledge and the reuse or recombination of the knowledge outline the innovation dynamics and focus on coevolution leading to intra-industrial collaboration. Nonetheless, the complexity in the triadic relationship between knowledge-innovation-coevolution needs to be resolved not only through the strategic focus of the firms, but also by means of strategic alliances among the industries. Industrial collaboration is primarily based on knowledge creation, resource-based evolution, and firms' innovative performance in order to drive economic growth in the underperformed markets. These collaborations promote knowledge output and design of technological innovation aimed at penetrating the market ecosystem (Tur et al., 2018). Therefore, based on the above discussion, the following proposition has been framed:

P_2: Effectiveness in inter-systemic alliance encourages coevolution to achieve pre-determined goals through strategic focus.

Knowledge-intensive firms face many challenges such as limited resources, risk identification and mitigation, balancing customization and standardization of product designs, and personalized customer attention strategies in order to gain market share in emerging economies. Therefore, enterprises are adopting more and more crowdsourcing strategies in order to gain innovative product designs, customers' product quality expectations, and user-acceptance criteria based on innovation and technology. Creation of new and innovative products based on crowdsourcing engages the enterprise with consumers intensively in a loop of process feedback, assigning technical layouts, and determining feasibility of the end product in order to surpass the market expectation on quality, innovativeness, and product performance. Also, the enterprise needs to take into account the knowledge foundations of the individuals, or the group of individuals, involved in the process of crowdsourcing, as there exists a substantial gap between the individual's knowledge application and the firm's product specificities (Jiao et al., 2021). The firm's ability to reduce this gap allows assuring the quality and performance of the co-designed product and an initial market share for starting the knowledge-intensive venture.

The firm's ability to motivate users to participate in the process of new product co-creation and manage their domain-specific knowledge in view of constraining biases from their professional ambiance, social environment, and cultural background paves the path for community-led crowdsourcing. In view of the social network theory presented by Dunn (1983), the co-creation and co-designing of new, innovative, and technological products are limited to the domain-specific knowledge of the individuals and the strength of their relationships on social networks. Such connectivity of individuals on social networks affects the new product efficiency, probability of high-quality, and an increase in inter-connectivity among the users and enterprise leading to the enhancement in knowledge-based skills (Hwang et al., 2019). The economic feasibility offered by crowdsourcing practices allows knowledge-intensive firms to focus on developing sales strategies, logistics and distribution, innovation-related issues and their mitigation, and enhancing organizational skills. Such outlook develops a strong intra-firm (employees and stakeholders) and inter-firm (user crowdsourcing) relationships. Taking into account the above discussion on crowdsourcing strategies implemented by knowledge-intensive firms, the following proposition has been proposed:

P₃: Crowdsourcing encourages co-creation and co-designing, and enhances organizational skills.

The intra-firm relationship involving employees and stakeholders promotes value creation for the knowledge-intensive firm and users. The intrinsic factors such as employee openness, customer-centric ability, service orientation, creativity, and technology-led creative outlook aid in value co-creation. These factors drive the behavior of the employees toward dynamic collaboration with the users and the stakeholders for building a holistic experience grid involving all the players in the process of knowledge-intensive co-creation (Chathoth et al., 2020). Knowledge-intensive firms acquire the ability to drive transformation among employees and users through motivation, strategic clarity, and employee empowerment to achieve effective management practices leading to organizational growth. Such ability of entrepreneurial leaders to drive transformation is founded on their intellectual capacity, influential nature, inspirational motivation, and uptight moral and ethical standards.

The level of enthusiasm and commitment of the employees in providing a continuous and sustainable effort to enhance organizational performance and growth can be considered as their engagement with the organization. The higher the level of employee engagement, the stronger their emotional connection with the organization. Such connection results in a low turnover rate, making employees committed and engaged to drive the firm's growth perspectives (Singh, 2019). Performance of motivated employees supports the evolution strategies implemented by the organizations. Evolution of a firm is based on the implementation of many attributes, upscaling technological platforms being one of the most critical phases. However, the evolution of firms resides mainly on the success of the interrelationship between employees, stakeholders, and technology. Transformational leadership supports collective decision-making ideology rather than traditional individualistic decision-making process. Hence transformational leadership not only promotes employee engagement, but also promotes technology acceptance within the organization's pre-determined processes. Therefore, taking into account the above discussion, the following proposition has been drafted:

P₄: Employee engagement and transformational leadership support co-evolution through technology-led organizational decisions.

Innovation-led firms in emerging markets tend to take advantage of consumer-to-consumer and consumer-to-developer communication (O'Hern et al., 2011) platforms to promote new products and services. Knowledge-intensive firms take advantage of user-generated content, as it can be accessed, easily accessed, and transformed into a community of users that share their perceptions on innovative products and services. However, it is imperative for knowledge-intensive firms to adequately administer user-generated contents, as it may benefit or hinder brand communication with equal intensity. Consumers are more involved with technological developments, sustainable approach, and fair pricing of innovative products and services, as they are knowledgeable and connected with the brand as well as society. Thus, the concepts of peer approval and social acceptance play a more important role than the mere functionality of the innovative products and services in the brand value perceived by the consumers (Ho-Dac, 2020). A case of Facebook, on managing user-generated content to identify the social concept of the users and identifying their orientation toward brand preferences can be discussed in order to determine the personality of consumers toward the brands. The governance of social media platforms plays a critical role in segregating fake information from real trends, leading to the generation of knowledge repositories. This has been especially witnessed during the COVID-19 pandemic where, user-generated content has played a critical role in the dissemination of knowledge, which was otherwise not disclosed by the public entities or news channels (Kim & Yemen, 2020). In view of the above review, the following proposition has been framed:

P₅: User-generated contents, perceived value, and social concept determine brand personality.

In the context of a crisis such as the COVID-19 pandemic, the innovation process is essential for economic growth, because innovations trigger market growth through the generation of new products or services that promote the development of different technology sectors and trigger empirical research associated with knowledge-intensive business services. This is important because knowledge-based production is, to a large extent, a great driver of productivity and economic growth. According to Corona-Treviño (2015), in reference to service innovation and evolution of economic thought, three evolutionary approaches can be distinguished: (1) assimilation, where innovation in services is considered similar to innovation in manufacturing; (2) demarcation, which considers that services are different and, therefore, require specific definitions and methods; (3) synthesis, where the combination of new and old theories and concepts is necessary for technological development. It can be distinguished that innovation arises from the convergence between technological development and knowledge services; each sector and each service consider different intensities of knowledge and innovative capacity, i.e., different rates of innovation that correspond to the intrinsic characteristics of a particular market. A practical application of knowledge-intensive business models in leveraging innovation through co-creation and dissemination of knowledge can be discussed using the case of FotoNation. FotoNation was founded in 2014 in Ireland, which based its business model in providing innovative digital photography-based solutions using an algorithm. FotoNation establishes knowledge repositories in various countries in Europe in order to build a competitive advantage through knowledge creation by offering an innovation solution regarding global knowledge networks, customer mobility, and technology acceptance (Kim et al., 2016).

In the new social and economic context caused by the pandemic, and according to Miles et al. (2021), the health crisis has caused knowledge-intensive services to direct their efforts toward the generation of information products such as blogs, news, webinars, podcasts, research, etc. Few exceptions directed their efforts toward accounting and consulting work and many others have developed work on supply chain problems, as these were affected by diseases, transport restrictions, and sudden imbalances in the supply and demand of their products. These variations in the provision of knowledge services represent a valuable opportunity to highlight and learn about the variables and mechanisms that would promote a transition toward a knowledge-based economy. In turn, the new structure of goods and services caused by the pandemic has shown that knowledge services are an important part of an integrated economy. The level of innovation can help overcome the health crisis. This study proposes that knowledge-intensive business services and their repercussions on the development of innovative services would enable the formation of the base for a real economic recovery based on the strengthening and growth of the internal capacities of the different sectors and niches of the new market affected by the health crisis. Under the current economic crisis, this opportunity is very valuable because it would allow us to anticipate trends and, therefore, true knowledge needs to maintain effective industrial resilience and achieve post-pandemic economic recovery. Therefore, in view of the above discussion, the following proposition has been drawn:

P$_6$: Knowledge-intensive business models generate innovations through co-creation and dissemination of knowledge.

The health crisis caused by COVID-19 has increased the pressure on organizations to generate disruptive elements that allow them to increase their skills and performance during the development of their products and/or services. In this sense, knowledge-intensive business services have been empirically shown to increase the company's performance by introducing practices that allow specialized external advice and promote the improvement of its processes and internal practices that have an impact on its final products. In these practices, human capital plays a very important role, as it is an intangible element and a source of competitive advantage including the elements that determine a positive influence affecting the final services of the company. The creation of capabilities within the human capital oriented toward the creation of an innovative culture is fundamental to offering quality and attractive services for the consumer.

With the vision of generating a sustained competitive advantage, companies must develop instruments that positively influence the generation of awareness, which improves innovative practices and processes. Depending on the degree of complexity that characterizes the processes, it is often convenient to involve external specialized knowledge, for which, knowledge-intensive business services are the best option. According to Dyer and McDonough (2001), external consulting aimed at this type of service allows capturing best practices, learn about new processes, improve customer satisfaction, and develop collaborative intelligence and competitive intelligence. According to Palacios-Marques et al. (2011), knowledge management is more than a set of management tools used sporadically, and a holistic approach should be considered that supports continuous learning and a business philosophy that includes a whole set of principles, processes, organizational structures and technological applications to achieve business objectives. At this point, human capital management in terms of its culture, behavior and the established work processes, with a people-based approach, becomes important.

P₇: Effective management of human capital and financial planning drive market competitiveness of knowledge-intensive innovations.

With reference to the above discussion, the success of effective human capital management depends, to a large extent, on the ability of the firm to successfully introduce practices, processes, routines, and individuals that allow increasing organizational capacity with a view to transfer and apply the new knowledge acquired. Knowledge-intensive business services mean that the company must be able to continuously learn and adopt a culture that allows it to adequately anticipate market changes. If achieved, an innovative culture is accomplished, that encourages the development of new knowledge and skills.

THEORETICAL MOTIVATION
Theory of Organization

Organizations are based on the core principles of knowledge dissemination, opportunity creation, and resource management. The peripheral principles of organizations tend to complement the core principles by reducing complexity, implementing a defined structure to organizations processes, and motivating stakeholders in order to assure customer satisfaction. The theory of organization tends to improve the success factors for knowledge-intensive organizations and implements risk management strategies to prevent any unforeseen issues (Feinberg, 2016). The relationship between the threats and opportunities perceived by the stakeholders acts as the foundation of the theory of organization. The diverse and complex nature of organizations challenges the core attributes surrounding the theory of organization due to resource limitations, crippled strategic outlook, myopic knowledge of consumer-market dynamics, and continuous diversity in consumer behavior (Starbuck, 2003).

Theory of organization discusses that organizations are open systems that coexist with leadership structure, employee engagement, and stakeholder management. Such an approach is based on the belief that there are many different ways to reach a goal, and it depends on the objectives of the organization to determine the critical path to do so. Knowledge-intensive firms tend to identify the most efficient path for attaining their objectives. These firms tend to use all available resources including the willingness of the customers and potential consumers in codesigning innovative products and services. Contingency theory discusses the implementation of an effective organizational structure in order to cater to the environmental needs (stakeholders, consumers, and market). Differentiation and integration are the two major attributes of contingency theory discussed by Lawrence and Lorsch (1967), which help the firm offer innovative products and services and seclude it from its competitors. Such differentiation offers an exclusive set of possibilities to enhance first-mover advantage in emerging economies. It also presents firms' undifferentiated opportunities to integrate the innovativeness with go-to-market strategies in order to offer customized products to cater to latent and incipient consumer needs.

Schumpeter's Theory of Economic Development

In current times, the role of innovation is necessary for business economic growth and development. However, the classical economic theory represented by the Keynesian postulates (Keynes, 1938), considered that the increase in productivity is related exclusively to the productive factors that arise from the labor force. This approach explains that economic development takes place only by physical capital and that there is no other differentiating element that better explains the economic development of institutions. However, different empirical studies observed that the physical capital and its productive factors were not enough to explain the progress of organizations, and that an additional, external element named "technical progress" supplemented the explanation for economic growth. This new paradigm assumes that most of the economic growth is due to a residual factor that explains to a greater extent (approximately in two-thirds) the differential growth of organizations (Solow, 1957). Hence, technological progress today is closely linked to innovation.

According to Olaya (2008), this new approach represented the beginning of the emergence of innovation economy and provided empirical evidence that economic development and business competitiveness were closely related to technological innovation. This new line of thought was a turning point for the emergence of contemporary economic thought that now includes research, development, and innovation as an economic process and not just a technological one. This is one of the main assumptions of Schumpeter's thought (Schumpeter, 1961) and establishes that innovative organizations recognize the current environmental conditions and generate disruptive elements based on these conditions, which allow them to develop products or services. These new postulates in the current economic model revealed a different way of understanding economic development, which follows three key elements: exogenous factors, workforce, and innovation. According to Schumpeter (1961), the third element (innovation) fosters extraordinary and long-term economic growth causing an initial imbalance in the market due to the modification of obsolete business models.

At the same time, the postulates of the Schumpeterian economic model assume that the structure of the company determines its business strategy, hence defining its role in the innovative process. It suggests that the knowledge, skills, and experience of the company are formed precisely from its routines and rules of behavior; that on many occasions, these would not be ready or would be insufficient to start the process of development and innovation. The knowledge and professional advice offered by external companies for the development of an innovative culture, and products, and services are the most important contribution of knowledge-intensive businesses. The Schumpeterian economic model highlights the role of an entrepreneur as an entity that is capable of adopting different levels of risk for the benefit of the company in addition to performing common management tasks. This implies that the profile of said entity must consider the following functional abilities typical of an entrepreneur; according to Emami (2017):

1. Appreciate the possibilities of innovation.
2. Overcome the socio-psychological barriers against the introduction of new things.
3. Direct the means of production into new channels.
4. Persuade the banker to provide him with necessary finance for innovations.
5. Induce other producers in his branch of activity for taking risks.
6. Create an environment conducive to the satisfaction of wants as the normal motive.
7. Provide leadership.
8. Take a high degree of risk in the economic world.

Consequently, the entrepreneur must also possess sufficient technical and financial knowledge that allows the correct allocation of resources for different undertakings. Adding to the understanding of the capacities that a company must develop to start the innovation process, Metcalfe (1994) indicates that these depend mainly on the routines established to understand the market surrounding them and anticipate changes. Consequently, the innovation process not only depends on technological development, but also on internal learning processes and the cooperation of external specialist agents to increase the probability of innovating. In summary, Schumpeterian postulates suggest that innovative knowledge is not a public good and is not innate to business growth. This means that innovation requires prior and specific knowledge with a cumulative and sequential nature that is not specific to each company and is located in other sectors or scientific disciplines that must interact to achieve the expected development. Under this argument, the knowledge-generating processes that yield innovation depend on the empirical knowledge possessed by external agents who can advise and guarantee the company a more relevant economic thought than a better positioning in the market.

Conceptual Model

A major challenge in the knowledge-intensive organization is to build a learning pool to assure the effectiveness of the cognitive learning process of the employees through observations and behavioral modeling. Hence, the pool of collective knowledge motivates the learners to cocreate through extensive knowledge sharing (Horsburgh & Ippolito, 2018) leading to the retention of knowledge and enhancement of collective intelligence (P_1). Knowledge-intensive organizations prefer to develop strategic alliances to gain access to new markets or accelerate the growth rate in the existing market. Such strategy aligns the organizational goals and objectives with the market needs leading to efficient sharing of resources and knowledge skills (Varadarajan & Cunningham, 1995). Most knowledge-intensive organizations develop effective business alliances in order to encourage coevolution by combining and connecting localized expertise to achieve pre-determined goals through strategic focus (P_2). These alliances promote long-term relationships rather than short-term transactional relationships to gain market competitiveness (Badaracco, 1991). Figure 9.1 represents a conceptual model, which explains the core dimensions, variables, and respective propositions of the study.

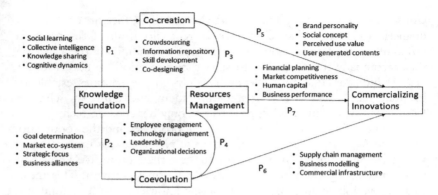

Fig. 9.1 Strategic growth perspectives in Knowledge-intensive firms (*Source* Authors)

Knowledge-intensive firms prefer crowdsourcing to encourage co-creation and codesigning strategies through enhanced organizational skills (P_3). Organizations that implement crowdsourcing initiatives drive open innovation to source new ideas and provide contemporary solutions for existing product or service-related issues. One of the reasons for knowledge-intensive firms to adopt crowdsourcing initiatives is to reduce costs and obtain easy access to experts and specialized skills (Ikediego et al., 2018). Apart from implementing crowdsourcing initiatives, knowledge-intensive firms also tend to engage employees and implement transformational leadership structures to support organizational evolution through technology-led decisions (P_4). These firms provide challenging, yet attainable, goals for employees and stakeholders by implementing a transformation-leadership style and encouraging employees and stakeholders to have a broader outlook (outside of self-interest) in order to achieve collective organizational goals. The induction of these holistic goals provides inspirational motivation for employees and drives cognitive reasoning in attaining the collective organizational goals (Lai et al., 2020).

Knowledge-intensive firms take advantage of user-generated content, value perceived by the consumers, and the social concept of the brand in order to determine brand personality (P_5). User-generated contents have an informative effect on consumers, which leads to a persuasive effect on consumers driving them to buy the products and services offered by these firms. The persuasive and informative effects are explained in the information processing theory (Riley et al., 1954), where the information generated by the users acts as a primary driver for finalizing the process of purchase (Colicev et al., 2019). Nonetheless, knowledge-intensive businesses tend to commercialize innovations through co-creation and dissemination of knowledge (P_6). Knowledge dissemination is a part of the knowledge-translation process, which consists of the creation and exchange of evidence-based involvement of stakeholders, consumers, and members of the co-creation community. The dissemination of knowledge advocates systematic dispersion of expertise and information to cocreate innovative products and services in emerging markets (Lafrenière et al., 2013).

In addition to the above discussion, effective management of human capital and financial planning in knowledge-intensive firms drive innovation and enhance market competitiveness (P_7). These firms acquire knowledge and apply it to promote incremental and process innovation to support the pre-determined goals and objectives for attaining organizational growth. Implementation of revenue-based remuneration for successful innovations acts as intrinsic motivation for employees and enhances the social concept of the brands promoted by the knowledge-intensive firms (Haneda & Ito, 2018).

General Discussion

The importance of co-creation and coevolution in any organization is to enhance the resource management process. Knowledge-intensive firms make use of the existing knowledge base of employees and stakeholders to offer innovative solutions with a degree of customization. These solutions rely on in-depth analysis, tacit consumer-market dynamics, and established competitive advantage. The study validates that social learning and cognitive dynamics play a crucial role in codesigning innovative products through crowdsourcing and knowledge-based skill development opportunities. The knowledge-management process employed by these firms helps in maximizing the reach of innovative solutions and replenishes the information repositories leading to enhanced competitive advantage. The core perspective of this study is the linkage between knowledge foundation and go-to-market approach of innovative firms in emerging markets. Also, the impact of this linkage in the post-pandemic era needs to be measured continuously, as the knowledge-intensive firms have implemented intrinsic and extrinsic learning tools in order to benefit from the knowledge networks. This study also aimed at developing a conceptual framework to highlight the interplay of knowledge resources, innovation, new ventures, and commercialization of innovative products and services in order to improve market share in the post-pandemic recovery process within emerging markets.

Learning plays a fundamental role in any organization (Chou & Ramser, 2019). The social and economic impacts caused by the current health crisis require organizations to develop disruptive skills and knowledge. Such attributes allow these organizations to face new perspectives to resist supply- and demand-shock due to the new consumption- and investment decisions caused by social distancing posing an impact on supply chains. This has forced companies to enhance their commercial networks and internal capacities which, according to Håkon (2020), depend on individual, organizational and interorganizational interactions. The latter is affected to a great extent by the uncertainty that the pandemic brings, and also by the scarcity of the knowledge necessary to deal with the current scenario. However, from an optimistic point-of-view, the pandemic offers a valuable opportunity for companies to adapt and recognize that it is possible to build new ventures and optimize financial resources through an adequate knowledge-management process. This process helps knowledge-intensive businesses orient new ventures toward the development of new sources of innovation and economic development.

Therefore, the role played by knowledge-intensive businesses today is very important. To overcome the pandemic at all its levels, a holistic and resilient vision that attends to current economic and market trends but, at the same time, cares about public health and new activities, must be considered. The health crisis has shown that knowledge-intensive businesses must respond to demand that meets the different dimensions of knowledge. Knowledge-intensive firms must provide services oriented toward the new consumption patterns caused by the pandemic and rely on the new sustainable practices and government. Such services of knowledge-intensive businesses could meet the demands originating from the interactive and collaborative activities of the current social context.

Managerial Implications

The disturbance in the economic activity due to the COVID-19 global pandemic has manifold implications. Knowledge-intensive organizations have had limited face-to-face interaction with the consumers leading to lack of direct feedback, evaluation of innovative solutions, and identification of problems. These organizations base their value proposition on the identification of problems, development of solutions, and dissemination of knowledge in order to gain consumer trust and build loyalty. Managers need to develop digital interactive platforms to diminish the negative effect of social distancing and other mobility restrictions implemented to contain the effect of the COVID-19 pandemic. Also, managers could benefit from developing more innovative solutions to accomplish the implementation of digital platform-based strategies toward market penetration, marketing, gaining consumer trust, and co-creation. Knowledge-intensive organizations can also support their communication strategies through interactive platform-based consultancy solutions to help consumers transition from traditional means of acquiring innovative products to digital platform-based marketplace. Nonetheless, managers need to facilitate work processes based on social distancing norms, maintaining hygienic facilities, and trained personnel to assure the pandemic-related resilience business plans.

Conclusion and Future Research Perspectives

Continuous innovation and process improvements have led to a sustainable outgrowth of knowledge-intensive firms in emerging markets. As any other emerging enterprise, these firms have limited resources, which make it difficult to promote innovative products and services with the same intensity, frequency, and reach as of the well-established enterprises. Knowledge-intensive firms depend on stakeholder involvement, crowdfunding strategies, and inclusive management style to implement critical market-oriented strategies in order to improve organizational performance. Such strategies tend to facilitate the firm's performance in reference to organizational complexities, consumer needs, resource management, economic recovery strategies, and marketability of innovative products and services. The philosophies of coevolution, co-designing, and co-creation involve consumers and stakeholders to identify consumer needs, enhance resource allocations, and improve the administrative and operational bi-directional dynamics. The information repositories are designed to reduce the learning curve of stakeholders and create a sustainable customer-market approach.

This study outlines a conceptual framework considering the interplay between the core and latent variables of knowledge-intensive firms, consumer participation through crowdsourcing and crowdfunding opportunities, and commercialization of innovation in emerging markets. It also discusses the impact of these strategies on the process of post-pandemic economic recovery from the point-of-view of improved market offering and customer involvement in the firm's process of innovation and commercialization. This study has reviewed some of the main issues faced by knowledge-intensive businesses services caused by the pandemic, where these will depend on different consumer segments and niches. Both segments represent the opportunities for new services and contemporary ways of working that will depend on the specialized knowledge arising as a necessity of the pandemic intended to reduce the impact of economic rebound on emerging markets. Hence, future research perspectives regarding the interrelation between leadership styles and customer-centric approach aimed at improving the firm's performance and revenue may be considered.

References

Badaracco, J. L., Jr. (1991). *The knowledge link: How firms compete through strategic alliances*. Harvard Business School Press.

Bandura, A. (1971). *Social learning theory*. General Learning Press.

Bergevoet, T., & van Tuijl, M. (2013). *De flexibele stad. Oplossingen voor leegstand en krimp*. noiuitgevers.

Bettencourt, L. A., Ostrom, A. L., Brown, S. W., & Roundtree, R. I. (2002). Client co-production in knowledge-intensive business services. *California Management Review, 44*(4), 100–128.

Bonomi, S., Za, S., De Marco, M., & Rossignoli, C. (2015). *Knowledge sharing and value co-creation: Designing a service system for fostering inter-generational cooperation*. In H. Nóvoa & M. Drăgoicea (Eds.), *Exploring services science*. IESS 2015. Lecture Notes in Business Information Processing (Vol. 201). Springer. https://doi.org/10.1007/978-3-319-14980-6_3

Chathoth, P. K., Harrington, R. J., Chan, E. S. W., Okumus, F., & Song, Z. (2020). Situational and personal factors influencing hospitality employee engagement in value co-creation. *International Journal of Hospitality Management, 91*(2), https://doi.org/10.1016/j.ijhm.2020.102687

Chou, S. Y., & Ramser, C. (2019). A multilevel model of organizational learning: Incorporating employee spontaneous workplace behaviors, leadership capital and knowledge management. *The Learning Organization., 26*(2), 132–145. https://doi.org/10.1108/TLO-10-2018-0168

Colicev, A., Kumar, A., & O'Connor, P. (2019). Modeling the relationship between firm and user generated content and the stages of the marketing funnel. *International Journal of Research in Marketing, 36*(1), 100–116. https://doi.org/10.1016/j.ijresmar.2018.09.005

Corona-Treviño, L. (2015). Innovation in knowledge-intensive business services (KIBS) in Mexico. 2015 Proceedings of PICMET'15: *Management of the Technology Age,* 897–904. https://doi.org/10.1109/PICMET.2015.7273237

Dunn, W. N. (1983). Social network theory. *Knowledge, 4*(3), 453–461. https://doi.org/10.1177/107554708300400306

Dyer, G., & McDonough, B. (2001, May). The state of KM. *Communicator eNewsletter*, pp. 1–4.

Emami F. (2017). *Schumpeter's theory of economic development: A study of the creative destruction and entrepreneurship effects on the economic growth.* https://papers.ssrn.com/sol3/papers.cfm?abstract_id=3153744

Feinberg, A. (2016). The theory of organization. In thermodynamic degradation science. In *Thermodynamic degradation science.* Wiley. https://doi.org/10.1002/9781119276258

Håkon, H. D. (2020). Interorganizational learning between knowledge-based entrepreneurial ventures responding to COVID-19. *The Learning Organization, 28*(2), 137–152. https://doi.org/10.1108/TLO-05-2020-0101

Haneda, S., & Ito, K. (2018). Organizational and human resource management and innovation: Which management practices are linked to product and/or process innovation? *Research Policy, 47*(1), 194–208.

Ho-Dac, N. N. (2020). The value of online user generated content in product development. *Journal of Business Research, 112*(1), 136–146. https://doi.org/10.1016/j.jbusres.2020.02.030

Horsburgh, J., & Ippolito, K. (2018). A skill to be worked at: Using social learning theory to explore the process of learning from role models in clinical settings. *BMC Medical Education, 18*(1), 156.

Hwang, E. H., Singh, P. V., & Argote, L. (2019). Jack of all, master of some: Information network and innovation in crowdsourcing communities. *Information System Research, 30*(2), 389–410. https://doi.org/10.2139/ssrn.2630826

Ikediego, H. O., Ilkan, M., Abubakar, A. M., & Victor Bekun, F. (2018). Crowd-sourcing (who, why and what). *International Journal of Crowd Science, 2*(1), 27–41.

Jääskeläinen, A., & Laihonen, H. (2013). Overcoming the specific performance measurement challenges of knowledge-intensive organizations. *International Journal of Productivity and Performance Management, 62*(4), 350–363. https://doi.org/10.1108/17410401311329607

Javalgi, R.(R). G., Gross, A. C., Joseph, B. W., & Granot, E. (2011). Assessing competitive advantage of emerging markets in knowledge intensive business services. *Journal of Business and Industrial Marketing, 26*(3), 171–180. https://doi.org/10.1108/08858621111115895

Jiao, Y., Wu, Y., & Lu, S. (2021). The role of crowdsourcing in product design: The moderating effect of user expertise and network connectivity. *Technology in Society, 64*, https://doi.org/10.1016/j.techsoc.2020.101496

Keynes, J. M. (1938). Lettere á R.F.Harrod. In *Collected writings of John Maynard Keynes XIV*. Macmillan.

Kim, T., & Yemen, G. (2020). *Facebook: Managing user-generated content* (pp. 1–10). Darden Business Publishing.

Kim, K. J., Lee, A., Monaghan, S., & Mudambi, R. (2016). *FotoNation: Leveraging international knowledge connectivity* (pp. 1–12). Ivey Publishing.

Klewitz, J., & Hansen, E. G. (2014). Sustainability-oriented innovation of SMEs: A systematic review. *Journal of Cleaner Production, 65*(1), 57–75.

Lafrenière, D., Menuz, V., Hurlimann, T., & Godard, B. (2013). Knowledge dissemination interventions: A literature review. *SAGE Open, 3*(1), 1–14. https://doi.org/10.1177/2158244019899085

Lai, F. Y., Tang, H. C., Lu, S. C., Lee, Y. C., & Lin, C. C. (2020). Transformational leadership and job performance: The mediating role of work engagement. *SAGE Open*. https://doi.org/10.1177/2158244019899085

Lawrence, P., & Lorsch, J. (1967). Differentiation and integration in complex organizations. *Administrative Science Quarterly, 12*(1), 1–30.

Matt O'Hern, M., Rindfleisch, A., Schweidel, D. A., & Antia, K. (2011). The impact of user-generated content on product innovation. *SSRN Electronic Journal*. https://doi.org/10.2139/ssrn.1843250

Metcalfe, J. (1994). Evolutionary economics and technology policy. *The Economic Journal, 104*(425), 931–944.

Miles, I. D., Belousova, V., Chichkanov, N., & Krayushkina, Z. (2021). Knowledge-intensive business services in time of crisis: The coronavirus pandemic. *Foresight, 23*(2), 125–153. https://doi.org/10.1108/FS-07-2020-0066

Millar, C. C. J. M., Lockett, M., & Mahon, J. F. (2016). Guest editorial: Knowledge-intensive organisations: On the frontiers of knowledge management. *Journal of Knowledge Management, 20*(5), 845–857.

Millar, C. C. J. M., Chen, S., & Waller, L. (2017). Leadership, knowledge and people in knowledge-intensive organisations: Implications for HRM theory and practice. *The International Journal of Human Resource Management, 28*(2), 261–275.

Nie, G., Xu, S., & Zhang, X. (2011). Research on the platform of enterprise coevolution based on the collective intelligence. In J. Zhang (Eds.), Applied informatics and communication. ICAIC 2011. *Communications in Computer and Information Science, 226*, 73–81.

Olaya, A. (2008). Economía de la innovación y del cambio tecnológico: una aproximación teórica desde el pensamiento schumpeteriano. *Revista Ciencias Estratégicas, 16*(20), 237–246.

Palacios-Marques, D., Gil-Pechuán, I., & Lim, S. (2011). Improving human capital through knowledge management practices in knowledge-intensive business services. *Service Businesses, 5*, 99. https://doi.org/10.1007/s11628-011-0104-z

Razzaq, S., Shujahat, M., Hussain, S., Nawaz, F., Wang, M., Ali, M., & Tehseen, S. (2019). Knowledge management, organizational commitment and knowledge-worker performance. *Business Process Management Journal, 25*(5), 923–947.

Riley, M. W., Hovland, C. I., Janis, I. L., & Kelley, H. H. (1954). Communication and persuasion: Psychological studies of opinion change. *American Sociological Review, 19*(3), 355.

Schumpeter, J. A. (1961). *The theory of economic development: An inquiry into profits, capital, credit, interest, and the business cycle*. Oxford University Press.

Siahtiri, V., Heirati, N., & O'Cass, A. (2020). Unlocking solution provision competence in knowledge-intensive business service firms. *Industrial Marketing Management, 87*(1), 117–127.

Singh, A. (2019). Role of transformational leadership in enhancing employee engagement: Evolving issues and direction for future research through literature review. *Proceedings of 10th international conference on digital strategies for organizational success*. http://dx.doi.org/10.2139/ssrn.3316331

Smith, M. A. (2021). Social learning and addiction. *Behavioural Brain Research, 398*. https://doi.org/10.1016/j.bbr.2020.112954

Solow, R. (1957). Technical change and aggregate production function. *Review of Economics and Statistics, 39*, 312–320.

Starbuck, W.H. (2003). The origins of organization Theory. In *Oxford handbook of organization theory: Meta-theoretical perspectives*. Oxford University Press.

Street, S. E., & Laland, K. N. (2016). Social learning, intelligence, and brain evolution. In S. V. Shepherd (Ed.), *The Wiley handbook of evolutionary neuroscience*. https://doi.org/10.1002/9781118316757.ch18

Swart, J., & Kinnie, N. (2003). Knowledge-intensive firms: The influence of the client on HR systems. *Human Resource Management Journal, 13*(3), 495–513. https://doi.org/10.1111/j.1748-8583.2003.tb00097.x

Tur, M. E., & Azagra-Caro, J. M. (2018). The coevolution of endogenous knowledge networks and knowledge creation. *Journal of Economic Behavior & Organization, 145*(1), 424–434. https://doi.org/10.1016/j.jebo.2017.11.023

Varadarajan, P. R., & Cunningham, M. H. (1995). Strategic alliances: A synthesis of conceptual foundations. *Journal of Academy of Marketing Science, 23*, 282. https://doi.org/10.1177/009207039502300408

von Schönfeld, K. C., Tan, W., Wiekens, C., Salet, W., & Janssen-Janssen, L. (2019). Social learning as an analytical lens for co-creative planning. *European Planning Studies, 27*(7), 1291–1313. https://doi.org/10.1080/09654313.2019.1579303

Wise, S., Paton, R. A., & Gegenhuber, T. (2012). Value co-creation through collective intelligence in the public sector: A review of US and European initiatives. *Vine, 42*(2), 251–276. https://doi.org/10.1108/03055721211227273

Woolley, A. W., Chabris, C. F., Pentland, A., Hashmi, N., & Malone, T. W. (2010). Evidence for a collective intelligence factor in the performance of human groups. *Science, 330*(6004), 686–688. https://doi.org/10.1126/science.1193147

CHAPTER 10

Communicating with Stakeholders via Twitter: From CSR to COVID-19

Jorge Arturo León y Vélez Avelar

INTRODUCTION

For nearly seven decades, thousands of studies have been related to Corporate Social Responsibility (CSR) with several different approaches that are not necessarily aligned one to another. However, there is no clear definition of CSR, but various studies organize its history, development, and definitions (Deggan & Soltys, 2007; Gray, 2002; Mathews, 1997). CSR is a topic that is increasingly gaining space in academics but also in businesses attendance, particularly in emerging economies such as Mexico. In the last years, many companies have recognized the importance of generating more benefits than just profits for stockholders, such

---

J. A. León y Vélez Avelar (✉)
Facultad de Ciencias Económicas Y Empresariales,
Universidad Panamericana, Mexico City, Mexico
e-mail: jorleon@up.edu.mx

© The Author(s), under exclusive license to Springer Nature Switzerland AG 2022
A. M. López-Fernández and A. Terán-Bustamante (eds.), *Business Recovery in Emerging Markets*, Palgrave Studies in Democracy, Innovation, and Entrepreneurship for Growth, https://doi.org/10.1007/978-3-030-91532-2_10

as contributing to society, placing these companies as socially responsible, and perceived as such by all stakeholders.

Companies' communication of their actions is critical and relevant labor. It becomes the way organizations can contact their different stakeholders to increase their efforts and be recognized as a generator of social value for society and customers. It is also essential to consider that the world has been subjected to a new technological revolution, starting with the internet and followed by the entry of social networks, which have generated a sharp increase in the adoption, communication, and research of CSR (Brown & Dacin, 1997; Kaplan & Haenlein, 2010; Tench & Jones, 2015; Welford, 2005).

Considering that, this research tries to find if companies are generating communication about social responsibility using digital media—specifically on Twitter—in an emerging economy, such as Mexico. The above is relevant because most of the studies that exist today have been carried out in developed countries (Maignan, 2001; Sen & Bhattacharya, 2001; Stanaland et al., 2011), so we need to explore whether those findings, variables, and their relationships are similar and can be generalized to other countries that continue in development, such as Mexico. Likewise, considering that social networks are a relatively new topic, there are still few practically implemented studies on this subject.

There are not many studies in terms of CSR communication and practically nothing in a quantitative perspective. Another essential variable to consider is that during 2020 the world was affected economically, socially, operationally, and health-wise by the Sars-Cov-2 virus (COVID-19) that generated a completely different way to do things worldwide. COVID-19 affected practically every country in the world, which generated many changes specifically in companies' behavior, relationships, and the importance of communicating their efforts and the content of those messages on social networks, considering those are great tools to communicate to stakeholders are carry out the message. Therefore, studying CSR communication in a developing country such as Mexico is a relevant topic in a specific moment such as 2020 regarding COVID-19, considering that these developing countries represent the fastest-growing economies and are the countries where there is a greater possibility of substantial changes in the future arising from globalization and potential investments and the challenge these countries have to the sustainable development agenda.

This chapter has three parts: the first part is a general study on the current literature regarding the topics of our research; then, in the second part, the methodology will be presented, and finally, the third includes the study carried out with a sample of 600 companies and the selection of tweets of 35 companies recognized as socially responsible in Mexico. The actual study includes an analysis of topics, content, and messages these companies shared during 2019 and 2020 while also comparing to analyze a difference during the COVID-19 time.

Literature Review

Corporate Social Responsibility

Corporate Social Responsibility (CSR) has shifted from an irrelevant idea to one of the most accepted concepts in the academic and business world in the past 20 years (Lee, 2008). However, different ideas and elements on the definition and analysis of CSR are generally aligned with the consideration of including additional objectives far more than just financial considerations in the company's KPIs. Some of CSR's main perspectives include:

- "It is businessmen's decisions and actions taken for reasons at least partially beyond the firm's direct economic and technical interest" (Davis, 1960)
- "It encompasses the economic, legal, ethical, and discretionary expectations that society has of organizations at a given point in time" (Carroll, 1999)
- "It is concerned with how an organization exceeds the minimum obligations to stakeholders specified through regulation and corporate governance" (Johnson & Scholes, 2002)
- "It is a commitment to improve community well-being through discretionary business practices and contributions of corporate resources" (Kotler & Lee, 2005).

Considering previous research (Dahlsrud, 2008), five dimensions of CSR activities could be defined: environmental, social, economic, stakeholder, and voluntariness. Similarly, Kim et al. (2014) proposed six categories of CSR, such as environmental stewardship, philanthropic contribution, educational commitments, community/employee involvement, public health commitments, and sponsorship of cultural/sports activities.

Communicating to Stakeholders

Reporting CSR, as other activities in the organization, has several advantages such as the improvement of the relationships with stakeholders, consumer satisfaction, brand loyalty, enhanced reputation, increase in collaborators' motivation and productivity, and a significant decrease in costs (Bhattacharya et al., 2011; European Commission, 2001). According to previous research, there is a relationship between the communication of social responsibility and stakeholders' perception with complex multiple correlations of different factors. A '4Is' framework has been developed to simplify the relationship (Crane & Glozer, 2016); this model is based on two variables—paradigm and audience—reduced to two discrete options that simplify and clarify the communication model.

The model (Crane & Glozer, 2016) determines that communication could have a functionalist essence, meaning the one that reflects reality in the best possible way, or it could try to build reality through the communication generated, which it has called constitutive. Examples of the functionalist essence are any information or news about a fact or action of the organization; on the other hand, the constitutive essence could be a campaign that generates a specific feeling or behavior in the consumer. On the other axis, this model recognizes that communication could be designed for internal stakeholders (internal newsletters or company-specific communications) or to external stakeholders (annual reports, web pages, and social networks); with this, a model is developed consisting of four quadrants bearing the following names:

- Interpretation: Internal Stakeholder/Constitutive
- Image: External Stakeholder/Constitutive
- Integration: Internal Stakeholder/Functionalist
- Identity: External Stakeholder/Functionalist

Remarkably, this study will analyze identity, which, according to the model proposed by Crane and Glozer (2016), is the reflection of reality—what the company wants to project—aimed to the external stakeholder, for which the use of social networks is a way of achieving engagement. It is also recognized that CSR communication can become a strong competitive advantage if it is aligned with its strategy (Saeidi et al., 2015); however, it is also important to segment the selection of the best channels to communicate.

Communication could be done in various ways such as products wrappers, information on company promotion, in traditional media, official reports, websites, and recently the inclusion of social networks such as Facebook and Twitter (Colleoni, 2013). Social media has become one of the most important communication channels in recent years, mainly because it allows a company to maintain close relationships with its stakeholders (Unerman & Bennett, 2004). Additionally, social media is multidirectional, meaning users can easily create, share, and even alter information (Friedman, 2006), and on social media, all content is easily accessible to anyone (Lee et al., 2013). Also, in recent years, corporations add social media as a tool to disclosure information. This phenomenon has caused stakeholders to go from being a passive element in communication that just receive information, as in traditional media, to active authorities that can combine what they want and feel, whenever they wish and by numerous channels taking more power in this communication process (Kent & Taylor, 2016).

CSR on Social Media

New technology and platforms, like social media, offer companies different possibilities to manage CSR communication, specifically as a tool to generate dialog with their stakeholders. In terms of new technology, digital cellphones generate a new generation that allows the creation and exchange of content generated by users and social interaction and communication. These networks have advantages worldwide popularity, low cost, and instantaneous communication (Crane & Glozer, 2016).

Social media, per se, does not make people social, but it can influence all the related actors of the company because it allows firms and stakeholders to share their ideas, opinions, experiences, likes, and dislikes instantly and globally at the comfort of their devices (Kent & Taylor, 2016). On Social Networks, everyone has a voice that can be translated into data; social media is inherently based on interactivity and is an attractive tool for organizations to develop dialogical communication (Oboler et al., 2012).

Studies about CSR communication and social media are not so common; the basis of this study is related to the analysis of social media platforms (Gómez & Borges-Tavárez, 2017) that analyze the frequency, content, and feedback of CSR messages on social media by top companies. However, this study must be adjusted to the reality of COVID-19 and the Mexican context. Another study (Lee et al., 2013) explains the importance of using social media for CSR, and a third one (López-Fernández & Rajagopal, 2015) explores how organizations can build the credibility of their CSR communication on social media and, as a result, found that promoting CSR activities generate greater credibility. Furthermore, other studies examined how a company's engagement in CSR influences word of mouth about the company (Vo et al., 2019). This chapter focuses on content analysis as a research method to explore companies' usage forms, ways, and ongoing conversations among the brand and its consumers. However, it is also crucial for public relations professionals to understand how consumers assess and react to an organization's messages disseminated through social media.

Twitter is a social network that allows users to publish what they are thinking at the exact moment they are thinking it. The information posted on Twitter, known as tweets, may contain photos, videos, or text. Each tweet can be reposted, which means that the number of users that can potentially see a tweet is massive; so, it should come to no surprise that millions of tweets are shared in real-time every day, considering that it is clear why many organizations use that tool to facilitate dialog between stakeholders and organizations (Gómez & Borges-Tavárez, 2017). This platform is not exempt from risks, such as the participation of activists opposed to the company, the distortion of the actions carried out in terms of social responsibility, or the consumer perceiving the communication as mere advertising without recognizing the social effort made (Chae & Park, 2018). Those risks could be reduced by eliminating any communication gap and engaging the audience in the conversation (Colleoni, 2013). Considering all the information, Twitter will be the medium of this study, considering it has become one of the preferred platforms to communicate CSR-related messages.

CSR in Mexico

As previously defined, there is much research regarding CSR in developed countries; however, a critical approach is to know if existing models are valid for emerging economies such as Mexico. For this research, we will use one of the most used models in emerging country research: the model of Carroll's Pyramid (Carroll, 1999; European Commission, 2001). In a simile to Maslow's model for human behavior, this model proposes that a company must first cover its economic needs, then the legal ones, followed by ethics respectively, to finely cover philanthropic and social ones. The four levels are linked to corporative social responsibility at different levels of engagement. However, some theories support that, in developing communities, philanthropy ranks second in the pyramid, as emerging countries require much more social collaboration, leaving legal and finally ethical ones in a third and fourth bracket (Visser, 2010); so, the model to follow would be:

- Economic responsibilities: Generating profits, creating well-paid jobs, and paying the corresponding taxes
- Philanthropic Responsibilities: Support social projects either internally or for communities
- Legal responsibilities: Ensuring a good relationship with the government
- Ethical responsibilities: Adopt codes of ethical governance aligned to global policies in this area

In Mexico, the most outstanding effort to certify the involvement of a company in CSR is made by the Mexican Center for Philanthropy (CEMEFI). CEMEFI is a civil association founded in 1988 that makes various efforts in the field of social responsibility and that in almost two decades has worked to generate a badge for socially responsible companies—distinctive ESR. Based on the reports delivered by companies, this badge is primarily aligned with the vision of the four pillars discussed. This model is based on 7-dimensional compliance steps, which are as follows (Cajiga, 2013):

1. Values, Transparency, and Governance: Linked to corporative issues, anti-corruption, competition, internal decision-making processes, promotion of social responsibility in its value chain, respect for intellectual property, among others.
2. Work practices in the company: well-paid jobs, equal opportunities, working conditions, life balance, human rights, among others.
3. Community development: Linked to the participation of the company in the community, job creation, the use of technology in product development and innovation, as well as investment in education and culture.

4. Environmental care: Aligned to the concept of sustainability, this fourth element seeks to analyze whether companies are collaborating to comply with global policies in this area, such as seeking to minimize effects on climate change, issues related to reforestation, care of natural areas, and education on environmental issues.
5. Human rights: This concept refers to the compliance and respect for employees, suppliers, and consumers' civil and political rights.
6. Suppliers: Ensure that adequate selection and evaluation of suppliers are available to comply with minimum elements of social responsibility.
7. Customers: Topics related to responsible consumption, health protection, but also to issues of customer service and form of conflict resolution, as well as the protection of personal data, are included in this variable.

This study will find the Carroll and the CEMEFI axis with the most used words in tweets during the pre-COVID-19 and the COVID-19 period.

Stakeholder Theory

One of the most widely used theories for the subject, developed by Freeman (1984), has been disseminated in hundreds of papers. It emphasizes that companies have more responsibilities than just generate profits for their shareholders, such as the continuity of the business and the satisfaction of customers, suppliers, and society (Crane & Glozer, 2016). According to this theory, communicating social responsibility is relevant because it is the way to inform various stakeholders of fulfilling the goals set. Also, research about two-way communication, like the one generated on social networks, generates greater involvement of stakeholders, allowing them to build communication and not only be receivers (Bhattacharya et al., 2011) as well as how communication strategies allow not only to inform but also to involve stakeholders in CSR actions.

Communication Theory

From a communication perspective, we could try to analyze the communication of CSR considering that communication theory analyzes the perspective to understand the forms and mechanisms that have been followed to generate adequate communication for the subject (March,

2007). For those authors, the generally accepted model is linked to the process of generating information (Go & Bortree, 2017). The current century has been specially analyzed from a cybernetic perspective, trying to recognize how organizations transmit messages, how those are disseminated by the media used, and how they are received by the audience (Pomering & Johnson, 2009).

METHODOLOGY

The study is descriptive and empirical based on companies with the ESR distinction that communicate with stakeholders via Twitter. Tweets from various companies were analyzed using content analysis methodology to find the elements of CSR most used in the communication of companies through such platform. Content analysis is recognized as a helpful tool for conducting research related to social networks; it is a systematic approach to extract meaningful information from text documents of any kind (Liao et al., 2017). This technique is growing in popularity among social networks' studies and could be used by humans reading the text and/or using computers to generate information about the corpora (Aureli, 2017). Computers are a valuable tool in quantitative text analysis (QTA) for communication and information flow through social media platforms considering that data increases in volume; QTA uses algorithms, often borrowed from computer science and statistics, to generate data analysis (Chew & Eysenbach, 2010).

The purpose of this study was to analyze the behavior of companies' CSR communication on Twitter. A sample of 600 companies, recognized with the badge of Socially Responsible Company (ESR) by the CEMEFI in 2020, has been used to perform this study. Of those companies, a manual search was carried out for Twitter accounts, looking at both the companies' web pages and direct inquiries on Twitter to find the official accounts. Results show that 467 of the 600 companies had an active Twitter account. That means that practically 80% of the companies with the socially responsible badge have Twitter. Then, the sample was reduced to 35 companies to generate the corpora of the study as the criteria defined to select companies also included those with accounts with more than 500 tweets in the 2019–2020 period, so it could be enough data to analyze it. The sample included small, medium, and large companies (See the complete list of companies in Table 10.1), from various sectors: Raw

Table 10.1 Complete list of companies analyzed by size, sector, and Tweets

Company	Twitter	Sector	Size	Number of tweets
Coca-Cola FEMSA	SomosCocaCola	Food/Beverage	Large	2526
Grupo Modelo	GrupoModelo_MX	Food/Beverage	Large	2148
Aguakan	DHCAGUAKAN	Services	Medium	2041
Holcim Mexico	Holcim_Mx	Raw material	Large	1953
L'Oréal Mexico	Lorealmexico	Care	Large	1734
Africam Safari	AfricamSafari	Entertainment	Medium	1726
Naturgy	Naturgy	Raw material	Large	1643
Adecco	AdeccoMexico	Services	Large	1634
Iberdrola México	Iberdrolamex	Raw material	Large	1625
Pepsico Internacional	PepsiCoMex	Food/Beverage	Large	1437
FEMSA Servicios	FEMSA	Food/Beverage	Large	1436
Grupo Bimbo	Grupo_Bimbo	Food/Beverage	Large	1217
Banco Azteca	BancoAzteca	Finance	Large	1193
Avon Cosmetics	AvonMexico	Care	Large	1158
Agnico Eagle México	Agnicoeagle	Raw material	Medium	1143
Bepensa	BepensaCorp	Food/Beverage	Large	1138
Toks	ToksMx	Food/Beverage	Medium	1118
Wal-Mart de México y Centroamérica	WalmartMXyCAM	Services	Large	1043
A.N.A. Compañía de Seguros	ANASeguros	Finance	Medium	1024
Citibanamex	Citibanamex	Finance	Large	938
BanBajío	BanBajioMX	Finance	Large	898
PETSTAR	Petstarmx	Services	Medium	891
General Motors de México	GeneralMotorsMx	Automobile	Large	864
Credito Real	CreditoRealMx	Finance	Medium	792

(continued)

Table 10.1 (continued)

Company	Twitter	Sector	Size	Number of tweets
Corporativo UNNE	CorporativoUNNE	Transportation	Large	694
Pullman de Morelos	PullmanDeMorOf	Transportation	Medium	589
Bio PAPPEL	BioPappel	Raw material	Medium	585
Grupo AlEn	GrupoAlEn	Raw material	Large	563
Braskem Idesa	BraskemIdesa	Raw material	Large	558
Grupo Dolphin Discovery	dolphindiscESP	Entertainment	Medium	549
Nuvoil	Nuvoil	Raw material	Large	518
3M	3MLatinoAmerica	Raw material	Large	515
ArcelorMittal México	ArcelorMittalMX	Raw material	Large	513
Morphoplast	Morphoplast	Raw material	Medium	503
Grupo CICE	grupo_cice	Transportation	Large	501

material, food and beverage, finance, services, transportation, personal care and recreation, and entertainment.

In 2019, a health pandemic caused by COVID-19 erupted worldwide. As has been analyzed, all health crises generate changes in social behavior (Chew & Eysenbach, 2010), notably this pandemic generated a total change in the action of society at the global level. Mexico was one of the most affected countries; with data from April 2021, it was the third country with the most deaths globally and the fifteenth in the number of reported contagions (Statista, 2020). On March 23rd, the pandemic's beginning was declared in Mexico which caused practically all businesses to turn to a virtual format, except for the essential ones. Considering that, throughout the study, the focus was also to determine if there were noticeable changes in behavior of social networks' management derived from the COVID-19 pandemic, two sets of data and information were defined. The first set (called PreCOVID) includes the period from April 2019 to March 2020, and the second (called COVID) includes the year related to the pandemic, that is, from April 2020 to March 2021.

The natural process to conduct the present study is by computer, generating a code in a programming language, in this case *R*, with a developed package such as quanteada. With R, a code was programmed to cleanse the database and eliminate common words such as adjectives, nouns, or pronouns, and then transform the data into a descriptive statistical analysis that could generate word frequency, word cloud, word association analysis, and other advanced content analysis; then, data was analyzed using descriptive statistic (Benoit et al., 2018). In the process of cleansing the data, the number of tweets was reduced from 39,408 tweets to around 24,000.

Findings and Discussion

Question 1: Is Twitter a social network for business communication?
Question 2: Are there any increases in the use of Twitter for business communications related to COVID-19?

According to Statista (2021), there are 81 million social media users in Mexico; 97% of those have Facebook and 57% Twitter, which means almost 1.5 times Facebook's penetration on Twitter in terms of users. However, according to the same study, Facebook is used 65% for conversations between friends, while Twitter is used 84% for information and connection with sources of information (Statista, 2021). With this framework as a reference, a first approach is whether companies use Twitter for communication purposes or just a mailbox to send and simulate receiving communication.

This first question can be answered by analyzing companies' accounts to find a tool where companies generate new messages (organic tweets) or only respond to questions from their stakeholders (replies to tweets). The second question tries to understand if an incremental behavior exists in the use of Twitter during the pandemic, as had already occurred, for example, in the COVID period (Chew & Eysenbach, 2010). To answer these questions, an analysis of messages originating from Twitter accounts has been carried out. Results, presented in Table 10.2, show that more than 50% of the messages in the two periods are organic; therefore, it can be concluded that the greater use of the tool is linked to the generation of communication by the company, followed by the interaction with stakeholders replying to the tweets when it is quoted. For the second question, it can also be observed in Table 10.2 that there is an increase of 46% in the total number of interactions during the COVID period, which is much bigger than the 24% of the two previous years (Statista, 2021),

Table 10.2 Source of tweets

	COVID		PreCOVID		Increase	
Organic	8116	57.18%	5765	59.69%	2351	40.78%
Retweets	1121	7.90%	1041	10.78%	80	7.68%
Replies	4956	34.92%	2852	29.53%	2104	73.77%
Total	14,193		9658		4535	46.96%

that allows affirming that there is an increase higher than usual during the year of the pandemic, without this implying a significant change in content generation proportions.

Question 3: What are companies talking about on Twitter regarding Social Responsibility during the COVID-19 pandemic?

As discussed previously in this document, communication, particularly CSR communication, is the way for companies to inform their stakeholders about their actions and what they want to know about them. A quantitative text analysis of the organic tweets of each sample was carried out. Results show the 100 most used words in each of the two samples, and those have been manually classified into nine categories: The first seven categories considering the elements presented on the ESR distinctive, an eighth category related to COVID, and a ninth related to general topics.

The result of this analysis is shown in Table 10.3 and indicates that the tweets are mainly related to a general vision of social responsibility and specifically with environmental and values axes, and these have no such relevant changes during COVID time. It's essential to consider the 830 occurrences of words related to COVID with cero in pre-COVID time, which allows us to affirm that COVID was a critical topic company were talking about during the pandemic.

Question 4: Which messages are best received by stakeholders? (Likes and retweets).

A similar analysis to the previous one was carried out with likes and retweets, trying to understand stakeholders' reactions to the messages

Table 10.3 Classification of tweet words according to ESR badge

Classification	COVID	Pre-COVID	Words like
Values, Transparency, and Governance	1225	931	Mexico, thanks, country
Work practices in the company	1013	723	Business, women, labor force
Community Development	583	612	Development, community, innovation, technology
Environmental Care	1776	1019	Water, world, environment, energy, planet
Human Rights	1256	464	Person, life, health, family, home
Suppliers	198	134	Collaborators
Customers	197	141	Customers, responsible consumption
COVID-19	830	0	COVID-19, pandemic, contingence
General	2503	1426	Commitment, program, actions, service, social, help, future, ESR, sustainability

primarily. To do so, the 500 most liked and retweeted messages were selected, and the same text analysis process was carried out with them. The results were classified based on the original message, whether it generated a positive or negative reaction in stakeholders. In this analysis, shown in Table 10.4, the following conclusions can be drawn: The main observation that can be noted is that tweets related to COVID were the ones that focused the primary attention of the stakeholders, representing 36% of the likes and 39% of the retweets, which is doubly significant considering that only 9% of the messages were related to this topic. These could show that COVID was the most impacting topic during 2020 for stakeholders. The gap obtained by COVID primarily resulted from the proportional decrease in likes and retweets related to "Values, transparency, and governance." Although they maintain very similar numbers in quantities, we know from the previous analysis that there was a significant increase in tweets, and this variable remains without movement. Another finding is a non-proportional interest in "Work practices in the company;" although 11% of the messages are related to this topic, only 5% of the likes and retweets are linked to this same variable.

Table 10.4 Likes and retweet analysis

Classification	Likes COVID	Likes Pre COVID	Retweet COVID	Retweet Pre COVID	Words like
Values, Transparency, Governance	154	152	160	164	Mexico, thanks, country, formexico
Work practices in the company	40	35	50	41	Business, women, inclusion
Community development	30	48	56	59	Development, community, technology
Environmental Care	149	87	181	81	Energyformexico, water, world, environment, energy, planet
Human Rights	107	64	157	45	Person, life, health, family, home
Suppliers	22	26	26	27	Collaborators
Customers	40	10	34	16	Customers, responsible consumption
COVID-19	398	10	599	10	COVID-19, pandemic, contingence, masks, respirators, n95, medical care
General	153	81	272	58	Commitment, program, actions, service, social, help, future, ESR, sustainability

Conclusions

In an exploratory way, the present study sought to understand the current situation of CSR communication of companies recognized as socially responsible (ESR), specifically in the framework of the COVID-19 crisis. In general, the chapter concludes that, during the COVID-19 period, there was an increase of practically 50% in the number of tweets generated by companies and that more than half of those were organic. That shows that companies, particularly in the COVID year, found a tool on Twitter to share information to their stakeholders. Likewise, it can be observed that according to the evaluation criteria, such as the ESR, environment related topics generated the most communication from companies. Specifically, words like water, world, environment, energy, and planet were the ones that appeared more often in the companies' organic tweets. The COVID-19 topic also caused the most reactions during the year, with the highest number of retweets and likes. It also was the topic with the highest proportion of company tweets and stakeholder reactions to them. Therefore, evidence shows that COVID-19 is a relevant issue for stakeholders who seek to know the companies' actions on this matter.

Companies' communication with their different stakeholders has always been a fundamental element; however, as presented in this document, virtuality has opened a space for interaction between the various actors and the company that results in more and more digital media being used to communicate actions carried out by the company.

As the study shows, communication has increased due to the pandemic, especially in actions related to COVID-19, which became one of the most communicated elements by companies and generated the most engagement in stakeholders measured in likes and shares. Despite the above, companies continued to talk mainly about environmental care, human rights, and institutional values, which are also the elements with the most engagement after COVID-19. Thus, these findings indicate that the commitment to CSR still stands as elemental for these companies. That is relevant because it allows us to identify that, in addition to the pandemic, companies continue to value the importance of carrying out and communicating socially responsible actions; their intent is to support the fulfillment of the 2030 agenda and the engagement with stakeholders which will drive the corresponding industries' recovery from the effects of the health crisis.

STUDY LIMITATIONS AND FUTURE RESEARCH DIRECTIONS

This study presents the analysis of Twitter communication in an exploratory way; however, it does not analyze their impact or whether these messages are aligned with the company's strategy. Therefore, future studies could be carried out to evaluate the reaction of consumers to know if the reactions and responses of the tweets (liking or disliking). The present study also does not cover stakeholders' feelings regarding companies' tweets, which could be studied later. Likewise, the present study was carried out with the tweets mainly from 2019 and 2020; however, in Mexico, a new wave of infection has emerged because of COVID-19's delta variant, and there is progress in terms of adult vaccination in which generates a return to normal social and labor activities. It could be interesting to analyze if the communication in this third wave and the return to normality is like the previous one. A study of feelings could be helpful for these purposes or conducting interviews with a sample of the stakeholders that interact in the tweets. Also, studies of what will happen after the health crisis could be interesting to know if there were definitive changes in the quantity and issues of the companies' communication or if these were temporary to the contingency.

References

Aureli, S. (2017). A comparison of content analysis usage and text mining in CSR corporate disclosure. *The International Journal of Digital Accounting Research, 17*, 1–32.

Benoit, K., Watanabe, K., Wang, H., Nulty, P., Obeng, A., Müller, S., & Matsuo, A. (2018). Quanteda: An R package for the quantitative analysis of textual data. *Journal of Open Source Software, 3*(30), 774–776.

Bhattacharya, C. B., Sen, S., & Korschun, D. (2011). *Leveraging corporate responsibility: The stakeholder route to maximizing business and social value.* Cambridge University Press.

Brown, T., & Dacin, P. (1997). The company and the product: Corporate associations and consumer product responses. *Journal of Marketing, 61*(1), 68–84.

Cajiga, J. F. (2013). *El concepto de la responsabilidad social empresarial.* CEMEFI. Retrieved June 30, 2021, from https://www.cemefi.org/esr/images/stories/pdf/esr/concepto_esr.pdf

Carroll, A. (1999). Corporate Social Responsibility: Evolution of a definitional construct. *Business and Society, 3*, 268–295.

Chae, B., & Park, E. (2018). Corporate Social Responsibility (CSR): A survey of topics and trends using Twitter data and topic modeling. *Sustainability, 10*(7), 2231.

Chew, C., & Eysenbach, G. (2010). Pandemics in the age of Twitter: Content analysis of Tweets during the 2009 H1N1 outbreak. *PLoS ONE, 5*(11), e14118. https://doi.org/10.1371/journal.pone.0014118

Colleoni, E. (2013). CSR communication strategies for organizational legitimacy in social media. *Corporate Communications: An International Journal, 18*(2), 228–248.

Crane, A., & Glozer, S. (2016). Researching corporate social responsibility communication: Themes, opportunities, and challenges. *Journal of Management Studies, 53*(7), 1223–1252. https://doi.org/10.1111/joms.12196

Dahlsrud, A. (2008). How Corporate Social Responsibility is defined: An analysis of 37 definitions. *Corporate Social Responsibility and Environmental Management, 15*, 1–13.

Davis, K. (1960). Can business afford to ignore Corporate Social Responsibilities. *California Management Review, 2*, 70–76.

Deggan, C., & Soltys, S. (2007). Social accounting research: An Australasian perspective. *Accounting Forum, 31*, 73–89.

European Commission. (2001). *Green paper: Promoting a European framework for Corporate Social Responsibility*. Commission of the European Communities. Retrieved June 30, 2021, from https://europarl.europa.eu/meetdocs/committees/deve/20020122/com(2001)366_en.pdf

Freeman, R. E. (1984). *Strategic management: A stakeholder approach*. Cambridge University Press.

Friedman, T. L. (2006). *The world is flat: A brief history of the twenty-first century* (Rev. ed.). Farrar, Straus, and Giroux.

Go, E., & Bortree, D. S. (2017). What and how to communicate CSR? The role of CSR fit, modality interactivity, and message interactivity on social networking sites. *Journal of Promotion Management, 23*(5), 727–747.

Gómez, L. M., & Borges-Tavárez, R. W. (2017). CSR online communication in Latin America: An analysis of social media platforms. In L. M. Gómez, R. W. Borges-Tavárez (Eds.), *Corporate Social Responsibility and corporate governance* (pp. 113–132). Emerald Publishing Limited.

Gray, R. (2002). The social accounting project and accounting, organisations and society: Privileging engagement, imaginings, new accountings and pragmatism over critique? *Accounting, Organisations and Society, 27*, 87–708.

Johnson, G., & Scholes, K. (2002). *Exploring corporate strategy: Text and cases* (6th ed., P. Hall, Ed.). *Financial Times*.

Kaplan, A., & Haenlein, M. (2010). Users of the world, unite! The challenges and opportunities of social media. *Business Horizons, 53*(1), 53–68.

Kent, M. L., & Taylor, M. (2016). From homo economicus to homo dialogicus: Rethinking social media use in CSR communication. *Public Relations Review, 42*(1), 60–67.

Kim, S., Kim, S.-Y., & Sung, K. H. (2014). Fortune 100 companies' Facebook strategies: Corporate ability versus social responsibility. *Journal of Communication Management, 18*, 343–362.

Kotler, P., & Lee, N. (2005). Best of breed: When it comes to gaining a market edge while supporting a social cause, "corporate social marketing" leads the pack. *Social Marketing Quarterly, 11*(3–4), 91–10.

Liao, P.-C., Xia, N.-N., Wu, C.-L., Zhang, X.-L., & Yeh, J.-L. (2017). Communicating the Corporate Social Responsibility (CSR) of international contractors: Content analysis of CSR reporting. *Journal of Cleaner Production, 156*, 327–336.

Lee, K., Oh, W.-Y., & Kim, N. (2013). Social media for socially responsible firms: Analysis of Fortune 500's Twitter profiles and their CSR/CSIR ratings. *Journal of Business Ethics, 118*, 791–806.

Lee, M.-D. P. (2008). A review of the theories of Corporate Social Responsibility: Its evolutionary path and the road ahead. *International Journal of Management Reviews, 10*(1), 53–73.

López-Fernández, A. M., & Rajagopal. (2015). Effect on stakeholders' perception of CSR: Analysis of information dynamics through social media. *Journal of Business Competition and Growth, 4*(1/2), 24–43.

Maignan, I. (2001). Consumers' perceptions of corporate social responsibilities: A cross-cultural comparison. *Journal of Business Ethics, 30*, 57–72.

March, J. G. (2007). The study of organizations and organizing since 1945. *Organization Studies, 28*, 9–19.

Mathews, M. (1997). Twenty-five years of social and environmental accounting research. *Accounting, Auditing & Accountability Journal, 10*(4), 481–531.

Oboler, A., Welsh, K., & Cruz, L. (2012). The danger of Big Data: Social media as computational social science. *First Monday, 17*, 7.

Pomering, A., & Johnson, L. W. (2009). Advertising corporate social responsibility initiatives to communicate corporate image: Inhibiting scepticism to enhance persuasion. *Corporate Communication: An International Journal, 14*, 420–439.

Saeidi, S. P., Sofian, S., Saeidi, P., Saeidi, S. P., & Saaeidi, S. A. (2015). How does Corporate Social Responsibility contribute to firm financial performance? The mediating role of competitive advantage, reputation, and customer satisfaction. *Journal of Business Research, 68*(2), 341–350.

Sen, S., & Bhattacharya, C. B. (2001). Does doing good always lead to doing better? Consumer reactions to Corporate Social Responsibility. *Journal of Marketing Research, 38*(2), 225–243.

Stanaland, A., Lwin, M., & Murphy, P. (2011). Consumer perceptions of the antecedents and consequences of Corporate Social Responsibility. *Journal of Business Ethics, 102*(1), 47–55.

Statista. (2020). *Coronavirus (COVID-19) in Mexico.* Retrieved June 30, 2021, from https://www.statista.com/study/71998/coronavirus-covid-19-in-mexico

Statista. (2021). *Social media usage in Mexico.* Retrived June 30, 2021, from https://www.statista.com/study/66866/social-media-usage-in-mexico

Tench, R., & Jones, B. (2015). Social media: The wild west of CSR Communications. *Social Responsibility Journal, 11*(2), 290–305.

Unerman, J., & Bennett, M. (2004). Increased stakeholder dialogue and the internet: Towards greater corporate accountability or reinforcing capitalist hegemony? *Accounting, 29*, 685–707.

Visser, W. (2010). The age of responsibility: CSR 2.0 and the new DNA of business. *Journal of Business Systems, Governance and Ethics, 5*, 7–22.

Vo, T. T., Xiao, X., & Ho, S. Y. (2019). How does corporate social responsibility engagement influence word of mouth on Twitter? Evidence from the airline industry. *Journal of Business Ethics, 157*, 525–542.

Welford, R. (2005). Corporate Social Responsibility in Europe, North America and Asia: 2004 survey results. *The Journal of Corporate Citizenship, 17*, 33–52.

CHAPTER 11

Unethical Supply Chains Delaying Recovery: Analyzing Pre and Mid COVID-19 Conditions

Andrée Marie López-Fernández and Alejandra Sánchez-Rosales

INTRODUCTION

All industries and sectors, to varying degrees, have been significantly impacted by the effects of the global health crisis caused by COVID-19; according to the World Economic Forum, as supply chains were disrupted, industries fell into crisis (Schell, 2020). Although the pandemic's effects could not have been entirely foreseen, it is clear that the many previous crises had evidenced the need for effective contingency and crisis planning to avoid intensifying negative collateral effects.

A. M. López-Fernández (✉) · A. Sánchez-Rosales
Facultad de Ciencias Económicas y Empresariales, Universidad Panamericana, Mexico City, Mexico

© The Author(s), under exclusive license to Springer Nature Switzerland AG 2022
A. M. López-Fernández and A. Terán-Bustamante (eds.), *Business Recovery in Emerging Markets*, Palgrave Studies in Democracy, Innovation, and Entrepreneurship for Growth, https://doi.org/10.1007/978-3-030-91532-2_11

In other words, organizations were justifiably unprepared for the disruption caused COVID-19, however, unjustifiably unprepared for a crisis. One of the predominant issues that has deepened and, for many, become more apparent, is the inequality pervading global supply chains, therefore, society at large.

Vaccines for COVID-19 are an important first step in managing the health crisis. However, in regards to the pandemic's effects, the Director-General of the World Health Organization (WHO) has stated that they "will be felt for decades to come" (UN News, 2020). The UN Deputy Secretary-General has posited that "Climate crisis, drought, hunger and heightened insecurity, are being exacerbated by the long-term economic effects of the inequality virus," and recovery entails effectively undertaking these challenges (UN News, 2021a). There are multiple variables correlating in these statements, yet, it has become unsurprisingly clear that inequity has and will most likely continue to burden the possibility of full recovery.

Prior to COVID-19, important advances had been made in equality globally; unfortunately, according to the OECD (2019), economies had not equally or evenly been distributing the benefits from their attested growth. Moreover, the pandemic has mercilessly revealed the significant gaps between haves and have-nots, among and within countries (UNDP, 2020). In other words, it has shed light on a preexisting social justice issue that carries unescapable damaging effects. Recovering from the effects of COVID-19, both physically and financially is greatly determined by privilege which is, both historically and currently, a birthright. Even though the virus does not discriminate, reality is that those of a certain gender, race, socioeconomic status, and birthplace share important advantages. In terms of inequality, those most vulnerable before the pandemic are still most at risk. The questions are: Is recovery even possible with the growing equality gap? And, is getting back to normal the best scenario?

The general objective of the study was to understand the reasons why recovery will take years to achieve. The specific objectives were to: (i) analyze the roles of organization dynamics and supply chains in the slow pace of recovery, and (ii) propose a model that may lead to organizational decision-making toward a socially responsible approach to supply chain governance. This chapter is sectioned as follows: section two includes a review of literature on the study's core constructs, section three encompasses a discussion on a conceptual model, section four includes concluding remarks, and the last section describes future research directions. The study contributes to social responsibility and supply chain literature, as well as to the understanding of pre-pandemic conditions that have exacerbated the slow pace of recovery from COVID-19.

Literature Review

Generalities on Inequality

Equality has been at the center of economic, social, political, legal, and philosophical discussions for decades. Ongoing debates on its importance, definition, and scope are perplexing; for one, these discussions tend to focus on what causes inequality rather than on the design and execution of strategic plans to successfully close the gap. Particularly in business, although there are legitimate claims of wrongdoings, unethical and non-socially responsible practices, it seems as though there is a greater intent on punishing those that do wrong, than a sense of pursuing global equality.

Distributive justice also referred to as economic justice (Phelps, 2018), according to Wagstaff (1994), is centered on the principals: equality, equity, and need. These principals indicate the manner in which "benefits and burdens" should be distributed (Rescher, 2002) in society. While equality refers to the access to same opportunities and resources, equity refers to just resources and opportunities to achieve equality. As such, equity, a principle of justice, is unprejudiced if resources and opportunities are distributed in accordance with particular efforts and contributions (Deutsch, 1985; Liebig et al., 2016); meaning that, the distribution is fair only if comparative to the effort (Rescher, 2002). Moreover, equity theory suggests that an individual's behavior and degree of satisfaction are weighed by what is considered equitable and, thus, fair; in such way that equity is a perception (Tyler & Smith, 1998) which significantly varies among individuals as well as social contexts. Even though equity is technically assessed mathematically, the results are not necessarily perceived to be proportional to their undertakings.

Equality impacts many aspects, including: income, employment, wealth (Graafland & Lous, 2018), health (Culyer & Wagstaff, 1993), education (Subrahmanian, 2005), democracy (Beer, 2009) security, safety, human rights (Donnelly, 2003), and overall opportunities. Therefore, inequality is the state of not being equal (UN, 2015a) in relation to any of the mentioned aspects. Inequality is a key deterrent for development and sustainability (Renouard & Lado, 2012), as it is a "Major source of injustice, a cause of poverty, and sometimes of conflict" (Stewart, 2013). Inequality, then, in its various forms directly impacts growth and development.

One of the major concerns related to the current health crisis, following infection and death rates, is heightening of inequality; that is, inequality on a global scale. According to Oxfam International, COVID-19 "exposed, fed off and increased existing inequalities of wealth, gender and race" (Berkhout et al., 2021). The issue is so pervasive that COVID-19 has been referred to as the "inequality virus" (Mohammed, 2021). Increased inequality has also been observed in various aspects including, but not limited to, learning opportunities (Jaeger & Blaabaek, 2020), technology, healthcare and public health (CDC, 2021; Myers, 2020), and gender relations (Czymara et al., 2021); further, for instance, those who were previously rich recovered in less than a year, while "hundreds of millions of people are being forced into poverty" and the "recovery for the world's poorest people could take over a decade" (Berkhout et al., 2021).

According to the World Economic Forum, country and organizational leaders should work toward a shared goal of just and inclusive economies (Schwab, 2020). Further, gender equality, particularly, continues to be a significant challenge for decision-makers around the world (Gazzola et al., 2016). Growth on its own is significantly associated with inequality (UN, 2015a), which means that for equality to be plausible, development is a must. For instance, in reference to the sustainable development goals (SDGs), lack of gender equality directly impacts other social development goals as it hinders progress (Tsumori, 2018). According to former Secretary-General Ban Ki-moon, the SDGs cannot be realized "without full and equal rights for half of the world's population, in law and in practice" (UN, 2015b). In order to achieve social growth and development, in other words, meet the seventeen sustainable development goals, gender equality is indispensable.

The Business of Equality

Corporate social responsibility (CSR) is an organization's approach to business whereby social, environmental, and financial performance are cultivated. It is usually associated with achievement of the Triple Bottom

Line (TBL) (Chandan & Das, 2017; Elkington, 1997) which focuses on the three Ps: people, profit, and planet. CSR has been described as multidimensional (Lindgreen et al., 2009), a complex construct, and an organization's commitment toward ethical behavior for the achievement of financial performance as well as society's and collaborators and their families' quality of life (Watts & Holme, 1999). For such matter, Feng et al. (2020) have posited that CSR "usually regarded as a complex and multidimensional concept that comprises a wide range of activities by a broad group of stakeholders;" therefore, CSR requires the active participation of internal and external stakeholders.

According to Isa (2012), CSR is an ongoing process, impacted by political interests, that focuses on the firm's policies, stakeholders, and the environment, and is derived from both personal and the firm's values. Stakeholders are those affected and that can affect the firm's business dynamics (Oluwafemi & Oyatoye, 2012); they are those that directly or indirectly impact the firm's "businesses' wealth-creating activities" (Evans & Sawyer, 2010). Just like operating without their participation is not possible, so is the effective engagement in CSR; in other words, achieving social, financial, and environmental performance requires stakeholders' proactive participation.

As successful stakeholder management entails ensuring their satisfaction, socially responsible firms develop policies aligned with their needs, wants, and requirements. As such, engagement in CSR is viable, as value is created and shared (Jonikas, 2012) with the active participation of stakeholders. Additionally, transparently communicating CSR policies with current and potential stakeholders have a significant impact on stakeholders' perception of the organization's image as well as the firm's performance (Maguire, 2011). Stakeholders need and want to know the firm's policies, practices, and results regarding its CSR; transparently sharing the latter informs their decision-making, as they value honesty (O'Connor & Meister, 2008). Engagement in CSR remains, for most organizations, a voluntary practice (Chandan & Das, 2017); however, that does not exempt them from complying with legal ethical standards, in other words, firms engaging in CSR ought to, at minimum, meet legal expectations. This means that socially responsible firms at the very least must comply with local and federal law of the location of operation and, in some cases, international guidelines.

Firms engaged in CSR certainly ensure diversity and inclusion in the organization; for one, not doing so may be discriminatory, and second, it makes good business sense. According to Artigas et al. (2013), for instance, gender diversity is not just a social issue but also a "business imperative." Diversity also enhances innovation; Østergaard et al. (2011) conducted a study and found that diversity in education, gender and a culture of diversity positively correlate with innovation and innovation performance. Furthermore, diversity has a positive impact on business growth of the firm in terms of market growth (Hewlett et al., 2013). Organizations that ensure gender equality are not only fair, but also positively impact their performance and that of the country (WGEA, 2018) in which they operate. For such reasons, organizations' procrastination worldwide on the matter is inconceivable.

The Business of Inequality

It is the organization's corporate philosophy and governance system which enable the firm to effectively impact gender equality in alignment with CSR objectives, strategies, and tactics. Meaning, it must be part of how the business operates, rather than a reasonable idea from one collaborator in one department at random intervals. Governance, the organization's system that controls its operations by means of laws, rules (Gillan & Starks, 1998), and standards, should extend outwards to address supply chain management, particularly when referring to focal companies given their power of influence over the entire supply chain. Organizations have begun to tackle social issues via CSR engagement aligned with corporate governance and supply chain governance; however, there still is work to be done.

There are many examples of the impact of diversity and inclusion, or lack thereof, on performance. Take, for example, the case of H&M in 2018. The firm launched a clothing line online; one of the pictures included a black child wearing a sweatshirt (hoodie) that said "Coolest monkey in the jungle" (Bever, 2018). Of course, social media backlash was immediate, and the firm apologized and took action to remove the picture and the item was no longer for sale (Bever, 2018). Consider how many collaborators were involved in this event. From design, manufacturing, marketing, advertisement, sales, etc. The saying on the sweatshirt first needed approval, then, the item was approved for sale, others booked and approved the models, others took the picture, and then the latter was deemed acceptable for others to upload on the website. The entire process was tone deaf. Many wondered, *what were they thinking?!* And, *who was in the room when this was approved?!* Perhaps the better questions are: who was not in the room? And, who did not have a say, and why?

Gender equality, for instance, is well associated with CSR strategies (Gazzola et al., 2016) and is overwhelmingly unattained. This has significant and negative effects on social growth and development which, in turn, certainly has a negative impact on business growth and development. In other words, designing and executing substantive actions to ensure gender equality makes good business sense. Davis and Geyfman (2015) have posited that in order to tackle the complexities of gender equality and achieve it, organizations must cultivate leadership that works toward the improvement of "work-life balance, developing future women leaders, and tackling unconscious bias." As firms must at the very least, especially those stating CSR engagement, fully comply with the extent of the law, unethical behavior is inexplicable. For instance, if the law is clear, why is equal pay so difficult to comprehend and execute?

By sector, women occupy 61.5% of services jobs, 13.5% in industry, and 25% in agriculture; further, 23% hold a position in Parliament and only 4% are CEOs of Fortune 500 firms (UN Women, 2021a); however, they also take on the burden of domestic work which is unpaid and unrecognized. The Organisation for Economic Co-operation and Development reported, in 2019, the gender wage gap ranging from 3.5% in Romania to 32.5% in Korea (OECD, 2021). And, according to UN Women (2021b), when compared to men's wages, women worldwide earn 77cents on the dollar. How can organizational leaders possibly continue to justify paying even a cent less? Moreover, the International Labour Organization has found that gender wage gaps are larger for women in management positions in 42 out of 93 studied countries (ILO, 2019).

Some firms have stated that they foster gender equality by means of their CSR engagement only to be actively practicing a form of social washing. For instance, according to Lange and Wyndham (2021), CSR practices in poor countries are more rhetorical than substantive. This statement is distinctively witnessed in the contrasting conditions of equality throughout global supply chains. Large, multinational, and very successful companies demonstrate significant dissonance as they consistently share annual reports on social responsibility, sustainability, social performance, etc., yet, continue to source irresponsibly.

It seems as though focal companies, firms at the far end of the supply chain providing to end consumers (Wang & Wood, 2016), are more than willing to source from organizations that exploit their workers and hire children; in other words, firms that engage in modern-day slavery. According to Donnelly (2003), "human rights are equal rights," as such, human beings have the same rights given their condition of being human. The issue, then, is not that some people do not have human rights, rather their rights are violated. Do organizational leaders really find these practices acceptable, an acceptable strategy? If not, then, why are there approximately 40.3 million people enslaved, 1 in 4 being children (Council on Foreign Relations, 2020), of which about 64% are working in the private sector (Freedom United, 2020)? The reality is that prominent and highly successful companies in technology, food and beverage, and clothing, among many others, operate in violation of human rights. Therefore, in such cases, supply chain governance is either non-existent, or not ethical or socially responsible. That being said, if firms do have supply chain governance that restricts business dynamics to ethical behavior, while sourcing from organizations that exploit their workers, do not ensure equal hire or pay, discriminate, etc., then, they are in violation of their own bylaws, as well as legal standards.

Inequality and COVID-19

Perry et al. (2021) found that COVID-19, like previous disasters, has particularly affected vulnerable groups. The latter being those "susceptible to physical or emotional injury or attack" (Van Kamp & Davies, 2013). Vaccine distribution has exposed one of the visible and stark effects of inequality; according to the head of the UN health agency, "The unequal distribution of vaccines is not only a moral outrage, but economically and epidemiologically self-defeating" (UN News, 2021b). Further, the Director-General of the WHO pointed out that "of the 832 million vaccine doses administered, 82% have gone to high or upper middle-income countries, while only 0.2% have been sent to their low-income peers" (UN News, 2021b). In other words, vaccination in the poorest countries accounts for about 1 out of every 500 people.

The slow and unequal pace of vaccination already has particular implications for growth and development. Consider those women and men that were sole bread earners and have passed away due to COVID-19; not only have their families lost a loved one, but they are now facing the very real and grave reality of poverty. A very similar scenario has been occurring with individuals furloughed and laid off at the beginning of the pandemic and has not found a steady paying job or have taken on jobs that put them at higher risk of infection. Too many have lost their income, their homes, therefore, the stability, access to resources and opportunities that not only directly impact them, but also their children's future, the generation that will largely deal with the consequences of the COVID-19 disruption.

In reference to workload, according to Raley et al. (2012), mothers tend to have a greater impact on their wages simply because they tend to select jobs that enable them to spend more time with their families, take on part-time jobs, or leave the labor market to do so. It would seem that with COVID-19 restrictions, men and women would be tackling home responsibilities equally, however, mothers are still performing the majority of domestic labor and childcare responsibilities (Ruppanner, 2020); in other words, mothers are taking on an extra 20 hours a week working from home (McKinsey & Company, 2020); such unequal conditions have also led to a perceived decrease in women's productivity (Feng & Savan, 2020).

In reference to job losses, the International Labour Organization (ILO) has stated that in 2020 unemployment losses amounted to 114 million jobs with women losing more jobs than men (ILO, 2021); that is, approximately 54% of jobs lost were held by women (Madgavkar et al., 2020). Therefore, although a significant number of women and men have lost their jobs, women have disproportionately left the labor market altogether (UNCTAD, 2021). Furthermore, women of color are significantly affected as they are more likely to be furloughed and laid off (McKinsey & Company, 2020). In the United States, in December 2020 alone, one hundred and forty thousand jobs were lost, all held by women; moreover, while they have lost a total of a hundred and fifty-six thousand jobs, men have gained sixteen thousand (Kurtz, 2021).

A long-lasting trajectory of business impunity relating to inequality lays the foundation for the current global reality. The number of years it will take to actually close the gender gap worldwide is overwhelming to say the least. According to PricewaterhouseCoopers (PWC), COVID-19 has caused a significant setback for women in the workplace and, therefore, work toward gender equality needs to be double the previous pace to revert the damage by 2030 (PWC, 2021). Table 11.1 includes data on the years it will take to close the gender gap per region. According to the World Economic Forum (WEF), at the current pace, it will take over one hundred and fifty years to close the gap globally; moreover, "40% of the wage gap, and over 50% of the income gap are still to be

Table 11.1 Years to close the gender gap per region

Region	Years to close the gender gap
Western Europe	54
Latin America and the Caribbean	59
South Asia	71 and a half
Sub-Saharan Africa	95
Eastern Europe and Central Asia	107
Middle East and North Africa	140
North America	151
East Asia and the Pacific	163

Source Developed with data from the WEF (Schwab, 2020)

bridged" (Schwab, 2020); a task particularly difficult in emerging markets and developing countries.

Therefore, inequality has created further crises in the midst of the health crisis; according to the CDC (2019), there is great need to be vigilant of and tend to the psychological impact of crises and, to do so, individuals need to be "empowered to take actions that will reduce their risk of harm." However, empowering individuals affected by inequality before and during the pandemic is complex to say the least.

Back to Normal?

The focus has been on returning back to normal, going back to how things were before COVID-19 impacted the world. According to Flaskerud (2021) the COVID-19 pandemic has been referred to as "the great pause" which implies a possibility of unpausing, resuming, and reverting to circumstances and conditions prior to the abrupt global health crisis. However, based on the information and data presented in the above sections: is *normal* the ideal state? Consider the following interaction during a virtual meeting, a year into the pandemic, into consideration, a man said: "Wow, it's been an entire year that I have not had to put up with the stress of hours in traffic to go back and forth from work;" a woman replied: "Wow, it's been a year that I have not had to put up with the stress, and fear of being sexually assaulted going to and from work."

Of course, many practices have changed for the better; for instance, we have learned that some meetings can be handled via email, business trips are not always necessary, paperless is a viable option, subjecting collaborators to hours in traffic to get to work and back home is inefficient and pointless, and home office does not necessarily mean a decrease in productivity (given the appropriate conditions), and collaborators need a work-life balance, among others. That said, bad practices have also emerged during this pandemic; for instance, work-personal life boundaries have been all but erased. Collaborators are working longer hours, simultaneously taking on work and home shifts. And, many workloads have simply increased; in some cases due to layoffs and in others due to modifications in the way operations are performed.

The changes that have emerged due to the pandemic notwithstanding, why would we want to go back to the way things were? Back to the reality of systemic violence, structured violence, pervasive inequality and discrimination, corruption, impunity, poverty, etc.? Organizational leaders, as government leaders, have a momentous opportunity to change the status quo and produce significant change. According to the OECD (2019), growth can be achieved without instigating or exacerbating inequality. It is needed neither to maintain nor increase growth at a micro or macro level, yet, equality is needed to enhance both business and social growth and development.

Recovering from the Crisis

Actually, the slow pace of recovery is strongly related to the pre-pandemic state of affairs. While it is true that the pandemic has exacerbated the issues that permeate society globally, such as inequality, pre-COVID-19 practices are at the root of industries' slow pace in recovering. Consider the following: in a pre-pandemic context, were collaborators across supply chains thriving? Did they have equal access to opportunities and resources? Were their needs being met? Did they perceive that their contributions and efforts were equitable with their wages, and work conditions?

Although it certainly does not seem outrageous to pay equally or provide equal resources and opportunities, inequality continues to be one of the most unrelenting issues that permeate societies worldwide. However, according to Carpentier et al. (2014), "Equality is not a matter of fate or chance," which means that effective policies can reverse the effects of inequality. For instance, Coury et al. (2020) have posited that organizations have an opportunity to make significant change by investing in a "flexible and empathetic workplace" and, by doing so, they may avoid unnecessary turnover, positively impact those collaborators that have been negatively impacted the most, and foster an organizational culture that ensures equal opportunities for women.

Industry and sector recovery are simply not possible if women are left behind, and working men, children, and women are still victims of modern-day slavery. Business impunity, involving all types of inequality, can be prevented as organizational leaders stop being mere profit maximizing bystanders. Firms engaged in CSR work with organizations across their supply chain to confirm the same conditions in their firms. Neglecting to take action across global supply chains is unethical and counteracts any CSR related policies and practices. For such matter, supply chain governance derived from corporate social responsibility is required for organizations to be able to sensibly and successfully recover from the COVID-19 crisis.

Resilience drives individuals to adapt well when challenged with crises; it is defined as a process by which individuals are able to face challenges and the "process of adapting well in the face of adversity or significant sources of stress" (Ernst et al., 2018). Individually, resilient people accept reality, they consider life meaningful, and are able to improvise (Coutu, 2002). And, organizational resilience has been defined as "The firm's ability to sense and correct maladaptive tendencies and cope positively with unexpected situations" (Ortiz-de-Mandojana & Bansal, 2016). Undoubtedly, facing and successfully recovering from the COVID-19 crisis will require organizations and their collaborators to be resilient; however, the organizations' practices across supply chains will also need to be properly addressed.

Global supply chains are complex systems of organizations, each with their own corporate philosophy; meaning their own form and sense of self-regulation (i.e., governance). As such, in any given supply chain, there are multiple missions, visions, policies, values and codes of conduct, objectives, strategies, and tactics in play. Governance entails coordinating and regulating activities by means of structures, policies, norms, and standards (Boström et al., 2015) which have been previously designed with the aim of guaranteeing accountability and transparency (Kariuki, 2019). Firms tend to limit their governance to their own organization, however, increased awareness of questionable and unethical practices across supply chains indicate the need for self-regulation and accountability, as well as for other firms in the supply chain to ensure ethical and socially responsible operations.

Corporate socially responsible supply chains (Sancha et al., 2016; Tang, 2018) have become common as, gradually, more organizations have begun to incorporate socially responsible standards and practices across supply chains (Mueller et al., 2009). For instance, sustainable supply chain governance is defined as the cooperation among organizations in the supply chain with the intent to improve social and environmental conditions across operations (Vermeulen & Kok, 2012); such cooperation would also impact social, environmental, and financial performance.

Amid the COVID-19 pandemic, some supply chains have been significantly debilitated, others deteriorated, and some are slowly trying to recover, a common effect of crises (Barman et al., 2021). According to Sharma et al. (2020), issues causing the latter include: "demand-supply mismatch, technology, and development of a resilient supply chain." And, many of them are in the current situation not only due to the virus, but also due to pre-pandemic conditions; hence, based on the above discussion, the following propositions have been framed:

P_1 Recovery from the COVID-19 pandemic requires a socially responsible resilient approach to supply chain governance.
P_2 A socially responsible resilient approach to supply chain governance has a positive impact on social growth and development.
P_3 Social growth and development derived from a socially responsible resilient supply chain governance positively impacts business growth and development.

MODEL DISCUSSION

It is easy to argue and claim accountability within the organization, yet, for some reason, intrinsically complex to assert accountability across global supply chains. When focal companies are questioned about the labor conditions of organizations closer to the end of the supply chain, they tend to shrug, lift their hands and claim exemption of responsibility due to outsourcing practices, and/or indirect affiliation with the companies' policies; in other words, they claim zero responsibility for their association with organizations that exploit their collaborators. However, there is an alternative that not only pursues accountability but fosters recovery through growth and development. Figure 11.1

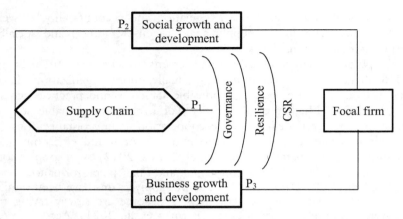

Fig. 11.1 Socially responsible resilient supply chain governance model (*Source* authors)

includes a conceptual model for socially responsible resilient supply chain governance.

Focal companies hold significant power and influence over the entire supply (Wang & Wood, 2016). Therefore, it is reasonable for them to establish how the supply chain ought to operate. Given current and pre-pandemic conditions across supply chains, successful recovery may not occur unless a genuine social responsibility approach is implemented to govern the entire supply chain (P_1). Resilience entails accepting reality before it materializes, which is possible by effectively developing, parallel to a strategic plan, a contingency plan and a crisis plan for various crisis-related scenarios. It also requires valuing human lives, and improvising when necessary to ensure goal achievement. Supply chain governance that is socially responsible and resilient, then, may have a positive effect on the social growth and development (P_2), of at least the communities surrounding each firm in the supply chain. There are multiple advantages to developing organizational policies and executing actions toward equality attainment. For instance, they increase diversity which impacts organizational performance, as well as collaborator satisfaction, commitment, work-life balance, and well-being which, in turn, positively impact the organizations' performance (Monks, 2007). When organizational performance is enhanced via social growth and development, business growth and development ensues (P_3).

Concluding Remarks

While corporate success brings good fortune through increased productivity and, in turn, financial and economic performance, it also burdens society with environmental destitution, inequality, and overall strain on social growth and development. Inequality has certainly been intensified by the global health pandemic, and at the very least been pushed to the forefront; however, many measures taken by organizational leaders across industries are indicative of pre-pandemic unethical management. As such, blaming related business downfalls on COVID-19 now seems to be more of a kneejerk reaction, than a critically analyzed statement.

Any firm enabling unethical behavior is ultimately rendered unethical and certainly not socially responsible. If the firm involved with such practices states to be engaged in corporate social responsibility, then their CSR practices are ineffective (New, 2015). In such cases, either organizations are not self-regulating or merely choose to ignore reality. In any case, their profit-based benefits are considered more relevant than human beings, their dignity (Shields, 2011), well-being, growth, development, and that of their families. The current pandemic is a clear opportunity for organizational leaders to make substantive changes to their supply chain governance to ensure that inequality is no longer an element of their strategy. Industries and sectors will certainly recover faster and more successfully if principles of justice—equality, equity and need—become core policies of CSR engagement. Furthermore, genuinely engaging in CSR drives both business and social growth and development which are desperately needed for a global recovery. Going back to *normal* ultimately means accepting the previous circumstances as the archetype; instead, this is an ideal moment to make *normal* obsolete. Certainly organizational leaders will see the benefit once they realize that competitive gain is not worth it if even one collaborator is subject to unlawful practices.

Future Research Directions

Future research could analyze the effects of a socially responsible supply chain on the eradication of inequality, at least regarding collaborators in the supply chains in question. Also, future research could focus on assessing the implications of socially responsible resilient supply chain governance on growth and development of the business as well as society, particularly the community surrounding the organizations in the supply chain.

References

Artigas, M., Novales-Flamarique, M., & Callegaro, H. (2013). *Women matter: A Latin American perspective. Unlocking women's potential to enhance corporate performance.* McKinsey & Company. Retrieved February 14, 2016, from http://www.mckinsey.com.br/LatAm4/Data/Women%20Matter%20Latin%20America.pdf

Barman, A., Das, R., & De, P. K. (2021). November). Impact of COVID-19 in food supply chain: Disruptions and recovery strategy. *Current Research in Behavioral Sciences, 2,* 1–5.

Beer, C. (2009). Democracy and gender equality. *Studies in Comparative International Development, 44*(3), 212–227.

Berkhout, E., Galasso, N., Lawson, M., Rivero Morales, P. A., Taneja, A., & Vázquez Pimentel, D. A. (2021, January 25). *The inequality virus: Bringing together a world torn apart by coronavirus through a fair, just and sustainable economy* (O. International, Editor) Retrieved May 17, 2021, from Policy Papers: https://www.oxfam.org/en/research/inequality-virus#:~:text=The%20virus%20has%20exposed%2C%20fed,individuals%20and%20corporations%20%E2%80%93%20are%20thriving

Bever, L. (2018, January 8). *H&M apologizes for showing black child wearing a 'monkey in the jungle' sweatshirt.* Retrieved April 8, 2021, from Business: https://www.washingtonpost.com/news/business/wp/2018/01/08/hm-apologizes-for-showing-black-child-wearing-a-monkey-in-the-jungle-sweatshirt/

Boström, M., Jönsson, A. M., Lockie, S., Mol, A. P., & Oosterveer, P. (2015). November). Sustainable and responsible supply chain governance: Challenges and opportunities. *Journal of Cleaner Production, 107,* 1–7.

Carpentier, C. L., Kozul-Wright, R., & Passos, F. D. (2014). Goal 10-why addressing inequality matters. *UN Chronichal, 51*(4). Retrieved May 7, 2021, from https://www.un.org/en/chronicle/article/goal-10-why-addressing-inequality-matters

CDC. (2019). *CERC: Psychology of a crisis.* Retrieved May 27, 2021, from https://emergency.cdc.gov/cerc/ppt/CERC_Psychology_of_a_Crisis.pdf

CDC. (2021, April 19). *Health equity considerations and racial and ethnic minority groups.* Retrieved May 17, 2021, from Work & School: https://www.cdc.gov/coronavirus/2019-ncov/community/health-equity/race-ethnicity.html

Chandan, H. C., & Das, R. (2017). Chapter 4—Evolution of responsible and sustainable corporate identity for Chinese firms. In E. Paulet & C. Rowley (Eds.), *The China business model: Originality and limits* (pp. 71–96). CP Chandos Publishing.

Council on Foreign Relations. (2020). *Modern slavery*. Retrieved October 23, 2020, from https://www.cfr.org/interactives/modern-slavery/#!/section1/item-1

Coury, S., Huang, J., Kumar, A., Prince, S., Krivkovich, A., & Yee, L. (2020, September 30). *Women in the workplace 2020*. Retrieved May 28, 2021, from https://www.mckinsey.com/featured-insights/diversity-and-inclusion/women-in-the-workplace

Coutu, D. L. (2002, May). How resilience works. *Harvard Business Review* (pp. 1–8). Retrieved May 16, 2021, from https://static1.squarespace.com/static/5d1536ab4e50dc0001a5f6e6/t/5ed49a11d1fbb47d97587bbf/1590991378838/HBR.Resilience03Couto.pdf

Culyer, A. J., & Wagstaff, A. (1993, December). Equity and equality in health and health care. *Journal of Health Economics, 12*(4), 431–457.

Czymara, C. S., Langenkamp, A., & Cano, T. (2021). Cause for concerns: Gender inequality in experiencing the COVID-19 lockdown in Germany. *European Societies, 23*, S68–S81. https://doi.org/10.1080/14616696.2020.1808692

Davis, L. M., & Geyfman, V. (2015). The glass door remains closed: Another look at gender inequality in undergraduate business schools. *Journal of Education for Business, 90*(2), 81–88.

Deutsch, M. (1985). *Distributive justice*. Yale University Press.

Donnelly, J. (2003). *Universal human rights in theory and practice*. Cornell University Press.

Elkington, J. (1997). *Cannibals with forks: The triple bottom line of 21st century business*. Capstone.

Ernst, R., Reed, S., & Welle, V. (2018, August). *Lesson plan: Practicing resilience*. Retrieved May 9, 2021, from American Psychological Association. https://www.apa.org/ed/precollege/topss/teaching-resources/practicing-resilience-lesson

Evans, N., & Sawyer, J. (2010). CSR and stakeholders of small businesses in regional South Australia. *Social Responsibility Journal, 6*(3), 433–451.

Feng, X., Groh, A., & Wang, Y. (2020, October 16). Board diversity and CSR. *Global Finance Journal*, 100578. doi:https://doi.org/10.1016/j.gfj.2020.100578

Feng, Z., & Savan, K. (2020, September). Covid-19 created a gender gap in perceived work productivity and job satisfaction: Implications for dual-career parents working from home. *Gender in Management, 35*(7/8), 719–736.

Flaskerud, J. H. (2021, April). Going back to normal. *Issues in Mental Health Nursing, 42*(11), 1078–1081. doi: https://doi.org/10.1080/016 12840.2021.1913001

Freedom United. (2020). *Freedom 101.* Retrieved October 9, 2020, from Learn: https://www.freedomunited.org/freedom-university/what-is-modern-slavery/

Gazzola, P., Sepashvili, E., & Pezzeti, R. (2016). CSR as a mean to promote gender equality. *Economia Aziendale Online, 7*(1), 95–99.

Gillan, S. L., & Starks, L. T. (1998). A survey of shareholder activism: Motivation and empirical evidence. *Contemporary Finance Digest, 2*(3), 10–34.

Graafland, J., & Lous, B. (2018). Economic freedom, income inequality and life satisfaction in OECD countries. *Journal of Happiness Studies, 19*, 2071–2093.

Hewlett, S. A., Marshall, M., & Sherbin, L. (2013, December). How diversity can drive innovation. *Harvard Business Review.* Retrieved April 2, 2021, from . https://static1.squarespace.com/static/5f335d8f379f9d38d30a78d6/t/607e6d66bd48400dba2c17da/1618898279248/How+Diversity+Drives+Innovation.PDF

ILO. (2019, September). *Beyond the glass ceiling: Why businesses need women at the top.* Retrieved April 2, 2021, from InfoStories. https://ilo.org/infost ories/en-GB/Stories/Employment/beyond-the-glass-ceiling#introduction

ILO. (2021, January 25). *ILo monitor: COVID-19 and the world of work* (7th ed.). Retrieved April 17, 2021, from https://www.ilo.org/wcmsp5/groups/public/---dgreports/---dcomm/documents/briefingnote/wcms_767028.pdf

Isa, S. M. (2012). Corporate social responsibility: What can we learn from the stakeholders. *Procedia—Social and Behavioral Sciences, 65*, 327–337.

Jaeger, M. M., & Blaabaek, E. H. (2020). August). Inequality in learning opportunities during Covid-19: Evidence from library takeout. *Research in Social Stratification and Mobility, 68*, 1–5.

Jonikas, D. (2012). Value creation through CSR at stakeholders level. *Corporate Social Responsibility, 17*(2), 693–698.

Kariuki, P. (2019). Monitoring and evaluation leadership through technology: The South African public-sector perspective. In S. O. Atiku (Ed.), *Contemporary multicultural orientations and practices for global leadership* (pp. 121–144). IGI Global.

Kurtz, A. (2021, January 9). *The US economy lost 140,000 jobs in December. All of them were held by women..* Retrieved April 5, 2021, CNN Business from: https://edition.cnn.com/2021/01/08/economy/women-job-los ses-pandemic/index.html

Lange, S., & Wyndham, V. (2021, January–February). Gender, regulation, and corporate social responsibility in the extractive sector: The case of Equinor's social investments in Tanzania. *Women's Studies International Forum, 84*, 102434. doi:https://doi.org/10.1016/j.wsif.2020.10243

Liebig, S., Hülle, S., & May, M. (2016). *Principles of the just distribution of benefits and burdens: The "basic social justice orientations" scale for measuring order-related social justice attitudes*. Retrieved April 28, 2021, from: SOEP papers on Multidisciplinary Panel Data Research. The German Socio-Economic Panel (SOEP).https://www.diw.de/documents/publikationen/73/diw_01.c.530548.de/diw_sp0831.pdf

Lindgreen, A., Swaen, V., & Maon, F. (2009). Introduction: Corporate Social Responsibility implementation. *Journal of Business Ethics, 85*, 251–256.

Madgavkar, A., White, O., Krishnan, M., Mahajan, D., & Azcue, X. (2020, July 15). *COVID-19 and gender equality: Countering the regressive effects.*. Retrieved April 17, 2021, from Mckinsey Global Institutehttps://cieg.unam.mx/covid-genero/pdf/reflexiones/academia/39covid19-gender-equality.pdf

Maguire, M. (2011). January). The future of corporate social responsibility reporting. *The Frederick S. Pardee Center for the Study of the Longer-Range Future, Issues in Brief, 19*, 1–8.

McKinsey & Company. (2020). *Women in the workplace*. Retrieved May 25, 2021, from https://wiw-report.s3.amazonaws.com/Women_in_the_Workplace_2020.pdf

Mohammed, A. (2021, April 15). *'Inequality virus' threatens 'catastrophe for all' unless crisis can be overcome together*. Retrieved May 7, 2021, from UN News: https://news.un.org/en/story/2021/04/1089872

Monks, K. (2007, July). *The business impact of equality and diversity. The international evidence.*. Retrieved April 16, 2021, from National Center for Partnership Performance http://www.tara.tcd.ie/bitstream/handle/2262/72579/NCPP_19_2007_bied_full_report.pdf?sequence=1&isAllowed=y

Mueller, M., dos Santos, V. G., & Seuring, S. (2009). The contribution of environmental and social standards towards ensuring legitimacy in supply chain governance. *Journal of Business Ethics, 89*, 509–523.

Myers, J. (2020, August 18). *5 things COVID-19 has taught us about inequality*. Retrieved April 22, 2021, from: World Economic Forum https://www.weforum.org/agenda/2020/08/5-things-covid-19-has-taught-us-about-inequality/

New, S. J. (2015). Modern slavery and the supply chain: The limits of corporate social responsibility? *Supply Chain Management, 20*(6), 697–707.

O'Connor, A., & Meister, M. (2008, March). Corporate social responsibility attribute rankings. *Public Relations Review, 34*(1), 49–50.

OECD. (2019). *Inequality. Social and wellfare issues*. Retrieved April 2, 2021, from https://www.oecd.org/social/inequality.htm

OECD. (2021). *Gender wage gap (indicator)*. Retrieved May 12, 2021, from OECD Data: https://data.oecd.org/earnwage/gender-wage-gap.htm

Oluwafemi, O. j., & Oyatoye, E. O. (2012). Corporate social responsibility: Are firms in Nigeria actually giving back or giving away? *International Journal of Business Excellence, 5*(1/2), 116–129.

Ortiz-de-Mandojana, N., & Bansal, P. (2016, August). The long-term benefits of organizational resilience through sustainable business practices. *Strategic Management Journal, 37*(8), 1615–1631.

Østergaard, C. R., Timmermans, B., & Kristinsson, K. (2011, April). Does a different view create something new? The effect of employee diversity on innovation. *Research Policy, 40*(3), 500–509.

Perry, B. L., Aronson, B., & Pescosolido, B. A. (2021). Pandemic precarity: COVID-19 is exposing and exacerbating inequalities in the American heartland. *Proceedings of the National Academy of Sciences of the United States of America, 118*(8), 1–6.

Phelps, E. S. (2018). Distributive justice. In M. P. Ltd, *The New Palgrave Dictionary of Economics* (p. 36). Palgrave Macmillan.

PWC. (2021, March 2). *COVID-19 is reversing the important gains made over the last decade for women in the workforce—PwC Women in Work Index*. Retrieved April 18, 2021, from https://www.pwc.com/gx/en/news-room/press-releases/2021/women-in-work-index-2021.html

Raley, S., Bianchi, S. M., & Wang, W. (2012, March). When do fathers care? Mothers' economic contribution and fathers' involvement in child care. *American journal of sociology, 117*(5), 1422–1459.

Renouard, C., & Lado, H. (2012). CSR and inequality in the Niger Delta (Nigeria). *Corporate Governance: THe International Journal of Business in Society, 12*(4), 472–484.

Rescher, N. (2002). *Fairness: Theory and practice of distributive justice*. Transaction Publishers.

Ruppanner, L. (2020). *Motherlands: How states in the U.S. push mothers out of employment*. Temple University Press.

Sancha, C., Gimenez, C., & Sierra, V. (2016, January). Achieving a socially responsible supply chain through assessment and collaboration. *Journal of Cleaner Production, 112*(3), 1934–1947.

Schell, C. (2020, September 30). *Here's how we need to change global supply chains after COVID-19*. Retrieved March 30, 2021, from Global Agenda https://www.weforum.org/agenda/2020/09/covid-19-crisis-change-global-supply-chains/

Schwab, K. (2020). *Global gender gap report 2020*. Retrieved April 30, 2021, from World Economic Forum: http://www3.weforum.org/docs/WEF_GGGR_2020.pdf

Sharma, A., Adhikary, A., & Borah, S. B. (2020). September). Covid-19's impact on supply chain decisions: Strategic insights from NASDAQ 100 firms using Twitter data. *Journal of Business Research, 117*, 443–449.

Shields, K. (2011). Labor exploitation. In P. Kaufmann, H. Kuch, C. Neuhaeuser, & E. Webster (Eds.), *Humiliation, degradation, dehumanization. library of ethics and applied philosophy* (Vol. 24, pp. 173–189). Springer.

Stewart, F. (2013). *Approaches towards inequality and inequity: Concepts, measures and policies* (Office of Research Discussion Paper No.2013–01). UNICEF Office of Research. Retrieved May 5, 2021, from https://www.unicef-irc.org/publications/pdf/stewart%20inequality_inequity_layout_fin.pdf

Subrahmanian, R. (2005, July). Gender equality in education: Definitions and measurements. *International Journal of Educational Development, 25*(4), 395–407.

Tang, C. S. (2018, January). Socially responsible supply chains in emerging markets: Some research opportunities. *Journal of Operations Management, 57*, 1–10.

Tsumori, H. (2018, March 28). *No gender equality, no SDGs*. UNDP. Retrieved May 8, 2021, from: https://www.asia-pacific.undp.org/content/rbap/en/home/blog/2018/3/28/No-Gender-Equality-no-SDGs.html

Tyler, T. R., & Smith, H. J. (1998). Social justice and social movements. In D. T. Gilbert, S. T. Fiske, & G. Lindzey, (Eds.), *The handbook of social psychology* (4th ed., Vol. 2, pp. 595–629). McGraw-Hill.

UN. (2015a, October 21). *Concepts of inequality. Development issues no. 1.*. Retrieved May 6, 2021, from Development strategy and policy analysis unit. Development policy and analysis division. Department of Economic and Social Affairs. https://www.un.org/en/development/desa/policy/wess/wess_dev_issues/dsp_policy_01.pdf

UN. (2015b, September 27). *Global goals cannot be achieved without ensuring gender equality and women's empowerment—UN chief*. Goal 5: Gender equality, News. Retrieved May 8, 2021, from: https://www.un.org/sustainabledevelopment/blog/2015/09/global-goals-cannot-be-achieved-without-ensuring-gender-equality-and-womens-empowerment-un-chief/#:~:text=As%20world%20leaders%20continued%20their,rights%20for%20half%20of%20the

UN News. (2020, August 1). *No end in sight to COVID crisis, and its impact will last for 'decades to come'*. Retrieved April 14, 2021, from Health: https://news.un.org/en/story/2020/08/106939

UN News. (2021a, April 15). *'Inequality virus' threatens 'catastrophe for all' unless crisis can be overcome together*. SDGs. Retrieved April 18, 2021, from: https://news.un.org/en/story/2021/04/1089872

UN News. (2021b, April 16). *Vaccine equity the 'challenge of our time', WHO chief declares, as governments call for solidarity, sharing*. Retrieved April 18, 2021, from Health: https://news.un.org/en/story/2021/04/1089972

UN Women. (2021a). *The issue: Women's economic empowerment in the changing world of work*. Retrieved May 28, 2021, from In Focus: CSW61: https://www.unwomen.org/en/news/in-focus/csw61

UN Women. (2021b). *Equal pay for work of equal value*. Retrieved May 28, 2021, from CSW61: https://www.unwomen.org/en/news/in-focus/csw61/equal-pay

UNCTAD. (2021, April 8). *Gender and unemployment: Lessons from the COVID-19 pandemic*. Retrieved April 18, 2021, from https://unctad.org/news/gender-and-unemployment-lessons-covid-19-pandemic

UNDP. (2020). *Coronavirus vs. inequality*. Retrieved April 28, 2021, from https://feature.undp.org/coronavirus-vs-inequality/

Van Kamp, I., & Davies, H. (2013). Noise and health in vulnerable groups: A review. *Noise and Health, 15*(64), 153–159.

Vermeulen, W., & Kok, M. (2012). November). Government interventions in sustainable supply chain governance: Experience in Dutch front-running cases. *Ecological Economics, 83*, 183–196.

Wagstaff, G. F. (1994). Equity, equality, and need: Three principles of justice or one? An analysis of "equity as desert." *Current Psychology, 13*(2), 138–152.

Wang, X., & Wood, L. C. (2016). The influence of supply chain sustainability practices on suppliers. In B. Christiansen (Ed.), *Handbook of research on global supply chain management* (pp. 531–544). IGI Global.

Watts, P., & Holme, R. (1999). *Corporate social responsibility: Meeting changing expectations*. World Business Council for Sustainable Development.

WGEA. (2018, November 12). *Workplace gender equality: The business case*. Retrieved May 1, 2021, from Publications: https://www.wgea.gov.au/publications/gender-equality-business-case

CHAPTER 12

The Pandemic Driving Socially Responsible Work-Family Performance in the Transportation Sector

Max Daniel Revuelta-López

INTRODUCTION

The pandemic has caused unimaginable and unplanned social changes; for some it has been a good experience while many others have not been so fortunate. For example, at an individual level, different stories can be told of success, failure, death, new beginnings, confusion, embracing life after being sick, love, fights, anguish, mistakes, anxiety, and creativity; the world today has changed (CEPAL, 2020a). At a macro level, according to the United Nations Economic Commission for Latin America and the Caribbean (CEPAL), "The global economy will undergo the deepest recession since the Second World War and per capita gross domestic

---

M. D. Revuelta-López (✉)
Universidad La Salle, Mexico City, Mexico
e-mail: max.revuelta@lasallistas.org.mx

© The Author(s), under exclusive license to Springer Nature Switzerland AG 2022
A. M. López-Fernández and A. Terán-Bustamante (eds.), *Business Recovery in Emerging Markets*, Palgrave Studies in Democracy, Innovation, and Entrepreneurship for Growth,
https://doi.org/10.1007/978-3-030-91532-2_12

product (GDP) will shrink in 90% of countries" (CEPAL, 2020b, p. 1) which is crucial to the functioning of the economy and society during the crisis caused by the pandemic.

Freight transportation is the main shipping mode in Mexico. In 2020, it represented 83.2% of domestic tonnage moved which contributed 3.96% to the Gross Domestic Product (GDP) and generated 2.73% of jobs nationwide (Berrones-Sanz, 2020). Due to the pandemic, the freight transportation industry dropped 14.8% in the GDP resulting in productivity decrease and profit collapse, which decreased between 41.0 and 50.0%. From a highway network perspective, the volume of cargo trucks fell 33.4%, while cross-border transportation reduction represented 11.1% (Ortega & Sánchez, 2021). In order to determine the impact the pandemic has had on small and micro freight transportation companies' billing level, the National Chamber of Freight Transportation (CANACAR, in Spanish) defined three levels of impact on small and micro-sized freight companies: approximately 15% had losses in their financial results of which some ceased operations; of the remaining 85%, 14.5% maintained their profit level and only 0.05% increased them (Ortega & Sánchez, 2021). Accordingly, the question is what is the social impact of COVID-19 on small and micro freight transportation companies?

This study focuses on how Corporate Social Responsibility promotes work-family balance as currently one of workers' most common challenges is balancing work and family activities. On the one hand, before the pandemic, the scale leaned toward work; to improve income, collaborators would work overtime, which encroached on what was previously exclusively family and personal time. This became the norm as certain competitive markets and companies increasingly demanded more focus on work activities in which new technologies had accelerated processes, impacting work habits. On the other hand, some family and personal situations demand more dedication than usual; such health-related situations become the sole priority, displacing work obligations. During the pandemic, most families have had to remain home for health and safety reasons, which has not meant the work-family balance has improved as now people work longer hours at home and health issues associated with sedentary lifestyle, anxiety, depression, and domestic violence have increased (CEPAL, 2020a).

Corporate Family Responsibility fosters work-family balance based on income and family wellbeing, elements that affect family performance.

The latter emerges because of the need to measure business objectives on family development, in this case, related to micro and small freight companies in Mexico during the pandemic. This study proposes an empirical assessment that considers the stability of family income, family wellbeing, work safety, and their environment. This is included in a company's objective toward good social performance that translates into putting its social mission in practice, which will result in the expected growth (Fernández & Rajagopal, 2014); as such, the family's influence on society during the pandemic must be taken into account.

Literature Review

Pandemic

From a series of cases of atypical pneumonia reported in Wuhan, China, in late December 2019, the etiological agent was identified as a new coronavirus, SARS-CoV-2, also known as COVID-19. From an isolated outbreak in a Chinese province, the virus quickly became a health emergency beyond State borders, and later spread over entire countries, becoming a pandemic (Mojica & Morales, 2020). The COVID-19 pandemic has negatively affected the global economy and its effects have continued in 2021. As of the third quarter of 2020, Mexico's GDP showed a -9.6% contraction, while the motor transportation industry's GDP was drastically affected by 12.8% decrease (INEGI, 2021). The data indicates that in times of crisis, such as a pandemic, the freight transportation industry's contraction has greater negative effects, compared to the country's economy contraction because cargo activity is based on demand. The industry's activities were forced to stop at the beginning of the pandemic as they were classified as "non-essential" by the government. It is important to stress that a great number of business activities were reduced beyond double digits, some reaching contractions over 40.0%, significantly affecting motor transportation fleets' proper functioning. Cargo is a means of transportation with transversal activity characteristics since it serves almost all trades. Some of the most affected industries by COVID-19 were: footwear manufacturing (-40.3%), leather tanning and finishing and leather, leather products, leather manufacturing and substitutes (-38.6%), clothing manufacturing (-37.8%), food and beverage preparation services (-31.7%), and cars and trucks manufacturing (-28.8%), among others (Berrones-Sanz, 2020).

Freight Companies in Mexico

Micro and small freight companies operate within the logistics and distribution process, moving goods from production to consumption centers. Proprietors usually own one or two trucks, have complete operational control and retain all profit and equipment, which means higher startup and operating costs. Management activities also rely on such proprietors; therefore, tasks and time optimization is mandatory to cut expenses and reduce costs (Campbell, 2016).

Those companies have a symbiotic relationship with families as the nucleus of society (López-Fernández & Rajagopal, 2014). Therefore, hiring companies shall operate within a framework of social responsibility purposes and strategies established in its corporate mission and vision (García & Revuelta, 2020); this converges with Corporate Family Responsibility (CFR) and firm performance (Fernández & Rajagopal, 2014). When the families of small and micro freight companies' collaborators are happy (toward high family performance), companies' operational and financial performance increases (López-Fernández & Rajagopal, 2014). Thus, the questions are: how has the pandemic conditioned small and micro freight firms for attaining work-family balance? And, how does it impact their profitability?

In Mexico, during the 80s, the owner-operator public transportation management model was launched in response to restrictions by the Communications and Transportation Secretariat, which grants federal freight transportation concessions (Robledo & Cano, 2020), according to which a private carrier could own a maximum of five units for each concession to provide federal cargo services. This meant that companies invested in private transportation, although it was not part of their core business (Rico, 1998). Moreover, the concession model was abrogated in 1988, when there were 1,997 small and micro freight companies with 2,996 vehicles (an average of 1.5 vehicles per company). Despite the concession model having been eliminated, by 1993, there were 7,108 small and micro freight companies with 10,116 vehicles (an average of 1.42 vehicles per company) (Rico, 1998). By 2012, there were 108,507 small and micro registered freight companies representing 89.4% of the total registered companies, with a fleet of 168,424 vehicles, representing 50.5% of the entire fleet in Mexico (an average of 1.55 vehicles per company) (SEPSA, 2014). The number of enterprises and vehicles has grown in the last decade; between 1980 and 2018, the number of businesses in the industry increased over 10.87 times, while the number of vehicles increased 6.9 times.

Work-Family Relationship

Work-family balance is a multidimensional construct defined in terms of influenced direction among work and family roles. That is, the influence and effect of work on family and vice versa (Frone, 2003). Social, economic, and political changes lead companies to greater involvement in work, family, and personal issues. The need for conciliation arises in work-family conflicts, which exist when productive role requirements are not mutually consistent with those of the personal role. This conflict generates tension for individuals exposing them to increased stress, thus lowering their productivity, and causing a negative impact on organizational performance (Benito-Osorio et al., 2014); therefore:

> H1: The pandemic's positive effect on Family Social Responsibility has improved the work-family balance driving the performance equity of hiring companies, small and micro freight companies, and their families.

Corporate Family Responsibility

Corporate Social Responsibility (CSR) describes what the company does and should be doing for society and the environment. Most CSR definitions include the voluntary integration of social and environmental concerns in their business operations and their relationships with their stakeholders. Being socially responsible is more than just fully complying with legal obligations, investing more in human capital, the environment, and relationships with small and micro freight companies (Correa-Jaramillo, 2007).

From an integral perspective, in the field of CSR, family has implications in the relationship between the company, its workers, and society. It recognizes the importance of the family in social *status quo* development through the need for reconciling family and work life. It is company's ethical and legal obligation to its collaborators within the framework of Corporate Social Responsibility. Then, family responsibility actions are taken in the company. Therefore, Corporate Family Responsibility implies the visibility of the employee and his/her family in goals and strategies, as a reality within the company and against which a commitment is maintained (Valdivieso, 2019). Thus, Corporate Family Responsibility focuses on and drives work-family balance, as a boost of family performance (Espinosa & Vírseda, 2018); hence:

> H2: If Corporate Family Responsibility increases during a pandemic, small and micro freight companies' work environment is improved, therefore, it drives equity.

Company Performance

Performance represents all objectively measurable achievements in a certain domain where performance is an outstanding achievement in a specific industry (Yucesoy & Barabási, 2016). The term performance implies at the same time three interpretations: action, result of action (when comparing its results to a benchmark), and success (Bourguignon, 1997b; Caruana & Niculescu-Mizil, 2004; Neely, 2020). The idea of performance defines how a person or group reaches a conclusion to achieve a goal (Yucesoy & Barabási, 2016). Performance is the result obtained the company's management, which imprints the organization and with characteristics of competitiveness, efficiency, and effectiveness (Taouab & Issor, 2019).

Performance can be considered the equivalent of competitiveness derived from differentiation (Verrue, 2014). Within the analysis of research on performance measurement frameworks, Coram et al. (2011), Abdel-Maksoud et al. (2016), and Omran et al. (2019), indicate that the measurement dimensions of a company's performance, small and micro freight companies and their families include financial and nonfinancial indicators. Productivity is the main nonfinancial indicator that Kotane and Kuzmina-Merlino (2011), Li et al. (2018) and Heizer et al. (2020), use and it is defined as the ratio or direct relationship between the goods or services resulting from a process and the inputs that entered the system.

Family Performance

Considering that a family's social and financial performance is a complementary term in a company, family performance can be defined as the way to measure compliance with corporate purposes in relation to the impact on the families of all interest groups (stakeholders) focused on the social mission of the company (Sesma et al., 2014; Valdivieso, 2019). The family, as a social institution, is a dynamic group adaptable to the environment in which it is found, integrating as a system to the company, emphasizing elements such as discipline, values, emotions, and competencies, that guide businesses (Alonso-Almeida et al., 2012; Chinchilla et al., 2016; Marquina et al., 2011; Valdivieso, 2019).

When considering the family dimension of the people who make up the organization, work and family life are reconciled, from the perspective of co-responsibility, by being considered a strategic and comprehensive management variable (Barroso, 2008). The outcome of implementing actions in favor of the family, such as work-family balance and improved work environment, is collaborator loyalty, greater willingness to carry out their tasks, and improved production (Valdivieso, 2019). Then, the hiring company can achieve business growth while appealing to collaborator needs and those of society (Porter & Kramer, 2006).

Family performance measures the way in which the company solves health problems, violence, conflict between work and family life, economic crises, natural disasters, terrorism, and war, which are the main stress-generating events in the family environment of interest groups (Malia, 2006). The World Health Organization (WHO, 1998) defined family health as the set of facts that determines and is determined by the ability to function effectively as a biosocial unit in the context of a culture and society; then, the concept transcends the physical and mental state of its members, as well as the healthy environment for the natural development of those who live within it (Louro, 2005). Thus, companies can include it within their family performance goals (Valdivieso, 2019); further, providing reasonable wages (Porter & Kramer, 2006), and reasonable family time (Marquina et al., 2011), would imply that family income and well-being are improved; hence:

H3: If Corporate Family Responsibility increases during a pandemic, small and micro freight companies' family income is improved, then it drives performance equity.

H4: If Corporate Family Responsibility increases during a pandemic, small and micro freight companies' family well-being is improved, then it drives performance equity.

Innovations for Poverty Action (IPA, 2020) defines social performance as "Effective translation of the mission of an institution into practice in accordance with the appropriate social values." Then, social performance measures the degree to which an organization achieves its mission and social purposes (Alonso-Almeida et al., 2012). Organizations use the probability of poverty index (PPI) to better understand their performance in the positive impact on the lives of people living in poverty through information, health services, employment opportunities, financing, or a combination of interventions (Ruiz, 2015).

Study Design

The general purpose of the study was to describe the pandemic's impact on work-family balance, considering equity of family and corporate responsibility through the Corporate Family Responsibility elements. This was made considering four framed hypotheses and a model developed to illustrate the relationship between the main study constructs and hypotheses. Figure 12.1 includes the study's hypotheses framework in which the conceptual model describes a virtuous cycle of Family Social Responsibility during the pandemic improving the performance equity of the hiring company, the freight enterprise, and families. Corporate Family

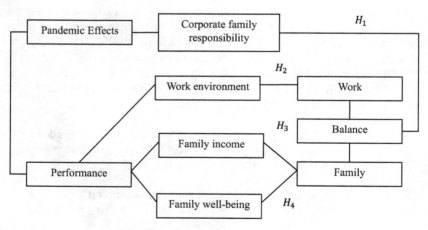

Fig. 12.1 Equity performance model

Responsibility has an impact on small and micro freight companies' work-family balance which, in turn, impacts families' performance; the latter, then, directly improves the hiring company's performance.

The exploratory study was designed and conducted through a quantitative method based on a systematic, purposeful, and rigorous methodology to generate and refine knowledge based on deductive reasoning (Maxim, 2002). A survey was developed and administered to a convenience sample of 607 from a total of 130,000 small and micro freight companies in the 32 states of Mexico. A structured survey was the study's instrument, it considered previous literature on the matter, the Mexican Official Standard, NOM-035-STPS-2018, which identifies, assesses, and prevents safety, security, and work-related risk factors (STPS, 2018), as well as variables proposed by Demarchi et al. (2015), regarding work-family dynamics as family revenue and well-being (Cronbach's alpha of 0.789). The survey was administered completely online due to the COVID-19 pandemic. Data was collected in October 2020, while the country's monitoring system placed the entire country on high-risk status. Data was analyzed through descriptive statistics, as well as regression and correlation analyses to test the corresponding hypotheses using SPSS Statistics software.

Findings and Discussion

The study variables zero in on the potential influence that certain aspects may have on small and micro freight companies' family performance in Mexico during the pandemic. Reflect both the transport service contracting companies' Corporate Family Responsibility and small and micro freight companies' family performance, in relation to the established work-family relationship. Table 12.1 summarizes variable definitions and descriptive statistics that in general explain small and micro freight companies' perspectives on the hiring company's behavior and the effects on their family's performance.

Multivariate regression results are exhibited in Table 12.2, indicating that the model well explains the dependent variable deviations, as 53.3% of the dependent variable variation is explained. Most significant variables are transportation-service contracting company's degree of Corporate Family Responsibility engagement, companies' importance to small and micro freight company's family well-being and transport-service contracting companies' respect and guarantee of small and micro

Table 12.1 Equity performance model descriptive statistics [$n = 607$]

Factor	Definition and scale	μ	σ
CEFT	Company encourages family time [1) completely agree-5) completely disagree]	3.62	1.267
IWAH	I work after hours [1) completely agree-5) completely disagree]	1.91	1.145
FWBP	Family well-being as a priority [1) completely agree-5) completely disagree]	1.3	0.632
CWFM	Coexistence with family during the meal [1) completely agree-5) completely disagree]	3.61	1.346
WFIC	Work-family integration commitment [1) completely agree-5) completely disagree]	3.06	1.259
RDWD	Rest during the workday [1) completely agree-5) completely disagree]	2.87	1.357
LIFS	Life insurance that guarantees family stability [1) completely agree-5) completely disagree]	3.88	1.233

Table 12.2 Equity performance model regression coefficients [$n = 607$]

R2: 0.533	Non-standardized coefficients		Standardized coefficients	t	Sig
D.V. CEFT	B	σ	β		
Constant	1.079	0.193		5.598	0.000
TFHF	−0.164	0.034	−0.148	−4.829	0.000
EBFP	−0.130	0.057	−0.065	−2.273	0.023
CECF	0.181	0.030	0.192	6.084	0.000
CITF	0.304	0.033	0.302	9.205	0.000
DDJT	0.195	0.030	0.209	6.590	0.000
SVEF	0.229	0.032	0.222	7.220	0.000

freight company's family rights during a pandemic. However, findings also show that the perception of transportation-service contracting company's positive impact on family performance is the least significant variable.

Correlation analysis results are included in Table 12.3. Results indicate that although not all variables correlate positively and significantly, not all correlations are strong. Two are moderate negative correlations (−0.5, −0.3), 7 are weak negative correlations (−0.3, 0), 4 are weak positive correlations (0, 0.3), 7 are moderate positive correlations (0.3, 0.5), and one are strong positive correlations (0.5, 1.0).

Table 12.3 Equity performance model correlation coefficients [$n = 607$]

	EFTF	TFHF	EBFP	CECF	CITF	DDJT	SVEF
EFTF	1						
TFHF	−0.389**	1					
EBFP	−0.113**	0.141**	1				
CECF	0.466**	−0.343**	−0.006	1			
CITF	0.573**	−0.281**	−0.014	0.340**	1		
DDJT	0.488**	−0.238**	0.041	0.321**	0.401**	1	
SVEF	0.465**	−0.139**	−0.137**	0.238**	0.357**	0.286**	1

**The correlation is significant at the 0.01 level (bilateral)

The first hypothesis assessed how the positive pandemic's effect on Family Social Responsibility has improved the work-family balance, thus driving the performance equity of hiring companies, small and micro freight companies, and families. The associated variables analyzed included transport-service contracting company's actions, in relation to small and micro freight companies, encourages family time (CEFT), I work after hours (IWAH), family well-being as a priority (FWBP), coexistence with family during the meal (CWFM), work-family integration commitment (WFIC), possibility to rest during the workday (RDWD), and life insurance that guarantees family stability (LIFS). The equation for H_1 is defined as:

$$\text{CEFT} = \beta_0 + \beta_1(\text{IWAH}) + \beta_2(\text{FWBP}) + \beta_3(\text{CWFM}) + \beta_4(\text{WFIC}) + \beta_5(\text{RDWD}) + \beta_6(\text{LIFS}) + u \tag{12.1}$$

$$\text{CEFT} = 1.079 - 0.164(\text{IWAH}) + 0.130(\text{FWBP}) + 0.181(\text{CWFM}) + 0.304(\text{WFIC}) + 0.195(\text{RDWD}) + 0.129(\text{LIFS}) \tag{12.2}$$

Moreover, results indicate that all variables increase in transport-service contracting companies' degree of Corporate Family Responsibility engagement, increases importance of small and micro freight companies' work-family balance, as well as the respect and guarantee of small and micro freight companies' family rights. As the transport-service contracting companies' importance to small and micro freight companies' family well-being increases, then so does its respect and guarantee that company encourages family time. It means that the greater the transport-service contracting company's Corporate Family Responsibility, the greater the positive impact on small and micro freight companies' work-family relationship; therefore, H_1 as framed is acceptable.

The second hypothesis assessed the positive impact of Corporate Family Responsibility increases during a pandemic, small and micro freight companies' work environment is improved, then it drives performance equity. Considering the same equation for H_2, the associated variables analyzed included company "encourages family time" (CEFT), transport-service contracting companies' importance to small and micro freight companies "they must not work overtime" (IWAH) and "work-family integration commitment" (WFIC).

Furthermore, results indicate that all variables have a strong and significant correlation. Meaning that, an increase in the transportation-service contracting companies' importance to "company encourages family time" (CEFT), increases its commitment to work-family integration. An increase in the transportation-service contracting company's commitment to work-family integration increases personal, work, and family development; and an increase in the transport-service contracting companies' Corporate Family Responsibility increases personal, work, and family development. As such, the greater the work-family relationship of the hiring company, the greater the small and micro freight companies' family performance; hence, H_2 as framed is acceptable.

The third hypothesis assessed that when the Corporate Family Responsibility increases during a pandemic, the small and micro freight companies' family income is improved, then it drives performance equity. Associated variables analyzed included the "company encourages family time" (CEFT), and they have "life insurance that guarantees the economic family stability" if the driver die (LIFS). Results indicate that an increase in the "company encourages family time," increases small and micro freight companies' positive perception of family performance and family performance impact on quality of life. Life insurance gives peace of mind to the family in the event of a fatal event. However, as can be seen, the corresponding variables were the least significant, have a decreasing effect on the dependent variable, and correlation coefficients are enough to perceive that their family performance, and its impact on quality of life, are positively associated with the hiring transport service contracting company's increases corporate family responsibility; therefore, H_3 as framed is acceptable.

Fourth hypothesis assessed that when Corporate Family Responsibility increases during a pandemic, small and micro freight companies' family well-being is improved, then it drives performance equity. Associated variables analyzed included the "company encourages family time," (CEFT) "family wellbeing as a priority" (FWBP) and "coexistence with family during the meal" (CWFM). Results indicate that an increase in "the company encourages family time," increases small and micro freight companies' positive perception of family income that increases the family performance impacting on quality of life. Furthermore, if most stakeholders do not work overtime and an increase in "coexistence with family during the meal" will mean love and loyalty to the company. In addition, therefore, H_4 is acceptable as framed.

Although hiring transportation-service contracting companies' Corporate Family Responsibility practices do have a positive effect on the balance of work-family relationship and the latter positively impacts family performance, small and micro freight companies do not perceive that their family's performance or its impact on quality of life are directly derived from above practices. Therefore, it is plausible that they are unaware that the benefits generated from the balance of work-family relationship stem from the hiring company's CFR. As such, micro transportation companies perceived those benefits do not, in turn, positively impact the hiring company.

Concluding Remarks

The fact that the secondary sector of the economy has contracted by 40% approximately had an impact on the transportation industry's distribution operations. This resulted in more time drivers spent at home with their families but did not necessarily boost the work-family balance. Therefore, in addition to reducing family income, if there is no Corporate Family Responsibility, there is no balance in the work-family relationship. Pandemic fostering the harmonious development of the person, whereby families, through Corporate Family Responsibility can assume their family and work responsibilities without one area being affected by the other, is essential to their development, confirming hypothesis one.

Further, the transportation-service contracting company can support small and micro freight companies to the extent that the corporate mission and vision establish initiatives that promote and facilitate management of their family responsibilities. To enhance the positive impact, rest time during work time should be matched to the family's financial stability, mentioned in hypothesis two. As such, the performance of hiring company, small and micro freight companies, and their family, occurs when Corporate Family Responsibility is strongly associated with the company's "encourages family time."

For the hiring company to improve their Corporate Family Responsibility in a pandemic, it ought to guarantee the balance of the work-family relationship and delegate efforts toward family welfare as well as respect as suggested by hypothesis three. To achieve this, it is imperative that the small and micro freight company does not work after hours, the perception that family well-being is a priority, boost the coexistence with family during the meal, achieve the work-family integration commitment, consider the possibility to rest during the workday and set up life insurance that guarantees family stability for a long time, as hypothesis four indicates.

Management in these transportation companies should carry out and control the necessary actions to improve family performance, through Corporate Family Responsibility, in Mexico. This implies the implementation of control methods and innovative alternatives to increase performance of the transport management area, of the small and micro freight companies and their families. Corporate Family Responsibility is a concept that seeks the integration of the work-family relationship within the concept of Corporate Social Responsibility (CSR); therefore, hiring transportation-service companies would need to align their CFR efforts with CSR engagement to have a positive correlation on and impact business growth of the transportation-service contracting company (Valdivieso, 2019).

As an effect of Corporate Family Responsibility during the pandemic, companies should effectively optimize family performance; small and micro freight companies would be positively impacted by increased revenue and reduced transport rates, through balanced work-family relationships (Fernández & Rajagopal, 2014). From a commercial point of view, this is a differentiating element in the market that will drive an increase in sales and the desire to work in these enterprises (Porter & Kramer, 2006).

Study Limitations and Future Research Directions

The study's main limitation is the size of the convenience sample with respect to the size of the population; findings are representative of the characteristics of the participants and for this reason cannot be generalized. Future research could include a mixed research method, and focus on other types of micro companies to identify potential cultural similarities and differences.

References

Abdel-Maksoud, A., Cheffi, W., & Ghoudi, K. (2016). The mediating effect of shop-floor involvement on relations between advanced management accounting practices and operational non-financial performance indicators. *The British Accounting Review,48*(2), 169–184.

Alonso-Almeida, M., Rodríguez, M., Cortez, K., & Abreu, J. (2012). La responsabilidad social corporativa y el desempeño financiero: un análisis en empresas mexicanas que cotizan en la bolsa. *Contaduría y administración, 57*(1), 53–77.

Barroso, F. (2008). La responsabilidad social empresarial: Un estudio en cuarenta empresas de la ciudad de Mérida, Yucatán. *Contaduría y Administración, 226,* 73–91.

Benito-Osorio, D., Muñoz-Aguado, L., & Villar, C. (2014). The impact of family and work-life balance policies on the performance of Spanish listed companies. *Cairn.info, 17*(4), 214–236.

Berrones-Sanz, L.(2020). Autotransporte de carga en México: producción y empleo. *Análisis Económico, 35*(90), 147–172.

Bourguignon, A. (1997a). Sous les pavés la plage...ou les multiples fonctions du vocabulaire comptable : L'exemple de la performance. *Comptabilité-Contrôle-Audit, 3*(1), 89–101.

Bourguignon, A. (1997b). The Various Functions of Accounting Language: An Example of Performance. *In Accounting Auditing Control, 3*(1), 89–101.

Campbell, A. (2016). *What Should an Owner-operator Do to Keep Organized?* Retrieved October 12, 2020, available at TruckingOffice. https://www.truckingoffice.com/blog/what-should-owner-operators-do-to-keep-organized/

Caruana, R., & Niculescu-Mizil, A. (2004). Data mining in metric space: An empirical analysis of supervised learning performance criteria. *ACM Press* (pp. 69–78).

CEPAL. (2020a). *Universalizing access to digital technologies to address the consequences of COVID-19.* CEPAL.

CEPAL. (2020b). *Addressing the growing impact of COVID-19 with a view to reactivation with equality: New projections*. CEPAL.

Chinchilla, N., Las-Heras, M., & Cruz, H. (2016). *Responsabilidad familiar corporativa*. Retrieved January 10, 2021, available at IESE. International Center for Work and Family: https://unis.edu.gt/wp-content/uploads/2018/08/IFREI-versio%CC%81n-conferencia-ilovepdf-compressed.pdf

Coram, P. J., Mock, T. J., & Monroe, G. S. (2011). Financial analysts' evaluation of enhanced disclosure of non-financial performance indicators. *The British Accounting Review, 43*(2), 87–101. https://doi.org/10.1016/j.bar.2011.02.001

Correa-Jaramillo, J. (2007). Evolución histórica de los conceptos de responsabilidad social empresarial y balance social. *Semestre Económico, 10*(20), 87–102.

Demarchi, G., Aguirre, M., Yela, N., & Viveros, E. (2015). Sobre la dinámica familiar. *Revisión Documental. Cultura Educación y Sociedad, 6*(2), 117–138.

Espinosa, M., & Vírseda, J. (2018). *Relaciones Familiares, afecto, valores y aprendizaje creador*. Amapsi Editorial.

Frone, M. R. (2003). Work-Family Balance. In J. C. Quick & L. E. Tetrick (Eds.), *Handbook of occupational health psychology* (pp. 143–162). American Psychological Association.

García, M., & Revuelta, M. (2020). *Planeación del proyecto de ocupación profesional* (tercera edición). Editorial Parmenia.

Heizer, J., Render, B., & Munson, C. (2020). *Operations management: Sustainability and supply chain management*. Pearson.

INEGI. (2021). *Producto Interno Bruto Trimestral. Año Base 2013*. Retrieved from Instituto Nacional de Estadística y Geografía (INEGI). https://www.inegi.org.mx/temas/pib/default.html#Tabulados

IPA. (2020). *Building a world*. Innovation for Poverty Action.

Kotane, I., & Kuzmina-Merlino, I. (2011). Non-financial indicators for evaluation of business activity. *European Integration Studies, 5*, 213–219.

Li, Y., Topal, E., & Ramazan, S. (2018). Optimising the long term mine landform progression and truck hour schedule in a large scale open pit mine using mixed integer programming. In R. Dimitrakopoulos (Ed.), *Advances in applied strategic mine planning* (pp. 669–686). Springer.

López-Fernández, A.M., & Rajagopal. (2014). Engaging stakeholders in co-creating corporate social responsibility: A study across industries in Mexico. *International Journal of Business Competition and Growth, 3*(3), 241–253.

Fernández, A.M.L, & Rajagopal. (2014). Convergence of corporate social responsibility and business growth: An analytical framework. *International Journal of Business Excellence, 7*(6), 791–806.

Louro, I. (2005, September–December). Modelo de la salud del grupo familiar. *Revista Cubana de Salud Pública, 31*(4), 332–337.

Malia, J. (2006). Basic concepts and models of family stress. *Stress, Trauma, and Crisis, 9*(3–4), 141–160.

Marquina, P., Goñi, N., Rizo-Patrón, C., Castro, R., Morice, J., Velásquez, I., & Villaseca, M. (2011). *Diagnóstico de la responsabilidad social en organizaciones Peruanas: Una aproximación interinstitucional y multidisciplinaria.* CENTRUM Católica.

Maxim, P. (2002). *Métodos cuantitativos aplicados a las ciencias sociales.* Oxford University Press.

Mojica, R., & Morales, M. (2020). Pandemia COVID-19, la nueva emergencia sanitaria de preocupación internacional: una revisión. *Semergen, 72*–84.

Neely, A. (2020). *Business performance measurement: Theory and practice.* Cambridge University Press.

Omran, M., Khallaf, A., Gleason, K., & Tahat, Y. (2019). Non-financial performance measures disclosure, quality strategy, and organizational financial performance: A mediating model. *Total Quality Management & Business Excellence, 32*(5–6), 652–675.

Ortega, M., & Sánchez, J. (2021). Efectos del Covid-19 en el transporte de carga terrestre en 2020. *Instituto Mexicano del Transporte, 166*–171.

Porter, M., & Kramer, M. (2006). Strategy & Society: The link between competitive advantage and corporate social responsibility. *Harvard Business Review, 84*(12), 78–92.

Rico, O. (1998). *Evolución de la industria del autotransporte de carga en México en el periodo 1988–1993.* Retrieved October 17, 2020, from Secretaría de Comunicaciones y Transportes. https://www.imt.mx/archivos/Publicaciones/PublicacionTecnica/pt100.pdf

Robledo, H. E., & Cano, L. (2020). De "el hombre-camión" al frente común de usuarios y operadores. *Encartes, 3*(5), 56–78.

Ruiz, M. (2015). *¿Qué entendemos por Calidad de Vida Familiar?* Retrieved May 12, 2021, from Inclúyeme. https://www.incluyeme.org/testimonios/que-entendemos-por-calidad-de-vida-familiar/

SEPSA. (2014). *Diagnóstico sobre la situación actual del sector del autotransporte de carga con un enfoque específico al hombre-camión y pequeños transportistas* Retrieved June 5, 2021, from tranferproject. http://transferproject.org/wp-content/uploads/2015/09/Reporte_Final_GIZ_Radiografia_mayo_2014.pdf

Sesma, J., Husted, B., & Banks, J. (2014). La medición del desempeño social empresarial a través de las redes sociales. *Contaduría y Administración, 59*(2), 121–143.

STPS. (2018). *Norma Oficial Mexicana NOM-035-STPS-2018, Factores de riesgo psicosocial en el trabajo-Identificación, análisis y prevención.* Retrieved February 23, 2021, from Diario Oficial de la Federación. https://www.dof.gob.mx/nota_detalle.php?codigo=5541828&fecha=23/10/2018

Taouab, O., & Issor, Z. (2019). Firm performance: Definition and measurement models. *European Scientific Journal, 15*(1), 93–106.

Valdivieso, E. (2019). La responsabilidad familiar empresarial en la gestión de empresas. Paradigmas y perspectiva jurídica. *IUS*, 116–139.

Verrue, J. (2014, June). *FA critical investigation of the Osterwalder business model canvas: An in-depth case study.* Retrieved available at Ghent University. https://biblio.ugent.be/publication/5712151/file/5712152.pdf

WHO (1998). *The world health report 1998 life in the 21st century A vision for all report of the director-general.* Retrieved from WHO. https://www.who.int/whr/1998/en/whr98_en.pdf

Yucesoy, B., & Barabási, A. (2016, April). Untangling performance from success. *EPJ Data Science, 5*(17). https://doi.org/10.1140/epjds/s13688-016-0079-z

CHAPTER 13

Machine Learning Sustainable Competitiveness for Global Recovery

Andrée Marie López-Fernández, Antonia Terán-Bustamante, and Antonieta Martínez-Velasco

INTRODUCTION

Competitiveness fosters more productive, innovative, and competitive organizations that contribute to the elevation of welfare and sustainability (Solleiro & Terán, 2014); given its economic and social impact, its analysis is important to understand how it can positively impact and boost society's quality of life. Competitiveness has been expanded to incorporate environmental and social aspects, fundamental to achieve long-term sustainability. However, win–win policies do not strictly depend on

A. M. López-Fernández (✉) · A. Terán-Bustamante
Facultad de Ciencias Económicas y Empresariales, Universidad Panamericana, Mexico City, Mexico

A. Martínez-Velasco
Facultad de Ingeniería, Universidad Panamericana, Mexico City, Mexico

© The Author(s), under exclusive license to Springer Nature Switzerland AG 2022
A. M. López-Fernández and A. Terán-Bustamante (eds.), *Business Recovery in Emerging Markets*, Palgrave Studies in Democracy, Innovation, and Entrepreneurship for Growth, https://doi.org/10.1007/978-3-030-91532-2_13

competitiveness; countries with same levels of competitiveness achieve different environmental and social results due to different priorities and political decisions. Therefore, environmental, social, and economic agendas should merge into a single inclusive and sustainable growth agenda (Schwab & Zahidi, 2020).

World and organizational leaders have been significantly focused on competitiveness as it is indicative of surpassing competitors and success. Hence, it is common for organizations and countries to measure their performance based on their competitiveness level. Multiple industries are still struggling to recover from the collateral effects of the COVID-19 pandemic, which has significantly impacted business and country growth and development. Today, more than ever, competitiveness entails much more than productivity; in fact, there are social and environmental elements that are key to its attainment. Thus, to achieve competitiveness, practices ought to be aligned with growth and development.

Sustainable development is only possible as social, environmental, and economic aspects are integrated into decision-making processes (Emas, 2015). The United Nations has stated that sustainable development is achieved by the effective interaction of its components: social development, economic development, and environmental protection (UN General Assembly, 1997). In 2013, Amartya Sen posited that the concept of sustainability should focus on human freedom (Sen, 2013); meaning, the "absence of coercive constraint" (Vásquez & McMahon, 2020).

COVID-19 has had many collateral effects; for instance, in some countries, advances in social development have fallen farther behind and halted in others, and the global economic recession (Schwab & Zahidi, 2020), the Great Recession, which has marked history as the worse since World War II (The World Bank, 2020), have significantly impacted global competitiveness. Naturally, COVID-19 has redirected attention toward tackling the virus and its effects' threats; unfortunately, this has also meant that work toward SDGs has stopped (Fenner & Cernev, 2021). Since progress prior to the pandemic was already insufficient (Tonne, 2021), today's pace puts current and future generations at great risk. When crises emerge, many decide to cut costs deemed unnecessary such as innovation given the limited resources; however, crises, as those originated by COVID-19, provide opportunities which can be effectively met with innovation (Wenzel et al., 2021). Organizational and government leaders are facing significant challenges, however, these are also opportunities to redesign and improve business models.

Organizations engaged in corporate social responsibility (CSR) work toward social and business growth and development by means of their social, financial, and environmental performance (Chandan & Das, 2017). They do so by delegating efforts toward current and potential stakeholders (Tokoro, 2007); thus, CSR enables sustainable development at micro-level. The question is: Which variables could be included in a comprehensive model for sustainable competitiveness that would guide organizations to proactively participate in its attainment and recover from the effects of the global health crisis, thus impacting global competitiveness?

Various global indexes serve as a system to rank countries in relation to their core concept with the aim of positioning economies in an ordinal fashion. Five global indexes were analyzed in the study: the Global Competitiveness Index, Global Sustainable development Goals, Global Innovation Index, Global Impunity Index, and Global Human Development Index. The general objective of the study was to evaluate the potential correlation between competitiveness and sustainable development for a global recovery. The specific objectives include the analysis of: (i) the most significant variables for the global indexes' achievement, (ii) whether countries' compliance across indexes is indicative of their global development attainment, (iii) if intersecting variables present the same degree of compliance across indexes, and (iv) the global indexes' significant variables that can be executed by organizations to drive global sustainable development.

Literature Review

Competitiveness

Competitiveness is a complex concept that has been studied from different approaches, and disciplines; its analysis is necessary to understand its factors and the way to promote it. Competitiveness' new focus is based on competitive advantages, which are dynamically created by businesspersons and governments through a set of strategies and actions, public policies, and interinstitutional relationships that seek to add value (Solleiro & Castañon, 2012). The US Competitiveness Policy Council has proposed a concept of competitiveness that refers to the ability of a national economy to produce benefits and services that surpass international market goals, while citizens reach a standard of growth and sustainable life (Competitiveness Policy Council, 1992; Solleiro & Castañon, 2012). Thus, the competitive environment implies a complex relationship among public policies and the relationship between companies and institutions in each sector.

Much time and effort has been spent attempting to differentiate the characteristics of micro- and macro-competitiveness. However, competitiveness emerging on a micro-level will certainly impact the degree of regional and country competitiveness. While prosperity is a main objective of competitiveness, it is commonly measured by means of productivity (Porter, 2004). The more progress is understood and achieved, the clearer it is that competitiveness can no longer be reached without social growth and development. In the sense that cost, market share, productivity, price, stock, and currency are no longer ideal and realistic indicators of competitive performance.

Atkinson (2013) posited that competitiveness is a ubiquitous concept, which makes sense since, regardless of the amount of definitions and their micro and/or macro emphasis, the variables tend to be well correlated. For instance, at a micro-level, competitiveness has been defined as the ability to be commercially successful by an increase in productivity, market share, and, thus, profitability (Filó, 2007). Louati (2018) posited that competitiveness refers to an organization's ability to deliver "products of higher value at equal or lower-cost and to build competitive positions that enable superior economic performance" than its competitors. Carayannis and Gonzalez (2003) have stated that competitiveness pertains to individuals, organizations, and countries alike. Therefore, it is not possible to understand a country's competitiveness without appreciating individuals and organizations' participation in its achievement, as well as the social, environmental, and economic conditions they endure.

At a macro-level, a Nation's competitiveness has been defined as its productivity and ability for growth (Ai & Ushakov, 2019) as well as proficiency to maintain and increase international market share while improving society's quality of life (Weng, 2019). The Global Competitive Index assesses 12 pillars that together describe a country's degree of competitiveness; that is, how close an economy is to the considered "ideal state or frontier" (Schwab, 2019). The pillars include: institutions, infrastructure, ICT adoption, macroeconomic stability, product market, labor market, financial system, market size, health, skills, business dynamism, and innovation capability (WEF, 2015).

Sustainability

It is a common misconception that sustainability is merely associated with the environment (Bansal & DesJardine, 2014), that it is reserved for the natural world. It makes sense as it is usually accompanied by concepts such as global warming, climate change, ozone layer depletion, deforestation, extinct species, and other major environmental issues. However, the environment is only one aspect of sustainability. In 1987, sustainability was defined by the World Commission on Environment and Development (WCED): Our Common Future Report, also known as the Brundtland Report, as the intent to "meet the needs of the present generation without compromising the ability of future generations to meet their own needs" (UN General Assembly, 1987). According to Sen (2013), the report emphasized justice across generations with a focus on human beings.

Brown et al. (1987) posited that sustainability is related to development and environmental management. And, according to Birdsall (2014), sustainability is a process by which environmental, sociocultural, and economic aspects interact to work on a given issue. As such, sustainability is typically related to the Triple Bottom Line: People, Planet, and Prosperity (Elkington, 1997), all elemental to organizational success. In other words, sustainability is concerned with economic, social, and environmental elements (Robins, 2006). The United Nations has defined development as the "multidimensional undertaking to achieve a higher quality of life for all people" (UN General Assembly, 1997); therefore, it is fitting that sustainable development "recognizes the interconnectedness of economic prosperity, environmental integrity, and social equity" (Gladwin et al., 1995); in other words, sustainable development is well associated with competitiveness.

In the year 2000, leaders from 189 UN member countries signed the now historic Millennium Declaration (SDGF, 2019), [A/RES/55/2] (UN, 2000), whereby they committed to the 8 Millennium Development Goals (MDGs) by 2015 (WHO, 2019). The goals' success laid in the fact that they were interrelated and addressed integrally; thus, the achievement of one goal would positively impact in the achievement of others. For instance, increased access and completion of primary education has direct impact in the eradication of extreme poverty, while the latter directly impacts the reduction of child mortality, etc. In September 2015, UN members approved the Agenda for Sustainable Development; 193

member countries signed "Transforming Our World: the 2030 Agenda for Sustainable Development," also known as the "2030 Agenda." The latter includes seventeen goals to be achieved by the year 2030, focused on sustainable development, and based on Human Rights and quality of life-leaving no one behind (Dugarova et al., 2017). The goals include: no poverty, zero hunger, good health and well-being, quality education, gender equality, clean water and sanitation, affordable and clean energy, decent work and economic growth, industry, innovation and infrastructure, reduced inequalities, sustainable cities and communities, responsible consumption and production, climate action, life below water, life on land, peace, justice, and strong institutions, and partnerships for the goals (Sachs et al., 2020).

Innovation

According to Sternberg et al. (2003), innovation is "the channeling of creativity so as to produce a creative idea and/or product to people that can and wish to use." The Oslo Manual (OECD, 2018) distinguishes between innovation as an outcome and the activities by which innovations come about. It defines an innovation as "a new or improved product or process (or combination thereof) that differs significantly from the unit's previous products or processes and that has been made available to potential users (product) or brought into use by the unit (process)" (OECD, 2018). Moreover, "innovation activities include all developmental, financial and commercial activities undertaken by a firm that are intended to result in an innovation for the firm" (OECD/Eurostat, 2018). Therefore, innovation is elemental to both business strategy and countries' growth (Dutta et al., 2020). According to Prahalad (2006), there are three particular concerns regarding innovation, including that emerging markets tend to have limited resources, institutional voids, and the characteristics and context of the bottom of the pyramid. That being said, these markets are also an important source of many types of innovations, including but not limited to frugal (Basu et al., 2013), reverse (Govindarajan & Ramamurti, 2011; Porter & Kramer, 2011), and sustainable innovations (Carrillo-Hermosilla et al., 2010). Therefore, innovation is elemental for SDG and competitiveness achievement. The Global Innovation Index (GII) evaluates innovation performance of 131 countries worldwide (WIPO, 2020) by providing and measuring 80 indicators (Dutta et al., 2020). The index includes an innovation input sub-index with 5 pillars (i.e. Institutions, human capital and research, infrastructure, market sophistication credit, and business sophistication) and an innovation output sub-index with 2 pillars (i.e., Knowledge and technology outputs and creative Outputs) (Dutta et al., 2020).

Impunity

According to the Business & Human Rights Resource Center (2017), impunity in organizations has significantly increased, particularly in relation to human rights abuses. For instance, violations of human rights go unchecked across supply chains as focal companies disassociate accountability from their associates' actions. This type of corporate impunity occurs in developing countries and emerging markets where regulatory authorities' efforts prove inadequate (Deva, 2012) and/or laws are less restrictive or vague. In 1997, the Commission on Human Rights' Report on the administration of justice and detainee human rights defined impunity as (Joinet, 1997):

> *The impossibility, de jure or de facto, of bringing the perpetuators of human rights violations to account – whether in criminal, civil, administrative or disciplinary proceedings – since they are not subject to any inquiry that might lead to their being accused, arrested, tried and, if found guilty, sentenced to appropriate penalties, and to making reparations to their victims.*

Therefore, impunity occurs when there is dissonance between the pursuit of justice and justice itself, when one party benefits from exemption of accountability; it is a significant hindrance to the execution of laws (OHCHR, 2011). For that matter, impunity is directly correlated with the violation of human rights and, as such, cannot coexist with competitiveness.

According to the Center for Impunity and Justice Studies (CESIJ), impunity is "a multidimensional phenomenon that goes beyond the analysis of crimes capable of being punished, such as homicide, and has three main dimensions: security, justice and human rights" (Le Clercq Ortega & Rodríguez Sánchez Lara, 2020). The objective of the Global Impunity Index (IGI) is to "quantitatively make visible the global problem of impunity and its relationship with other complex phenomena such as inequality, corruption and violence (Le Clercq Ortega & Rodríguez Sánchez Lara, 2020)." The latter is done by comparing levels of impunity worldwide in relation to the structure and function of security and justice systems and human rights. The index includes three general dimensions (i.e., structural dimension, functional dimension, and human rights) that together describe the degree of impunity of a country; in 2020, the dimensions of 69 economies were evaluated (Le Clercq Ortega & Rodríguez Sánchez Lara, 2020).

Human Development

Organizations have stake in society and the environment, therefore, neglecting their distress is counterproductive. Schmidheiny and Business Council for Sustainable Development (1998) have posited that "corporate leaders who ignore economic, political or social changes will lead their companies to failure." That said, according to Hopkins (2007), organizations can impact social development via CSR engagement and obtain benefits, including improved image, financial performance, collaborator motivation, innovation, creativity, improved risk management and stakeholder management, consumer preference, among others. Development is a concept constructed on context, where at some point, development means sufficient income and GDP, and in another context it means poverty reduction, equality, and freedom. According to the UNDP (2020a), human development encompasses "expanding the richness of human life, rather than simply the richness of the economy in which human beings live. It is an approach that is focused on people and their opportunities and choices." As such, human development is elemental for the achievement of competitiveness. In accordance with the Human Development Index, there are three dimensions, health, education, and standard of living, which together describe the degree of development of a country (UNDP, 2020b); the indicators are: population trends, health outcomes, education achievements, national income and resource composition, work and employment, human security, human and capital mobility, perceptions of wellbeing, and fundamental human rights treaties' status (UNDP, 2020c); in 2020, 195 economies were evaluated (UNDP, 2020b).

Competitiveness and Sustainability

According to the World Economic Forum, competitiveness as a part sustainability is defined as "the set of institutions, policies and factors that make a nation productive over the longer term while ensuring social and environmental sustainability" (Cann, 2016; Corrigan et al., 2014). Therefore, sustainable competitiveness implies the attainment of balanced economic, social, and environmental elements, which may not be achieved if any of these elements are not proactively sought out, measured, and fulfilled. Therefore, in order to achieve competitiveness, there should be equal levels of sustainable development, human development, and innovation. Further, for there to be synergy of the latter, impunity should be a non-issue. In this approach, the perceived trade-offs between economic, social, and environmental factors can be mitigated by adopting a holistic and longer-term approach to growth (Schwab & Zahidi, 2020).

Study Design

The general objective of the study was to evaluate the potential correlation between competitiveness and sustainable development toward global recovery. In order to do so, the study was conducted with a mixed-method approach: quantitative and qualitative analyses were carried out using machine learning and content analysis. A univariate analysis was executed to determine the most relevant values for each index. Next, a correlation analysis was executed to determine the degree of the indexes' indicator association. Correlations were calculated based on Pearson's correlation scores for all characteristic pairs in the data set. Only the most relevant variables were considered. The ranking considers the target variable in the dataset and scores the attributes according to their correlation with the target variable (index value); the higher the value, the greater the relevance to the regression.

In order to determine if the countries listed were behaving in a similar manner, a k-Means machine learning technique was implemented to identify potential clusters for each index. A Silhouette metric was used to assess and verify cluster veracity; said metric includes a value between 0 and 1 which indicates a country's probability of being part of a specific cluster. These metrics contrast average distance to elements in the same cluster with the average distance to elements in other clusters. The method used to initiate the clustering process was k-Means + (first center is selected randomly, the subsequent are chosen from the remaining points with probability proportioned to squared distance from the closest center). A value above 0.5 was acceptable to confirm countries' appropriate fit in their corresponding cluster.

Results

Variables Triggering Competitiveness

The correlation analysis for the GCI revealed the indicators significant to the corresponding regression. The top twenty indicators, which had a greater impact on the overall attainment of global competitiveness or the "ideal state" of competitiveness (Schwab, 2019), and the corresponding scores by relevance are as follows:

- Reliability of water supply (643.74)
- Border clearance efficiency (430.06)
- Patent applications (425.00)
- Internet users (355.30)
- Fixed-broadband Internet subscriptions (338.27)
- Intellectual property protection (333.44)
- Efficiency of air transport services (327.56)
- Incidence of corruption (317.44)
- Strength of auditing and accounting standards (317.38)
- Active labor market policies (314.54)
- Health life expectancy (286.22)
- Property rights (281.97)
- Digital skills-active population (281.94)
- e-participation (280.24)
- International co-inventions (278.31)
- Debt dynamics (271.31)
- School life expectancy (268.61)
- Exposure to unsafe drinking water (260.84)
- Buyer sophistication (253.56)
- SME financing (253.36).

Clustering Competitive Economies

Potential similarities among economies are evaluated in association with the top 20 variables that best describe global competitiveness. Results show that there were 8 major clusters by which countries were grouped; meaning that, economies belonging to each cluster depict similarities among them and, as a group, differ from the other seven clusters. Table 13.1 depicts the countries that have been associated in each of the 8 clusters along with their corresponding level of competitiveness. The clusters

Table 13.1 GCI cluster analysis

Country	C	GCI 4.0	Country	C	GCI 4.0	Country	C	GCI 4.0
Chile	C1	70.53	Angola	C2	38.11	Australia	C3	78.74
China	C1	73.90	Burundi	C2	40.25	Austria	C3	76.60
Cyprus	C1	66.38	Benin	C2	45.82	Belgium	C3	76.38
Czech Republic	C1	70.85	Burkina Faso	C2	43.42	Canada	C3	79.59
Spain	C1	75.27	Cote d'Ivoire	C2	48.14	Switzerland	C3	82.32
Estonia	C1	70.90	Cameroon	C2	46.01	Germany	C3	81.79
Hungary	C1	65.07	Congo, Democratic Rep.	C2	36.13	Denmark	C3	81.17
Italy	C1	71.52	Gabon	C2	47.46	Finland	C3	80.24
Lithuania	C1	68.35	Haiti	C2	36.34	France	C3	78.80
Latvia	C1	66.98	Lesotho	C2	42.90	United Kingdom	C3	81.20
Malta	C1	68.54	Madagascar	C2	42.85	Hong Kong SAR	C3	83.14
Poland	C1	68.89	Mali	C2	43.59	Ireland	C3	75.11
Portugal	C1	70.44	Mozambique	C2	38.07	Iceland	C3	74.71
Slovak Republic	C1	66.77	Mauritania	C2	40.91	Israel	C3	76.74
Slovenia	C1	70.20	Malawi	C2	43.70	Japan	C3	82.27
Uruguay	C1	63.46	Nigeria	C2	48.32	Korea, Rep.	C3	79.61
			Chad	C2	35.08	Luxembourg	C3	77.02
Country	C	GCI 4.0	Yemen	C2	35.50	Netherlands	C3	82.39
Armenia	C4	61.27	Zambia	C2	46.51	Norway	C3	78.05
Dominican Republic	C4	58.31	Zimbabwe	C2	44.24	New Zealand	C3	76.74
Egypt	C4	54.54				Singapore	C3	84.78
Indonesia	C4	64.62	Country	C	GCI 4.0	Sweden	C3	81.24
India	C4	61.36	Bangladesh	C5	52.12	Taiwan, China	C3	80.24
Jamaica	C4	58.25	Botswana	C5	55.49	United States	C3	83.67
Jordan	C4	60.93	Ethiopia	C5	44.37			
Sri Lanka	C4	57.10	Ghana	C5	51.19	Country	C	GCI 4.0
Morocco	C4	60.00	Guinea	C5	46.13	Albania	C6	57.61
Panama	C4	61.63	Gambia, The	C5	45.92	Bosnia and Herzegovina	C6	54.73
Philippines	C4	61.86	Guatemala	C5	53.51	Bolivia	C6	51.80
Thailand	C4	68.11	Honduras	C5	52.62	Brazil	C6	60.92
South Africa	C4	62.43	Kenya	C5	54.14	Cape Verde	C6	50.83
			Cambodia	C5	52.08	Algeria	C6	56.25
Country	C	GCI 4.0	Lao PDR	C5	50.10	Ecuador	C6	55.73
Argentina	C7	57.20	Namibia	C5	54.46	Iran, Islamic Rep.	C6	52.96
Bulgaria	C7	64.89	Nepal	C5	51.57	Kyrgyz Republic	C6	53.99
Barbados	C7	58.90	Pakistan	C5	51.35	Lebanon	C6	56.28
Brunei Darussalam	C7	62.75	Rwanda	C5	52.82	Moldova	C6	56.74
Colombia	C7	62.73	Senegal	C5	49.68	Macedonia, FYR	C6	57.32
Costa Rica	C7	62.00	Eswatini	C5	46.43	Mongolia	C6	52.61
Georgia	C7	60.61	Tajikistan	C5	52.39	Nicaragua	C6	51.52
Greece	C7	62.58	Tanzania	C5	48.19	Peru	C6	61.66
Croatia	C7	61.93	Uganda	C5	48.93	Paraguay	C6	53.63
Kazakhstan	C7	62.94				El Salvador	C6	52.57
Kuwait	C7	65.10	Country	C	GCI 4.0	Tunisia	C6	56.40
Mexico	C7	64.94	United Arab Emirates	C8	75.00	Ukraine	C6	56.99
Montenegro	C7	60.82	Azerbaijan	C8	62.71	Venezuela	C6	41.82
Mauritius	C7	64.26	Bahrain	C8	65.37	Viet Nam	C6	61.54
Romania	C7	64.35	Malaysia	C8	74.60			
Russian Federation	C7	66.73	Oman	C8	63.60			
Serbia	C7	60.85	Qatar	C8	72.86			
Seychelles	C7	59.59	Saudi Arabia	C8	70.02			
Trinidad and Tobago	C7	58.30						
Turkey	C7	62.13						

Source Own elaboration with data from Schwab (2019)

with more countries were 5 and 6 followed by cluster 8; however, countries with the largest and best water-access infrastructure are in cluster three, which corresponds to the countries with the highest incomes.

Countries tend to shift index positions in the index from year to year; this would suggest that achieving sustained competitiveness is not as straightforward as complying with the GCI's Pillar indicators. Results show that countries grouped in cluster three rated the highest; in other words, they were the most competitive countries and, thus, should account for the best practices; however, not all countries in cluster three account for the highest compliance with water reliability, yet did comply with a threshold of at least 70% compliance.

Variables Triggering Sustainability

The intent was to develop the same analysis for the SDGs, however, due to data paucity, a qualitative analysis was developed on the basis of the "traffic light" results (i.e. red: score is decreasing; orange: score is stagnant or increasing below 50%; yellow: score increased 50% or more, yet below the goal itself; green: score is increasing toward the goal or remains at goal achievement; gray: insufficient data), as well as the overall the countries' SDG index (Sachs et al., 2020). Best practices regarding sustainable development are visible by countries with green status goals. Results indicate that only 4 countries did not have a score or any goals rated in green. 22% had an overall score for sustainable development, but did not have any green goals. 12% had no overall score, yet had green goals; from these, 26% had 2 green goals and 74% had 1. Thus, it is interesting that these countries did not have a score. It was thought that the reason was because they accounted for too many goals without information, however, the number of goals without information varies from zero to eleven; therefore, the motive remains unclear. 64% had at least 1 green goal, of which 56% only had 1 green goal, 33% had 2, 6% had 3, and only 1% had 5 and 6 green goals. Finally, it is noteworthy that no countries had a green status for goals 2 and 14.

In order to determine association of best practices between competitiveness and SDGs, the countries with 70% or better GCI compliance were considered for analysis. These countries were selected because they were the most competitive countries and should, therefore, also be on track for SDG achievement. However, results indicate that the most competitive countries are not highly compliant with the goals; in fact, only 1 has 5 green goals. The top ten counties are: Denmark, Sweden, Finland, France, Austria, Germany, Czech Republic, Norway, Netherlands, and Estonia; moreover, there was paucity in data for Hong Kong SAR and Taiwan, China.

Variables Triggering Innovation

The correlation analysis for the GII revealed the indicators significant to the corresponding regression. The twenty indicators that had greater impact on overall attainment of Global innovativeness, and their corresponding scores by relevance are as follows:

- ICT use (535.87)
- Government effectiveness (472.69)
- ICT access (361.33)
- Regulatory quality (356.78)
- Country code top-level domains (346.92)
- Generic top-level domains (331.70)
- Online e-participation (267.01)
- Rule of law (266.71)
- Government's online service (260.89)
- Environmental performance (243.00)
- Citable documents H index (199.95)
- Political and operational stability (180.14)
- Scientific and technical publications (164.63)
- Patent applications by origin (163.82)
- ISO 14001 environmental certificates (156.26)
- QS university ranking average score top 3 universities (155.65)
- Ease of resolving insolvency (155.37)
- ISO 9001 quality certificates (145.78)
- Tertiary enrollment (140.01)
- Patent families filed in at least two offices (137.49).

Clustering Innovative Economies

Potential similarities among economies were evaluated on the basis of the top 20 variables that best describe global innovativeness. Results show that, in 2020, there were 8 major clusters by which countries were grouped. Table 13.2 depicts the countries that have been associated in each of the 8 clusters. The cluster with more countries were clusters 4 and 1 followed by clusters 6 and 7. Results show that countries grouped in cluster 4, the largest cluster, rated highest; in other words, they were the most innovative countries and, thus, should account for the best practices. Although not all countries in said cluster had the highest compliance with the top twenty indicators, they did comply with a threshold of at least 70% compliance.

Table 13.2 GII cluster analysis

Country	C	GII
United Republic of Tanzania	C1	25.57
Honduras	C1	22.95
Guatemala	C1	22.35
Tajikistan	C1	22.23
Cambodia	C1	21.46
Malawi	C1	21.44
Côte d'Ivoire	C1	21.24
Lao People's Democratic Republic	C1	20.65
Uganda	C1	20.54
Madagascar	C1	20.40
Bangladesh	C1	20.39
Nigeria	C1	20.13
Burkina Faso	C1	20.00
Cameroon	C1	19.98
Zambia	C1	19.39
Mali	C1	19.15
Mozambique	C1	18.70
Togo	C1	18.54
Benin	C1	18.13
Ethiopia	C1	18.06
Niger	C1	17.82
Myanmar	C1	17.74
Guinea	C1	17.32

Country	C	GII
United Arab Emirates	C2	41.79
Thailand	C2	36.68
Montenegro	C2	35.39
Mauritius	C2	34.35
Costa Rica	C2	33.51
Qatar	C2	30.81
Brunei Darussalam	C2	29.82
Panama	C2	29.04
Kuwait	C2	28.40
Bahrain	C2	28.37
Albania	C2	27.12
Oman	C2	26.50
Trinidad and Tobago	C2	24.14

Country	C	GII
Mongolia	C3	33.41
Jamaica	C3	29.10
Azerbaijan	C3	27.23
Indonesia	C3	26.49
Botswana	C3	25.43
Dominican Republic	C3	25.10
Rwanda	C3	25.06
El Salvador	C3	24.85
Paraguay	C3	24.14
Cabo Verde	C3	23.86
Sri Lanka	C3	23.78
Senegal	C3	23.75
Namibia	C3	22.51
Ghana	C3	22.28

Country	C	GII
Switzerland	C4	66.08
Sweden	C4	62.47
United States of America	C4	60.56
United Kingdom	C4	59.78
Netherlands	C4	58.76
Denmark	C4	57.53
Finland	C4	57.02
Singapore	C4	56.61
Germany	C4	56.55
Republic of Korea	C4	56.11
Hong Kong, China	C4	54.24
France	C4	53.66
Israel	C4	53.55
Ireland	C4	53.05
Japan	C4	52.70
Canada	C4	52.26
Luxembourg	C4	50.84
Austria	C4	50.13
Norway	C4	49.29
Iceland	C4	49.23
Belgium	C4	49.13
Australia	C4	48.35
Estonia	C4	48.28
New Zealand	C4	47.01
Malta	C4	46.39
Spain	C4	45.60
Portugal	C4	43.51

Country	C	GII
Ukraine	C5	36.32
Armenia	C5	32.64
Georgia	C5	31.78
Saudi Arabia	C5	30.94
Iran	C5	30.89
Bosnia and Herzegovina	C5	28.99
Jordan	C5	27.79

Country	C	GII
Czech Republic	C7	48.34
Italy	C7	45.74
Cyprus	C7	45.67
Slovenia	C7	42.91
Malaysia	C7	42.42
Hungary	C7	41.53
Latvia	C7	41.11
Bulgaria	C7	39.98
Poland	C7	39.95
Slovakia	C7	39.70
Lithuania	C7	39.18
Croatia	C7	37.27
Greece	C7	36.79
Romania	C7	35.95
Serbia	C7	34.33
Chile	C7	33.86
North Macedonia	C7	33.43
Uruguay	C7	30.84

Country	C	GII
China	C6	53.28
Viet Nam	C6	37.12
Russian Federation	C6	35.63
India	C6	35.59
Philippines	C6	35.19
Turkey	C6	34.90
Mexico	C6	33.60
Republic of Moldova	C6	32.98
South Africa	C6	32.67
Brazil	C6	31.94
Belarus	C6	31.27
Tunisia	C6	31.21
Colombia	C6	30.84
Morocco	C6	28.97
Peru	C6	28.79
Kazakhstan	C6	28.56
Argentina	C6	28.33

Country	C	GII
Kenya	C8	26.13
Lebanon	C8	26.02
Uzbekistan	C8	24.54
Kyrgyzstan	C8	24.51
Nepal	C8	24.35
Egypt	C8	24.23
Ecuador	C8	24.11
Bolivia	C8	22.41
Pakistan	C8	22.31
Zimbabwe	C8	19.97
Algeria	C8	19.48
Yemen	C8	13.56

Source Own elaboration with data from Dutta et al. (2020)

Variables Triggering Impunity

The correlation analysis for the IGI revealed the indicators significant to the corresponding regression. The twelve indicators which had a greater impact on the overall impunity of the countries and the corresponding scores by relevance are as follows:

- Region (0.493)
- Professional judges and magistrates per 100,000 inhabitants (0.363)
- Police per 100,000 inhabitants (0.329)
- Percentage of incarcerated without sentence (0.318)
- People before courts/number of judges (0.267)
- Personnel in prisons/total inmates (0.223)
- People before courts/ number of prosecutors (0.208)
- Human rights (0.178)
- Imprisoned /convicted (0.148)
- Incarcerated for homicide /total homicides (0.147)
- People before courts/people in formal contact with police (0.134)
- Personnel in prisons/total capacity of prisons (0.134).

Clustering Economies Exempt from Punishment

Potential similarities among economies are evaluated based on the top 12 variables that best describe global impunity. Results show that there were 7 major clusters by which countries were grouped. Table 13.3 depicts the countries associated in each of the 7 clusters along with their corresponding level of impunity. The clusters with more countries were 2 and 4 followed by cluster 1. Findings indicate that countries grouped in cluster four, the second largest cluster, rated highest; in other words, they were the least exempt of punishment and, thus, should account for the best practices; however, not all countries in said cluster account for the highest compliance the most relevant variables.

Variables Triggering Human Development

The correlation analysis for the HDI revealed the indicators significant to the corresponding regression. The five indicators, which had a greater impact on overall Global human development attainment, are: life expectancy at birth (0.113), mean years of schooling (0.113), expected years of schooling (0.093), GNI per capita rank minus HDI rank (0.079), and gross national income per capita (0.061).

Clustering Economies on Human Development

Potential similarities among economies are evaluated using the top 5 variables that best describe global human development. Results show that, in 2020, there were 8 major clusters by which countries were grouped. Table

Table 13.3 IGI cluster analysis

Country	C	IGI
Armenia	C1	48.72
Azerbaijan	C1	54.56
Cameroon	C1	47.87
Ecuador	C1	48.17
Georgia	C1	40.51
Kazakhstan	C1	48.30
Kyrgyzstan	C1	51.80
Nepal	C1	51.94
Republic of Korea	C1	37.71
Singapore	C1	44.89
State of Palestine	C1	47.79

Country	C	IGI
Austria	C4	37.24
Belgium	C4	32.97
Canada	C4	45.66
Estonia	C4	31.36
Finland	C4	32.90
France	C4	36.06
Germany	C4	32.46
Iceland	C4	31.03
Italy	C4	33.78
Japan	C4	37.67
Mongolia	C4	35.02
Netherlands	C4	29.76
Norway	C4	27.36
Spain	C4	34.81
Sweden	C4	25.94
Switzerland	C4	38.42
UK (England & Wales)	C4	32.49
UK (Northern Ireland)	C4	36.61
UK (Scotland)	C4	36.09

Country	C	IGI
Albania	C2	32.12
Bahrain	C2	46.37
Belarus	C2	41.17
Bosnia and Herzegovina	C2	25.31
Bulgaria	C2	31.37
Croatia	C2	20.46
Greece	C2	24.05
Hungary	C2	28.34
Kosovo under UNSCR	C2	47.69
Latvia	C2	33.14
Liechtenstein	C2	47.83
Lithuania	C2	35.78
Montenegro	C2	31.71
Poland	C2	37.20
Portugal	C2	33.06
Republic of Moldova	C2	44.29
Romania	C2	28.89
Russian Federation	C2	46.74
Serbia	C2	30.97
Slovakia	C2	32.73
Slovenia	C2	20.26

Country	C	IGI
Chile	C5	47.63
Denmark	C5	38.82
Thailand	C5	62.82
Turkey	C5	46.17

Country	C	IGI
Barbados	C3	40.48
Colombia	C3	46.88
Costa Rica	C3	39.51
Guatemala	C3	49.66
Guyana	C3	52.07
Honduras	C3	59.69
Mexico	C3	49.67
Panama	C3	42.54
Paraguay	C3	53.15
Peru	C3	48.31

Country	C	IGI
Algeria	C6	57.63
Morocco	C6	58.04

Country	C	IGI
United States of America	C7	40.21

Source Own elaboration with data from Le Clercq Ortega and Rodríguez Sánchez Lara (2020)

13.4 depicts the countries that have been associated in each of the 8 clusters. The clusters with more member countries were 1 and 4 followed by 3 and 2. Findings suggest that the lower the score on human development, the lower the score on life expectancy at birth. However, countries not positioned in the highest cluster did account for a relatively high compliance with life expectancy at birth; the latter is consistent with the fact that it is the most relevant variable for human development. Results show that countries grouped in cluster 2 rated highest; in other words, countries with the highest scores in human development and, thus, should account for the best practices. While none of the countries in cluster 2 scored one hundred percent on compliance with most relevant variable, they did meet a threshold of at least seventy percent compliance.

Table 13.4 HDI cluster analysis

Country	C	HDI
Panama	C1	81.5
Bahamas	C1	81.4
Malaysia	C1	81
Mauritius	C1	80.4
Seychelles	C1	79.6
Trinidad and Tobago	C1	79.6
Mexico	C1	77.9
Saint Kitts and Nevis	C1	77.9
Antigua and Barbuda	C1	77.8
Thailand	C1	77.7
North Macedonia	C1	77.4
Colombia	C1	76.7
Brazil	C1	76.5
China	C1	76.1
Saint Lucia	C1	75.9
Dominican Republic	C1	75.6
Lebanon	C1	74.4
Maldives	C1	74
Saint Vincent and the Grenadines	C1	73.8
Suriname	C1	73.8
Botswana	C1	73.5
Paraguay	C1	72.8
Libya	C1	72.4
Indonesia	C1	71.8
South Africa	C1	70.9
Egypt	C1	70.7
Viet Nam	C1	70.4
Morocco	C1	68.6
Guyana	C1	68.2
Iraq	C1	67.4
El Salvador	C1	67.3
Cabo Verde	C1	66.5
Guatemala	C1	66.3
Bhutan	C1	65.4

Country	C	HDI
Norway	C2	95.7
Ireland	C2	95.5
Switzerland	C2	95.5
Hong Kong, China (SAR)	C2	94.9
Iceland	C2	94.9
Germany	C2	94.7
Sweden	C2	94.5
Australia	C2	94.4
Netherlands	C2	94.4
Denmark	C2	94
Finland	C2	93.8
United Kingdom	C2	93.2
Belgium	C2	93.1
New Zealand	C2	93.1
Canada	C2	92.9
United States	C2	92.6
Austria	C2	92.2
Israel	C2	91.9
Japan	C2	91.9
Slovenia	C2	91.7
Korea (Republic of)	C2	91.6
Spain	C2	90.4
France	C2	90.1
Czechia	C2	90
Malta	C2	89.5
Italy	C2	89.2
Greece	C2	88.8

Country	C	HDI
Nicaragua	C3	66
India	C3	64.5
Honduras	C3	63.4
Bangladesh	C3	63.2
Kiribati	C3	63
Sao Tome and Principe	C3	62.5
Micronesia	C3	62
Ghana	C3	61.1
Vanuatu	C3	60.9
Timor-Leste	C3	60.6
Nepal	C3	60.2
Kenya	C3	60.1
Cambodia	C3	59.4
Zambia	C3	58.4
Myanmar	C3	58.3
Congo	C3	57.4
Zimbabwe	C3	57.1
Solomon Islands	C3	56.7
Syrian Arab Republic	C3	56.7
Cameroon	C3	56.3
Comoros	C3	55.4
Benin	C3	54.5
Uganda	C3	54.4
Rwanda	C3	54.3
Tanzania	C3	52.9
Madagascar	C3	52.8
Togo	C3	51.5
Afghanistan	C3	51.1
Haiti	C3	51
Malawi	C3	48.3

Country	C	HDI
Montenegro	C4	82.9
Palau	C4	82.6
Belarus	C4	82.3
Barbados	C4	81.4
Georgia	C4	81.2
Serbia	C4	80.6
Albania	C4	79.5
Cuba	C4	78.3
Iran	C4	78.3
Sri Lanka	C4	78.2
Bosnia and Herzegovina	C4	78
Ukraine	C4	77.9
Peru	C4	77.7
Armenia	C4	77.6
Ecuador	C4	75.9
Azerbaijan	C4	75.6
Moldova	C4	75
Algeria	C4	74.8
Fiji	C4	74.3
Dominica	C4	74.2
Tunisia	C4	74
Mongolia	C4	73.7
Jamaica	C4	73.4
Jordan	C4	72.9
Tonga	C4	72.5
Uzbekistan	C4	72
Bolivia	C4	71.8
Philippines	C4	71.8
Belize	C4	71.6
Samoa	C4	71.5
Venezuela	C4	71.1
Palestine	C4	70.8
Marshall Islands	C4	70.4
Kyrgyzstan	C4	69.7
Tajikistan	C4	66.8

Country	C	HDI
Turkmenistan	C5	71.5
Gabon	C5	70.3
Namibia	C5	64.6
Lao People's Democratic Republic	C5	61.3
Eswatini	C5	61.1
Equatorial Guinea	C5	59.2
Angola	C5	58.1
Nigeria	C5	53.9
Côte d'Ivoire	C5	53.8
Lesotho	C5	52.7

Country	C	HDI
Singapore	C6	93.8
Liechtenstein	C6	91.9
Luxembourg	C6	91.6
United Arab Emirates	C6	89
Andorra	C6	86.8
Qatar	C6	84.8
Brunei Darussalam	C6	83.8
Kuwait	C6	80.6

Country	C	HDI
Estonia	C7	89.2
Cyprus	C7	88.7
Lithuania	C7	88.2
Poland	C7	88
Latvia	C7	86.6
Portugal	C7	86.4
Slovakia	C7	86
Hungary	C7	85.4
Saudi Arabia	C7	85.4
Bahrain	C7	85.2
Chile	C7	85.1
Croatia	C7	85.1
Argentina	C7	84.5
Romania	C7	82.8
Kazakhstan	C7	82.5
Russian Federation	C7	82.4
Turkey	C7	82
Uruguay	C7	81.7
Bulgaria	C7	81.6
Oman	C7	81.3
Costa Rica	C7	81
Grenada	C7	77.9

Country	C	HDI
Pakistan	C8	55.7
Papua New Guinea	C8	55.5
Mauritania	C8	54.6
Djibouti	C8	52.4
Senegal	C8	51.2
Sudan	C8	51
Gambia	C8	49.6
Ethiopia	C8	48.5
Guinea-Bissau	C8	48
Guinea	C8	47.7
Yemen	C8	47
Eritrea	C8	45.9
Mozambique	C8	45.6
Burkina Faso	C8	45.2
Sierra Leone	C8	45.2
Mali	C8	43.4
South Sudan	C8	43.3
Chad	C8	39.8
Central African Republic	C8	39.7
Niger	C8	39.4

Source Developed by authors with data from UNDP (2020b)

Discussion

Best practices across indexes are most likely associated with the top 10 countries in each index. Findings showed that only 2 countries made the top 10 for all 5 indexes: The Netherlands and Sweden; Denmark made the top 10 in 4 indexes. Switzerland, Germany, and Norway made the top 10 in 3 indexes, Singapore, the United States, Hong Kong, United Kingdom, and Finland ranked high in 2 indexes, and the rest only in 1. Hong Kong SAR, and Taiwan, China, are considered high performing in regard to competitiveness; however, there is no SDG achievement information for them. Switzerland, the United States, United Kingdom, and Singapore, which are in the top 10 on Competitiveness and Innovation indexes, did not make the top 10 on SDGs. It is noteworthy that only half of countries ranking high on human development are among the top 10 of the other indexes. The following are the top ten countries in each index:

GCI	SDGs	GII	IGI	HDI
1. Singapore SAR	1. Denmark	1. Switzerland	1. Slovenia	1. Norway
2. United States	2. Sweden	2. Sweden	2. Croatia	2. Ireland
3. Hong Kong	3. Finland	3. United States	3. Greece	3. Switzerland
4. Netherlands	4. France	4. United Kingdom	4. Bosnia and Herzegovina	4. Hong Kong SAR
5. Switzerland	5. Austria	5. Netherlands	5. Sweden	5. Iceland
6. Japan	6. Germany	6. Denmark	6. Norway	6. Germany
7. Germany	7. Czech Republic	7. Finland	7. Hungary	7. Sweden
8. Sweden	8. Norway	8. Singapore	8. Romania	8. Australia
9. United Kingdom	9. Netherlands	9. Germany	9. Netherlands	9. Netherlands
10. Denmark	10. Estonia	10. Republic of Korea	10. Serbia	10. Denmark

Given competitiveness' definition, it would be expected that the most competitive countries would also rank high in other global indexes sharing common variables. Gabriela Ramos, Chief of Staff and Sherpa to the G20, has posited that it "is not only unacceptable and unsustainable ethically or socially, inequality also impacts the prospects of higher productivity and growth" (OECD, 2018). According to the quantitative and qualitative results, there is significant variable overlap in each index, which begs the question, why are competitive countries not ranking higher in other indexes?

It makes sense that water supply reliability is the most relevant variable when describing competitiveness, since it is described as the absence of fluctuations/interruptions (Schwab, 2019), and water supply unreliability significantly burdens households and negatively impacts the population's health, especially for the poorest countries (Majuru et al., 2016), as well as poorest and neglected areas in developing and developed countries. According to the Human Development Report, both "water and sanitation are essential for human development" and are a human right (UN General Assembly, 2010). In other words, access to water is essential to the attainment of competitiveness.

If competitiveness is the conjunction of the best economic, social, and environmental conditions, then, it would be expected that the most competitive countries effectively tend to these three key aspects. When analyzing the top 20 variables, it is noteworthy that Pillars 10 and 11 are not included in the most significant variables which are descriptive of Global Competitiveness. Variables with 70% or higher compliance that could be tackled at an organizational level to promote micro- and macro-competitiveness include: research and development, innovation, stakeholder relationship, training and development, effective management, auditing, and anti-corruption.

According to the results, the most competitive countries with higher SDG achievement are significantly lagging in: zero hunger, responsible consumption and production, climate action, life below water, and partnerships toward the goals, respectively. Further, these countries only show an increasing score for goal 1, no poverty. The SDGs have been previously studied, and Morton et al. (2017) argued that there is further need to create conditions that would enable an adequate approach to all goals. The latter is apparent because: (i) There is insufficient data for a significant statistical analysis for the last three years, and (ii) even the most competitive countries are nowhere close to achieving the SDGs. Interestingly, all SDG variables can be applied in an organization with an adjusted scope. In other words, organizational leaders may aim to achieve them within the limits of their surrounding community and, in turn, positively impact sustainable development at local and global levels. For instance, a study held by PricewaterhouseCoopers, in 2018, found that 54% had aligned the SDGs with their business strategies, and 60% mention the goals in their CSR reports (Scott & McGill, 2018).

Innovation is an important element in the pursuit of competitiveness as well as sustainable development, thus, the most competitive countries and those with high sustainable development achievement are expected to rank high on the innovation global index sharing common variables. According to Rexhepi et al., (2013), organizations' competencies stem from social responsibility and innovation; therefore, it makes good business sense to converge innovativeness with socially responsible strategic objectives in order to achieve business and social growth and development. It was also found that the variables effectively applicable to organizations include: regulatory quality, ICT use and access, environmental performance, ISO 14001 environmental certificates, and ISO 9001 quality certificates.

Inequality, corruption, and the rule of law significantly correlate with impunity (Le Clercq Ortega & Rodríguez Sánchez Lara, 2020); therefore, organizations may take on variables related to inequality, corruption, in addition to human rights, to positively impact the reduction of impunity. This will significantly impact trust which, in regard to firms, is essential in terms of reputation, and license to operate (Goodman, 2006). Further, "inequality, discrimination and unjust power relations" directly and negatively impact development (WHO, 2010). In terms of human development, it was also found that organizations may take on variables related to health, schooling, and income.

Model Analysis

According to Goodman (2006), successful firms effectively align their operations with "human and labor rights, environmental standards, anti-corruption and transparency"; thus, it makes sense that global competitiveness, sustainable and human development, innovation, and impunity be significantly impacted by firms' alignment with their attainment. Thus, if organizational and government leaders have shared goals associated with each index, global sustainable competitiveness is plausible. Moreover, such alignment may certainly be key to a global efficient and effective recovery in response to the pandemic and collateral crises. Firms may certainly impact all three aspects; however, in order to do so effectively, according to Hutchins et al. (2019), there is a particular need for the development of a social sustainability measurement. Interestingly, all applicable variables, from each index, may be well aligned with organizations' engagement in corporate social responsibility, that is, the approach to business dynamics for and by society to attain social, financial, and environmental performance.

The general objective of this study was to evaluate the potential correlation between competitiveness and sustainable development with the intention to scale previous actions for a comprehensive approach to organizational sustainable competitiveness toward global recovery. Thus, a conceptual framework was developed to illustrate the relationship among the study's constructs and relevant variables applicable for organizational achievement. Figure 13.1 includes the conceptual framework. It describes firms engaging in corporate social responsibility which can address a series of indicators related to global indexes: innovation, human development, sustainability, impunity, and competitiveness. In such way that firms may aid in a country's economic and social recovery from the effects of COVID-19 by managing effectively and designing and executing strategies aligned with: the seventeen sustainable development goals, quality control, information and communication technology, anticorruption, innovation, research and development, effective stakeholder relationship, and equal and fair income. By doing so, firms may positively impact the country's sustainable development, innovation, competitiveness, impunity, and human development, and, in turn, impact global sustainable development.

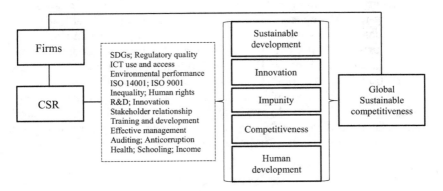

Fig. 13.1 Global sustainable competitiveness framework

Concluding Remarks

In a constantly evolving world, where unexpected changes are the rule rather than the exception, the COVID-19 pandemic has highlighted an urgent need for all countries to strengthen strategic, scientific-technological capacities with a strong emphasis on sustainability, focusing on environmental issues, human rights, and impunity, to achieve a higher quality of life for the population. Grouping countries regarding their environmental, human rights, impunity, sustainability, and innovation performance is a beneficial quantitative approach that enables evaluation of regions requiring support to improve substantive aspects of the population's quality of life. Doing so allows working groups focused on improving global living conditions to promote regional improvement.

The study's results indicate a potential correlation between competitiveness and sustainable development toward global recovery. In addition, through this research, the relevance of digitization is evidenced by highlighting the importance of adopting information and communication technologies, as well as the relevant role of governments and institutions in making adequate policies to combat impunity and human rights violations. Further, findings show that, in the context of the pandemic, governments must prioritize large-scale actions and work to ensure that public institutions include governance principles to recover their citizens' confidence, hence, the prevalence of common ownership and eradication of corruption. Moreover, they must work with organizational leaders to ensure that they too are working toward sustained growth and development. Currently, most countries' efforts are focused on tending to the health crisis caused by COVID-19; yet, this juncture offers an opportunity to transform economic systems so they are productive, innovative, competitive, and sustainable. Social growth and development are only achievable if all interested parties participate in its attainment; for such matter, firms need to be proactive in their CSR efforts to positively impact global indexes and, in turn, influence global sustainable competitiveness.

References

Ai, T. H., & Ushakov, D. (2019). Taxation regime and macroeconomic systems' dynamics. In D. Ushakov, *Global trends of modernization in budgeting and finance* (pp. 225–240). IGI Global.

Atkinson, R. D. (2013, August). *Competitiveness, innovation and productivity: Clearing up the confusion.* Retrieved January 18, 2021, from http://www2.itif.org/2013-competitiveness-innovation-productivity-clearing-up-confusion.pdf

Bansal, P., & DesJardine, M. R. (2014). Business sustainability: It is about time. *Strategic Organization, 12*(1), 70–78.

Basu, R. R., Banerjee, P. M., & Sweeny, E. G. (2013). Frugal innovation: Core competencies to address global sustainability. *Journal of Management for Global Sustainability, 1*(2), 63–82.

Birdsall, S. (2014). Measuring student teachers' understandings and self-awareness of sustainability. *Environmental Education Research, 20*(6), 814–835.

Brown, B. J., Hanson, M. E., Liverman, D. M., & Merideth, R. W., Jr. (1987). Global sustainability: Toward definition. *Environmental Management, 11*(6), 713–719.

Business & Human Rights Resource Center. (2017). *Corporate impunity is common & remedy for victims is rare. Corporate legal accountability annual briefing.* Retrieved January 11, 2021, from https://media.business-humanrights.org/media/documents/files/documents/CLA_AB_Final_Apr_2017.pdf

Cann, O. (2016, September 27). *What is competitiveness?* Retrieved January 23, 2021, from Competitiveness framework. https://www.weforum.org/agenda/2016/09/what-is-competitiveness/

Carayannis, E. G., & Gonzalez, E. (2003). Creativity and innovation = Competitiveness? When, how, and why. In L. V. Shavinina (Ed.), *The international handbook on innovation* (pp. 587–606). Elsevier Science.

Carrillo-Hermosilla, J., del Río, P., & Könnölä, T. (2010). Diversity of eco-innovations: Reflections from selected case studies. *Journal of Cleaner Production, 18*(10), 1073–1083.

Chandan, H. C., & Das, R. (2017). Chapter 4 - Evolution of responsible and sustainable corporate identity for Chinese firms. In E. Paulet, & C. Rowley (Eds.), *The China business model. Originality and limits* (pp. 71–96). CP Chandos Publishing.

Competitiveness Policy Council. (1992). *Building a competitive America.* In First Report to the President and the Congress.

Corrigan, G., Crotti, R., Hanouz, M. D., & Serin, C. (2014). *Defining sustainable competitiveness.* Retrieved January 22, 2021, from Reports. https://reports.weforum.org/global-competitiveness-report-2014-2015/defining-sustainable-competitiveness/

Deva, S. (2012). *Regulating corporate human rights violations: Humanizing business.* Routledge.

Dugarova, E., Slay, B., Papa, J., & Marnie, S. (2017). *Leaving no one behind in implementing the 2030 Agenda for sustainable development: Roma inclusion in Europe*. Retrieved January 16, 2021, from United Nations Development Programme: https://www.undp.org/content/dam/rbec/docs/LeavingNoOneBehindinthe2030Agenda_Roma%20inclusion%20in%20Europe.pdf

Dutta, S., Lanvin, B., & Wunsch-Vincent, S. (2020). *The global innovation index 2020: Who will finance innovation?* Cornell University, INSEAD, & WIPO.

Elkington, J. (1997). *Cannibals with forks: The triple bottom line of 21st century business*. Capstone.

Emas, R. (2015). *The concept of sustainable development: Definition and defining*. Retrieved December 25, 2020, from United Nations: https://sustainabledevelopment.un.org/content/documents/5839GSDR%202015_SD_concept_definiton_rev.pdf

Fenner, R., & Cernev, T. (2021, April). The implications of the Covid-19 pandemic for delivering the Sustainable Development Goals. *Futures, 28*, 102726. doi:https://doi.org/10.1016/j.futures.2021.102726

Filó, C. (2007). Territorial competitiveness and the human factors. *International Conference of Territorial Intelligence*, (pp. 323–336). CAENTI.

Gladwin, T. N., Kennelly, J. J., & Krause, T.-S. (1995). Shifting paradigms for sustainable development: Implications for management theory and research. *Academy of Management Review, 20*(4), 874–907.

Goodman, M. B. (2006). The role of business in public diplomacy. *Journal of Business Strategy, 27*(3), 5–7.

Govindarajan, V., & Ramamurti, R. (2011, November). Reverse innovation, emerging markets, and global strategy. *Global Strategy Journal, 1*(3–4), 191–205.

Hopkins, M. (2007). *Corporate social responsibility and international development: Is business the solution?* Earthscan.

Hutchins, M. J., Richter, J. S., Henry, M. L., & Sutherland, J. W. (2019, March). Development of indicators for the social dimension of sustainability in a U.S. business context. *Journal of Cleaner Production, 212*(1), 687–697.

Joinet, L. (1997). *Annex II. Set of principles for the protection and promotion of human rights through action to combat impunity*. The administration of justice and human rights of detainees. Commission of Human Rights. Retrieved January 12, 2021, from http://hrlibrary.umn.edu/demo/RightsofDetainees_Joinet.pdf

Le Clercq Ortega, J. A., & Rodríguez Sánchez Lara, G. (2020). *Índice Global de Impunidad. Escalas de impunidad en el mundo. Índice Global de Impunidad 2020 (IGI-2020)*. Fundación Universidad de las Américas. Retrieved October 7, 2020, from https://www.casede.org/index.php/biblioteca-casede-2-0/autores-casede/gerardo-rodriguez-sanchez-lara/574-indice-global-de-impunidad-2020/file

Louati, F. (2018). Knowledge management and the competitiveness of learning organizations. In A. Malheiro, F. Ribeiro, G. L. Jamil, J. P. Rascao, & O. Mealha, *Handbook of research on knowledge management for contemporary business environments* (pp. 64–85). IGI Global.

Majuru, B., Suhrcke, M., & Hunter, P. R. (2016, December). How do households respond to unreliable water supplies? A systematic review. *International Journal of Environmental Research and Public Health, 13*(12), 1222. doi:https://doi.org/10.3390/ijerph13121222

Morton, S., Pencheon, D., & Squires, N. (2017, October). Sustainable Development Goals (SDGs), and their implementation: A national global framework for health, development and equity needs a systems approach at every level. *British Medical Bulletin, 124*(1), 81–90.

OECD. (2018, June 15). *A broken social elevator? How to promote social mobility. Overview and main findings.* Retrieved April 29, 2019, from https://www.oecd.org/social/soc/Social-mobility-2018-Overview-MainFindings.pdf

OECD, Eurostat. (2018). *Oslo manual 2018: Guidelines for collecting, reporting and using data on innovation* (4th ed.). The Measurement of Scientific.

OHCHR. (2011). *Impunity and the rule of law. Combating impunity and strengthening accountability, the rule of law and democratic society.* Office of the United Nations High Commissioner for Human Rights. Retrieved January 12, 2021, from https://www2.ohchr.org/english/ohchrreport2011/web_version/ohchr_report2011_web/allegati/10_Impunity.pdf

Porter, M. E. (2004). *Building the microeconomic foundations of prosperity: Findings from the microeconomic competitiveness index.* Palgrave Macmillan.

Porter, M. E., & Kramer, M. R. (2011, January–February). Creating shared value. How to reinvent capitalism-and unleash the wave of innovation and growth. *Harvard Business Review, 89*(1–2), 62–77.

Prahalad, C. K. (2006). *The fortune at the bottom of the pyramid. Eradicating poverty through profit.* Wharton School Publishing.

Rexhepi, G., Kurtishi, S., & Bexheti, G. (2013, April). Corporate social responsibility (CSR) and innovation–The drivers of business growth? *Procedia-Social and Behavioral Sciences, 75*(3), 532–541.

Robins, F. (2006, March). The challenge of TBL: A responsibility to whom? *Business and Society Review, 111*(1), 1–14.

Sachs, J., Schmidt-Traub, G., Kroll, C., Lafortune, G., Fuller, G., & Woelm, F. (2020). *The sustainable development goals and COVID-19.* Sustainable Development Report 2020. Cambridge University Press

Schmidheiny, S., Council, B., & for Sustainability. (1998). *Changing course: A global business perspective on development and the environment.* The MIT Press.

Schwab, K. (2018). *The global competitiveness report.* Retrieved February 20, 2020, from World Economic Forum. http://www3.weforum.org/docs/GCR2018/05FullReport/TheGlobalCompetitivenessReport2018.pdf

Schwab, K. (2019). *The global competitiveness report*. Retrieved February 20, 2020, from World Economic Forum. http://www3.weforum.org/docs/WEF_TheGlobalCompetitivenessReport2019.pdf

Schwab, K., & Zahidi, S. (2020). *The global competitiveness report. How countries are performing on the road to recovery*. Retrieved May 19, 2021, from Special Edition 2020: World Economic Forum. http://www3.weforum.org/docs/WEF_TheGlobalCompetitivenessReport2020.pdf

Scott, L., & McGill, A. (2018). *From promise to reality: Does business really care about the SDGs? And what needs to happen to turn words into action*. Retrieved September 10, 2020, from SDG Reporting Challenge 2018: https://www.pwc.com/gx/en/sustainability/SDG/sdg-reporting-2018.pdf

SDGF. (2019). *Millennium development goals*. Retrieved June 10, 2019, from Sustainable Development Goals Fund: https://www.sdgfund.org/mdgs-sdgs

Sen, A. (2013). The ends and means of sustainability. *Journal of Human Development and Capabilities. A Multi-Disciplinary Journal for People-Centered Development, 14*(1), 6–20.

Solleiro, J. L., & Castañon, R. I. (2012). Competitividad, innovación y transferencia de tecnología en México. *Información Comercial Española, ICE: Revista De Economía, 869*, 149–162.

Solleiro, J.L., & Terán-Bustamante, A. (2014). Elementos clave en la competitividad: aspectos teóricos. In *La competitividad de la industria farmacéutica en el Estado de México*. Cambio Tec, COMECYT, UNAM, CONACYT

Sternberg, R. J., Pretz, J. E., & Kaufman, J. C. (2003). Chapter 9. Types of innovation. In L. V. Shavinina, *The international handbook on innovation* (pp. 158–169). Oxford: Elsevier Science Ltd.

Sustainable Development Report. (2020). *Country Profiles*. Retrieved November 14, 2020, from https://dashboards.sdgindex.org/profiles

The World Bank. (2020, June 8). *COVID-19 to Plunge Global Economy into Worst Recession since World War II*. Retrieved May 19, 2021, from https://www.worldbank.org/en/news/press-release/2020/06/08/covid-19-to-plunge-global-economy-into-worst-recession-since-world-war-ii

Tokoro, N. (2007). Stakeholders and corporate social responsibility (CSR): A new perspective on the structure of relationships. *Asian Business & Management, 6*(2), 143–162.

Tonne, C. (2021, February). Lessons from the COVID-19 pandemic for accelerating sustainable development. *Environmental Research, 193*, 110482.

UN. (2000, September 8). *Millennium Summit of the United Nations*. Retrieved September 12, 2018, from Millenium Declaration: http://www.un.org/en/development/devagenda/millennium.shtml

UN General Assembly. (1987, August 4). *Resolution A/42/427*. Retrieved January 13, 2021, from Report of the World Commission on Environment and Development: https://undocs.org/en/A/42/427

UN General Assembly. (1997, October 15). *Resolution A/RES/51/240*. Retrieved January 14, 2021, from https://undocs.org/pdf?symbol=en/A/RES/51/240

UN General Assembly. (2010, July 28). *Resolution A/RES/64/292*. Retrieved August 20, 2020, from Sixty-fourth session. Agenda item 48: https://documents-dds-ny.un.org/doc/UNDOC/GEN/N09/479/35/PDF/N0947935.pdf?OpenElement

UNDP. (2020a). *What is human development?* Retrieved January 14, 2021, from About Human Development: http://hdr.undp.org/en/humandev

UNDP. (2020b). *Human Development Report 2020. The next frontier Human development and the Anthropocene*. New York: United Nations Development Programme. Retrieved January 16, 2021, from http://hdr.undp.org/sites/default/files/hdr2020.pdf

UNDP. (2020c). *Technical notes*. Retrieved January 16, 2021, from Human Development Report 2020: http://hdr.undp.org/sites/default/files/hdr2020_technical_notes.pdf

Vásquez, I., & McMahon, F. (2020). *The Human Freedom Index 2020 . A global measurement of personal, civil, and economic freedom*. Washington, DC: The Cato Institute and The Fraser Institute. Retrieved January 17, 2021, from The Cato Institute and The Fraser Institute: https://www.cato.org/sites/cato.org/files/2021-03/human-freedom-index-2020.pdf

WEF. (2015). *The 12 pillars of competitiveness*. Retrived April 22, 2019, from World Economic Forum. Methodology: http://reports.weforum.org/global-competitiveness-report-2014-2015/methodology/

Weng, P. W. (2019). Destination competitiveness: An antecedent or the result of destination brand equity? In R. Hashim, M. H. Hanafiah, & M. R. Jamaluddin, *Positioning and branding tourism destinations for global competitiveness* (pp. 49–73). Hershey: IGI Global.

Wenzel, M., Stanske, S., & Lieberman, M. B. (2021, February). Strategic responses to crisis. *Strategic Management Journal, 42*(2), O16-O27. doi:https://doi.org/10.1002/smj.3161

WHO. (2010). *A human rights-based approach to health*. Retrieved May 23, 2021, from https://www.who.int/hhr/news/hrba_to_health2.pdf

WHO. (2019). *Millennium Development Goals (MDGs)*. Retrieved June 10, 2019, from World Health Organization: https://www.who.int/topics/millennium_development_goals/about/en/

WIPO. (2020). *Global Innovation Index (GII)*. Retrieved October 17, 2020, from Resources: https://www.wipo.int/global_innovation_index/en/

Index

A
Automotive sector, 13, 45

B
Bankruptcy, 2, 4, 54, 110, 112, 113, 116–119, 121–124
Bayesian Network (BNs), 136–139, 146, 147, 150
Business growth and development, 207, 213, 214, 243
Business model, 4, 50, 123, 124, 129–135, 142–145, 150, 158, 159, 166, 170, 242
Business Model Innovation (BMI), 4, 130–135, 139, 140, 145–151

C
Coevolution, 159, 162, 163, 171, 173
Cointegration, 32, 34, 35
Company classification, 4, 123, 124
Company performance, 228

Competitiveness, 5, 13, 49, 50, 131–133, 168, 169, 171, 173, 228, 241–252, 258–262
Competitive performance, 54, 244
Consumer behavior, 168
Consumer expectations, 20
Consumer goods (I.G), 28, 34, 36–38
Consumer privacy, 52
Consumer satisfaction, 184
Corporate social responsibility (CSR), 5, 181, 183, 204, 212, 215, 224, 227, 236, 243, 261
    engagement, 184, 186, 205–207, 215, 236, 248
Crisis, 2–16, 18, 19, 42, 62–64, 73, 77–79, 89, 98, 110, 112, 116, 121, 123, 130, 165, 167, 195, 201, 202, 211, 212, 214, 224, 225
Customer engagement, 158

D

Decision-making, 2–4, 49, 131, 136, 137, 142, 162, 164, 187, 202, 205, 242
Developing countries/nations, 9, 11, 182, 210, 247
Distributive justice, 203

E

Economic circular systems, 158
Economic cycle, 113
Economic development, 9, 159, 169, 170, 174, 242
Economic growth, 10–12, 14, 17, 20, 63, 112–116, 118, 121, 162, 163, 165, 166, 169, 170, 246
Economic performance, 3, 11, 115, 116, 122, 123, 215, 244
Economic reactivation, 9, 13, 20, 48
Economic recession, 4, 12, 13, 110, 111, 113, 162, 242
Economic sector, 11, 13, 14, 16, 17, 47, 110, 111, 118, 119, 121, 122
Education, 1, 3, 4, 15, 19, 42, 45, 48, 53, 55, 57, 58, 67, 114–116, 118, 183, 187, 188, 203, 206, 245, 246, 248
Emerging economies, 8–10, 12, 14–16, 19, 158, 159, 162, 169, 181, 186
  markets, 163
Employee engagement, 158, 164, 165, 168
Employment recovery, 65, 76
Entrepreneur, entrepreneurship, 121, 133, 145, 170, 171
Environmental performance, 5, 205, 243, 253, 260, 261
Equity performance, 230, 232, 233
Ethical behavior, 205, 208
  standards, 164, 205

F

Face to face interaction, 4
Family performance, 5, 224, 226, 228, 229, 231, 232, 234–236
Financial sector, 15, 115
5G network, 3, 42, 43, 48, 54
5G technologies, 42, 45

G

Gender employment gap, 78
Gender equality, 204, 206, 207, 209, 246
Gender equity, 3
Gender gap, 3, 66, 78, 79, 209, 210
Gender skills, 62, 63, 65–67, 71, 72, 76, 78
Global recovery, 5, 215, 243, 249, 261, 262
Global sustainable competitiveness, 260–262
Governance, 18, 132, 144, 165, 183, 187, 194, 195, 206, 212

H

Health crisis, 2, 7–9, 19, 20, 47, 61, 159, 166, 167, 174, 196, 197, 201, 202, 204, 210, 243, 262
Higher education sector, 85
Human development, 5, 7, 248, 249, 255, 256, 258–261
Human rights, 48, 187, 188, 194–196, 203, 208, 246–248, 255, 259, 260, 262

I

Imports, goods, 2, 25–29, 31, 36–38
Impunity, 5, 209, 211, 212, 247–249, 254, 255, 260–262
Industrial sector, 15, 16, 18, 51
Industry 4.0, 3, 53, 57

Inequality, 5, 8, 16, 53, 202–204, 208–212, 215, 247, 258, 260
Innovation, 2–5, 42, 43, 47–49, 52, 69, 112, 130–133, 135, 139, 145, 150, 158–160, 162–176, 187, 194, 206, 242, 244, 246–249, 259–262
Internet of things, 42, 43, 45, 46, 53, 58

J
Job recovery, 62, 65

K
Keynesian theory/Keynesian model, 10–12
Knowledge-intensive business models, 159, 166, 167
Knowledge intensive organizations/firms, 172, 175
Knowledge sharing, 162, 171

L
Leadership, 162, 168, 170, 176, 207
  entrepreneurial, 164
  transformational, 164, 165, 172
Lockdown, 1, 5, 6, 8, 85, 86, 90, 110, 111, 121–124

M
Machine learning, 46, 58, 148, 249
Marketing, 133, 143, 145, 146, 175, 206
Micro, small and medium companies, enterprises, 110, 114, 120, 121

O
Organizational performance, 3, 5, 158, 164, 175, 214, 227

P
Policy making, 112
Policy strategies, 112
Primary sector, 16, 19
Private sector, 14, 16, 51, 208
Public health, 19, 174, 183, 204
Public health communication, 3, 87, 90, 101
Public health restrictions, 114
Public policy, 2, 3, 10, 13, 47, 48, 57, 161

R
Resilience, 142, 167, 175, 212, 214
Resource management, 159, 162, 168, 173, 175

S
Schumpeterian economic model, 170
Secondary sector, 2, 9, 10, 14–19, 235
Social distancing, 3–5, 13, 18, 65, 88, 89, 114, 123, 160, 174, 175
Social growth and development, 5, 6, 204, 207, 211, 213–215, 244, 260, 262
Social learning, 158, 161, 162, 173
Social media, 5, 90, 92, 165, 185, 186, 192, 206
  networks, 46, 163, 182, 184–186, 188, 189, 191
Social performance, 207, 225, 230
Social responsibility, 2, 4, 57, 182, 184, 186–188, 193, 203, 207, 214, 226, 260
Social Value Orientation (SVO), 3, 87–92, 94–98, 101
Stakeholders, 3, 5, 47, 158, 161, 162, 164, 168, 169, 172, 173, 175, 176, 182–186, 188, 189,

192–197, 205, 227, 228, 235, 243, 259, 261
management, 168, 205, 248
Supply chain, 5, 17, 134, 166, 174, 201–203, 206, 207, 211–216, 247
global supply chain, 5, 202, 207, 212, 213
Supply chain governance, 5, 202, 206, 208, 212–216
Sustainability, 57, 123, 144, 188, 194, 195, 204, 207, 241, 242, 245, 248, 249, 260–262
Sustainable development goals (SDGs), 5, 204, 242, 246, 252, 258–261
Systemic crisis, 7, 13, 14, 16, 18, 19

T
Technology sector, 166

Transportation sector, 123, 223
Trust, 3, 87, 89–92, 94–98, 100–102, 175, 260

V
Vaccination, 86, 98, 99, 109, 197, 208
Value creation, 143, 144, 164
co-creation, 164
Value proposal, 131–134, 143, 151
VAT collection, 23–25, 27–29, 34, 36–38

W
Well-being, 3, 158, 183, 214, 215, 224, 225, 229, 231–233, 235, 236, 246, 248
Work-family performance, 224, 227
Work-personal life, 211

CPSIA information can be obtained
at www.ICGtesting.com
Printed in the USA
LVHW082142260122
709537LV00004B/57